BRITAIN'S ECONOMIC MIR...

During the 1980s successive Conservative governments wrought dramatic changes in the conduct of British economic policy. The prescriptions of 'Keynesianism', once unchallenged as the theoretical orthodoxy, have been turned on their head. Privatization, deregulation and market liberalization have replaced prices and incomes controls and state intervention. Rigid targets – first for the money supply, then for the exchange rate – have swept away the earlier discretionary approach to demand management. Whichever political party is in power, the impact of these changes on the shape of British economic policy is bound to endure.

Britain's Economic Miracle assesses changes in economic policy and their impact on the economy. It is divided into two parts. Part I focuses on the macroeconomy, with chapters on the core issues of growth, inflation, unemployment and the balance of payments. Part II concentrates on the key micro issues, including privatization, taxation and regional issues. In his introduction the editor provides the background to these chapters by examining the theoretical basis of the different policy innovations and by exploring the analytical models appropriate to the study of economic policy.

The book is based on chapters which appeared in *Economics* but all have been updated to take account of recent developments. It is clear, accessible and non-technical throughout.

Nigel Healey is Lecturer in Economics and Director of the Centre for European Economic Studies at the University of Leicester. He has wide teaching experience both in this country and abroad and is the author of several books, the most recent of which is *The Macroeconomic Environment* (1992). He has been the editor of *Economics*, the journal of the Economics Association, since 1990.

BRITAIN'S ECONOMIC MIRACLE

Myth or reality?

Edited by Nigel M. Healey

London and New York

First published 1993
by Routledge
11 New Fetter Lane, London EC4P 4EE

Simultaneously published in the USA and Canada
by Routledge
a division of Routledge, Chapman and Hall Inc.
29 West 35th Street, New York, NY 10001

Typeset in Garamond by Witwell Ltd, Southport
Printed and bound in Great Britain by
Biddles Ltd, Guildford and King's Lynn

British Library Cataloguing in Publication Data

*A catalogue reference for this book is available from the British
Library.*

ISBN 0–415–08157–2 (hbk)
0–415–08158–0 (pbk)

*Library of Congress Cataloging in Publication Data has been
applied for.*

ISBN 0–415–08157–2 (hbk)
0–415–08158–0 (pbk)

For Ken and Yvonne

CONTENTS

CONTENTS

ILLUSTRATIONS

FIGURES

TABLES

CONTRIBUTORS

David Blackaby	Lecturer in Economics at the University College of Swansea
Andrew Britton	Director of the National Institute of Economic and Social Research
Nigel Healey	Lecturer in Economics at the University of Leicester and Economics Editor of *Economics*
Lester Hunt	Lecturer in Economics at the University of Surrey
Peter Johnson	Lecturer in Economics at the University of Durham.
Kent Matthews	Senior Lecturer at Cardiff Business School
Geoffrey Maynard	Visiting Professor of Economics at the University of Reading and Economic Advisor at Investcorp International Ltd
David Parker	Senior Lecturer in Business Economics at Cranfield Management School and Research Fellow at the University of York
Ian Paterson	Lecturer in Economics at Heriot-Watt University.
Ken Richards	Senior Lecturer in Accounting at the University College of Wales, Aberystwyth
Phil Robins	Principal Lecturer and Head of Studies in Business Management and Administration at Trinity and All Saints College, University of Leeds
Leslie Simpson	Lecturer in Economics at Heriot-Watt University
John Wells	University Lecturer in Economics at the University of Cambridge

PREFACE

Nigel M. Healey

The last fifteen years have seen dramatic changes in the conduct of British macroeconomic policy. The policy prescriptions of 'Keynesianism', once unchallenged as the theoretical orthodoxy in macroeconomics, have been turned on their head. In their place, the Conservative government which took office in 1979 introduced the radical programmes recommended by the new classical school of thought. Privatisation, deregulation and market liberalisation replaced prices and incomes controls and state interventionism. Rigid 'rules' or targets – first for the money supply, then for the exchange rate – swept away the earlier, discretionary approach to demand-management policy.

Whichever political party governs in the future, the impact of these profound changes on the shape of British macroeconomic policy is certain to endure. Major ideological battles have been fought and won. The electorate now appears to accept that government has no business running productive enterprises or fixing prices and wages for the private sector; that governments cannot permanently hold down unemployment by pumping demand into the economy; and that the primary role of government is to control inflation. It is difficult to envisage a future government turning the clock back to the days when the public sector controlled Britain's major industries and when price and wage increases were set by ministerial edict and chancellors adjusted the fiscal stance thrice-yearly to regulate demand. Moreover, external developments have served to cement many of the most important changes in domestic policy. The spectacular collapse of communism in Eastern Europe has shattered any lingering, popular faith in the principles of state interventionism which underpinned yesterday's supply-side policy; and Britain's membership of the

European Monetary System will oblige tomorrow's government to continue with a rigid, non-inflationary demand-management policy, leaving little scope for once-fashionable 'fine-tuning'.

This book is about the changing face of British macroeconomic policy. The chapters that follow explain the theoretical basis of contemporary macroeconomic policy, highlighting the breaks with the former Keynesian orthodoxy (Chapter 1). They examine the effects of the new policies on Britain's macroeconomic performance (Chapters 2 to 7) and discuss some of the most pressing microeconomic issues thrown up by their implementation (Chapters 8 to 13). Apart from Chapter 1, all of the chapters in this book originally appeared as articles in *Economics*, the national journal of the Economics Association. The majority were commissioned by Rosalind Levacic during her term as Editor of the journal's Economics Section, although some of the earlier pieces came under the editorial scrutiny of her predecessor, Professor Frank Livesey. I owe an enormous debt to both these eminent colleagues. As the latest Editor to tread in their footsteps, I have taken over the role of cajoling and nagging the authors of the most recent articles: I thank them for their remarkable patience.

All the articles have been revised and updated to take account of developments since they first appeared. Thanks are particularly due to Phil Robins (Chapter 8) and Ken Richards (Chapter 12), who rewrote large parts of their original manuscripts at very short notice. Otherwise, I have interpreted my present editorial duties broadly, taking over the task of redrafting and cross-referencing the remaining chapters (wherever possible and appropriate) and standardising the terminology used. I have endeavoured to respect the original tone and content as far as possible. For any errors of commission or omission in the revised chapters, I alone am responsible. I would like to thank Eve Healey, who heroically retyped Chapters 2 to 13, and my son, Daniel, who tolerated my long absences during the preparation of this book and almost never switched off my computer in protest. Finally, I would like to thank my colleagues and friends at the University of Leicester for their support and the members and officers of the Economics Association (especially the General Editor of *Economics*, Peter Maunder), without whom this book would not have been possible.

ABBREVIATIONS

ACAS	Advisory, Concilation and Arbitration Service
APF	aggregate production function
BES	Business Expansion Scheme
CAD	computer-aided design
CBI	Confederation of British Industry
CGT	Capital Gains Tax
CTT	Capital Transfer Tax
DLT	Development Land Tax
EAS	Enterprise Allowance Scheme
ECU	European Currency Unit
EMS	European Monetary System
ERM	Exchange Rate Mechanism
GDP	Gross Domestic Product
GHS	General Household Survey
IFS	Institute of Fiscal Studies
LRAS	long-run aggregate supply
MRP	marginal revenue product
MTFS	Medium-Term Financial Strategy
NIESR	National Institute of Economic and Social Research
OFGAS	Office of Gas Supply
OFTEL	Office of Telecommunications
OFWAT	Office of Water Supplies
PEP	Personal Equity Plan
PPF	production possibility frontier
PSBR	public sector borrowing requirement
PSDR	publis sector debt repayment
R&D	research and development
RPI	retail price index
SBLGS	Small Business Loan Guarantee Scheme
SRAS	short-run aggregate supply
SRPC	short-run Phillips Curve
TUC	Trade Union Congress
VAT	Value Added Tax

1

FROM KEYNESIAN DEMAND MANAGEMENT TO THATCHERISM

Nigel M. Healey

INTRODUCTION

In November 1990, Margaret Thatcher resigned as Prime Minister, bringing to an end one of the most remarkable political careers of modern times. During her eleven years in office, her government transformed the face of British macroeconomic policy, shattering the 'postwar consensus' that had grown up since 1945. Prior to 1979, successive governments had sought to maintain aggregate demand at a level sufficient to achieve 'full employment'. In other words, demand-management policy had been directed towards 'real' macroeconomic objectives for output and employment. In contrast, 'supply-side' policies (i.e. policies designed to influence private sector decisions to produce goods and services) had primarily taken the form of rules and regulations, notably controls that limited the size of wage and price increases which companies were permitted to make.

Mrs Thatcher's government was elected on the basis of a programme which was diametrically opposed to the economic philosophy of the postwar consensus between the two major political parties. The incoming administration rejected the notion that demand management could be systematically used to promote high levels of output and employment, arguing that such a strategy was a recipe for ever-accelerating inflation. The new government advanced the (then) radical proposition that fiscal and monetary policies should be directed towards re-establishing price stability, regardless of the short-run costs in terms of falling output and higher unemployment. Mrs Thatcher's ministers also claimed that postwar supply-side policies had been fundamentally misconceived, suffocating the 'wealth-creating' market economy with bureaucratic 'red-tape'. Turning conventional wisdom on its head, the Thatcher government

1

contended that the only way of revitalising the real economy, thereby returning to the high rate of economic growth and low rates of unemployment enjoyed in the 1950s and 1960s, was to sweep away the paraphernalia of state interventionism with a revolutionary programme of privatisation, deregulation and market liberalisation.

Although macroeconomic policy has evolved considerably since 1979, the early Thatcher years have left a lasting impression on subsequent developments. The once-rigid 'monetary targets', which were intended to lock demand-management policy on to a non-inflationary path, have given way to membership of the European Monetary System (EMS). By joining the EMS as a full member in October 1990, Britain implicitly agreed to tie its domestic monetary policy stance to the stance pursued by the European Community's lowest-inflation member, Germany (Artis, 1991). Zero inflation has been replaced by 'German inflation' as the target of demand-management policy. But the use of demand-management policy to achieve 'nominal' objectives for the rate of inflation – rather than 'real' objectives for output and employment – has endured and (given Britain's commitment to the EMS) will continue to shape macroeconomic policy for the rest of the decade.

Supply-side policy, which has also been in a constant state of flux since 1979, nevertheless retains almost no point of tangency with the past. The intellectual baggage of the postwar consensus, which included nationalisation, state planning, and prices and incomes controls, is now disowned by all the mainstream political parties. Recent events in Eastern Europe and the Soviet Union, which have been interpreted across the political spectrum as evidence of the failure of central planning to replace the role of the 'invisible hand' (i.e. the price signals generated by a free market economy), have hastened the retreat from state interventionism. While concern about the environment has raised fears about the costs of uncontrolled economic growth, contemporary proposals to create a 'greener' society are almost universally predicated on assumptions of private ownership of capital and minimalist government controls.

The effects of this dramatic shift in the objectives and conduct of economic policy have not unsurprisingly provoked enormous controversy (e.g. Green, 1989). Many commentators have claimed that the economic benefits that apparently flowed from 'Thatcherism' have been illusory and that, once the distortions injected into the statistical data by a deep recession between 1979–82 and an unchecked boom between 1982–9 are stripped out, Britain's underlying performance is either little changed or actually worse than before. In contrast, supporters of the post-1979 policies maintain that Britain has undergone an 'economic renaissance' which, once the present recession has run its course, will ensure permanently higher growth rates and lower unemployment levels. Others concede that national living standards have increased at a faster rate since 1979 but, harking back to a 'gentler, more caring' era, fear that the social costs in terms of greater social and regional inequalities have proved unacceptably high.

This book explores the development of economic policy in Britain since 1979 and considers many of these important debates (see also Campbell *et al.*, 1989). Part I (Chapters 2 to 7) offers different interpretations of the macroeconomic impact of recent policy, in terms of its effects on inflation, unemployment, economic growth and the balance of payments. Part II (Chapters 8 to 13) concentrates on a range of contemporary microeconomic issues – for example, the effects of privatisation, the changing distribution of income and the 'North–South' divide. The role of the present chapter is to provide a theoretical 'lens' through which subsequent chapters can be viewed. It examines the Keynesian theories that underpinned the era of demand management between 1945 and 1979 and, within the context of the aggregate supply and demand framework, contrasts this body of thought with the new classical macroeconomics that has come to dominate British policymaking since 1979. In particular, it introduces readers to the major theoretical innovations and controversies of recent years – 'rule' versus 'discretion', 'monetary targets', 'credibility' and 'supply-side economics' – and prepares the ground for the chapters that follow.

THE KEYNESIAN 45-DEGREE LINE DIAGRAM

The approach to macroeconomic policy that characterised the period 1945–79 is captured by the familiar, 'Keynesian' 45-degree line diagram (see Figure 1.1). The 45-degree line shows points at which there is equilibrium in the 'goods market', that is, where planned expenditure (E) is equal to output (Y). Unless planned expenditure (E) – which comprises the sum of household consumption (C), corporate investment (I), government spending (G) and net exports (X-M) – is equal to output (Y), there will be disequilibrium in the sense that the business sector will find its inventories (i.e. stocks of unsold goods) rising or falling in an unintended fashion. Under such circumstances, firms will tend to adjust current output in the light of

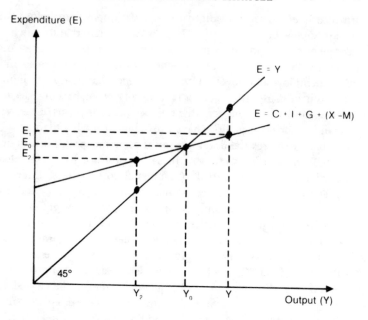

Figure 1.1 Equilibrium in the 45-degree line diagram

actual sales in the previous time period. But because the process of producing output generates an equivalent income for the household sector – in the form of profits, interest, rent and wages – as firms change output, households will be forced to revise their consumption plans, so that the business sector again finds itself with a level of output inappropriate to the level of planned expenditure.

We can use the 45-degree line diagram to illustrate this interaction between firms adjusting output and households altering consumption. The expenditure schedule ($E = C + I + G + (X-M)$) in Figure 1.1 shows how planned expenditure (E) varies with current output or income (Y). Although investment (I), government spending (G) and exports (X) are conventionally assumed to be exogenous (i.e. determined by forces outside the model), because consumption (C) and imports (M) are influenced by current income, total expenditure varies with income. Specifically, the higher the level of income, the higher the level of consumption and imports. Since the increase in consumption (which adds to expenditure) must necessarily be at least as large as the increase in imports (which reduces expenditure on domestic output), the former effect normally far outweighs the latter and the expenditure function is upward-sloping; that is, total expenditure rises with income.

By superimposing the expenditure schedule on the 45-degree line, we can see that there is only one point at which planned expenditure and output are equal (E_0, Y_0). Above Y_0 at Y_1, planned expenditure (E_1) would be lower than output. Inventories would rise and firms would cut back output (and income); expenditure would fall (but by less than the reduction in income) and the economy would gradually converge on E_0, Y_0. The same sequence of events would take place in reverse if the economy were initially at a level of income below Y_0 at Y_2, planned expenditure (E_2) would be higher than output, inventories would fall, and the business sector would step up production, adding to income and expenditure and driving the economy back to E_0, Y_0.

THE POLITICAL ECONOMY OF THE 45-DEGREE LINE DIAGRAM

Several major conclusions can be drawn from this simple model. First, there is no reason why the equilibrium level of income (or output) on which the economy converges should be consistent with the government's policy objectives. All other things equal, output and employment are closely related. Suppose that in Figure 1.2, Y_F is the level of output consistent with 'full employment' in the labour market (NB the relationship between output and employment is explored more fully below). With the economy in equilibrium at E_0, Y_0, there is clearly considerable unemployment. Second, the model suggests that a key reason for fluctuations in the levels of output and employment may be random shifts in the exogenous components of planned expenditure. For example, investment is greatly influenced by the state of business confidence, which is notoriously unstable over time. Suppose that a rise in interest rates (the cost of borrowing) triggers a collapse in business confidence. This could cause a sharp fall in investment, shifting the expenditure schedule in Figure 1.2 downwards from $E = C + I_0 + G + (X-M)$ to $E = C + I_1 + G + (X-M)$, pushing the equilibrium level of output further away (from Y_F to Y_1. The same downward shift in the expenditure schedule could result, all other things equal, from a slump in exports, perhaps following a recession in foreign markets.

Finally, because (i) the economy can lodge at equilibrium levels of

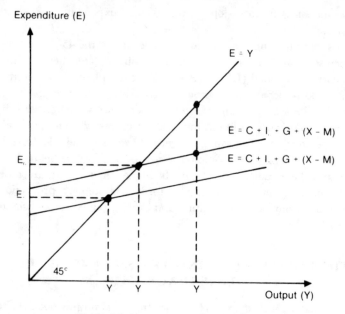

Figure 1.2 Investment and unemployment

output below full employment and (ii) investment and (possibly) exports may change in a way that gives rise to undesirable fluctuations in output and employment, the 45-degree line model suggests that the government should take responsibility for managing the economy. The government can alter its spending plans to raise or lower the expenditure schedule, propelling the equilibrium level of income to Y_F and thereby avoiding prolonged periods of high unemployment (see Figure 1.3). And it can 'fine-tune' its own spending plans to neutralise the random changes in investment and exports which would otherwise tend to drive the economy away from full employment. Note that the government could achieve the same 'stabilisation' of income through the use of tax policy. This would work by changing the share of income pre-empted by the government in the form of taxes, causing households to increase or reduce the proportion of any change in income that they spend buying firms' output ('the marginal propensity to consume'). A tax cut would increase the marginal propensity to consume, making the expenditure schedule steeper so that it intersected the 45-degree line at Y_F rather than Y_0 (see Figure 1.3); and vice versa, in the case of a tax increase.

6

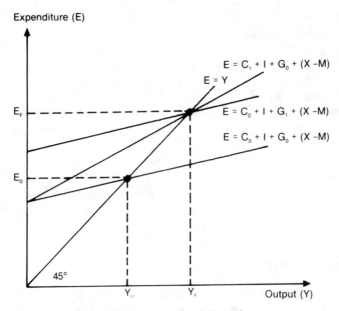

Figure 1.3 Fine-tuning for full employment

THE POSTWAR CONSENSUS

In the 1950s and 1960s, successive governments took the message of the 45-degree line model to heart. Reflecting the growing political influence of 'Keynesian' ideas, the wartime coalition government published the famous 'White Paper on Employment' in 1944, committing future peacetime governments to take responsibility for stabilising income at its full-employment level. Over the following thirty-five years, 'discretionary' fiscal policy (i.e. frequent changes in government spending and taxes) became the main policy tool for keeping the economy at a permanently high level of employment. During this period, monetary policy played an essentially supporting role. While it was recognised that corporate investment could be influenced by changing interest rates (so that expenditure could be boosted by a cut in interest rates rather than government spending increases or tax reductions), it was generally reckoned that the final effects on income were weak and unpredictable when compared with the impact of fiscal measures.

The 1950s and 1960s were the high point of the so-called 'postwar consensus' between the political parties. Both Labour and Conserva-

7

tive governments subscribed to the view that the maintenance of full employment through the use of discretionary demand-management policies was the basic role of macroeconomic policy. Between 1950 and 1966, unemployment averaged 2 per cent, never rising above half-a-million. It appeared that the days of mass unemployment were over. And while the two main political parties disagreed over the amount of nationalisation and the extent of the welfare state, even in this sphere of policy, the differences between them were essentially of degree rather than kind. Then, just when it seemed that the process of controlling the economy had been perfected, cracks in the postwar consensus – and in the basic Keynesian theory that underpinned it – began to emerge. Levering open these cracks was the acceleration in inflation during the late 1960s and the inability of the 45-degree line framework to offer convincing solutions.

DEMAND-PULL VERSUS COST-PUSH INFLATION

The simple 45-degree line model assumes away prices and wages, taking them as exogenously determined. To the extent that a theory of inflation can be incorporated into the model, it only applies to the special case in which the expenditure function shifts up so far that the equilibrium level of output is greater than the full-employment level of output. Under these circumstances, the model predicts that the result will be 'demand-pull' inflation. Because the economy cannot physically produce more output than the full-employment level (Y_F), the attempt to spend more than the economy can produce thus bids up prices and wages. The inflationary episode continues for as long as equilibrium output remains above the full-employment level. Thus, in the 45-degree line model, inflation can only occur at full employment. Gradually during the 1960s, as inflation began to accelerate despite levels of income that were clearly below full employment, this deficiency in the model became increasingly exposed.

Keynesian economists developed alternative theories of inflation, arguing that prices and wages were set by monopolistic firms and trade unions, so that they could rise in the absence of any demand-side influences. (Recall that a monopoly producer maximises profit by restricting output and charging higher prices than firms acting in competition with one other.) Initially reassured by such theories, governments introduced prices and incomes policies during the 1960s, in an attempt to curb 'cost-push' inflation at its source. The results were disappointing, however, with the policies causing damaging distortions to the economy, and prices and wages typically accelerating in 'catch-up' fashion as soon as the controls were lifted.

FROM THE 45-DEGREE LINE DIAGRAM TO AGGREGATE SUPPLY AND DEMAND

The 45-degree line diagram is, in many respects, a curious model, since it compresses together aggregate supply and demand in a way that makes it difficult to disentangle changes in prices and output. By separating out the aggregate demand and supply schedules implicit in the 45-degree line model, we can lay the foundations for a more comprehensive framework (see also Ghatak *et al.*, 1992). Take aggregate supply first. We have seen that the model assumes that, up to the full-employment level of output, firms supply whatever output is demanded without any increase in the price level. In other words, up to full employment, output is wholly demand-determined and the aggregate supply schedule is horizontal (i.e. perfectly elastic) at the exogenously-given price level. Once the full-employment level of income is reached, by definition the economy cannot produce any more output. At full employment, therefore, the aggregate supply schedule becomes vertical. Combining the two ranges of the aggregate supply schedule gives a backward 'L' shape for the complete aggregate supply schedule (see Figure 1.4).

Now consider aggregate demand. We have seen that the 45-degree line model assumes that prices and wages are exogenously determined. In other words, the planned expenditure function is drawn for a given price level. In Figure 1.5a, let us assume that this price level is P_0. With the price level at P_0, the equilibrium level of output predicted by the model is Y_0. Now, suppose that the price level were not P_0 but some higher price level, P_1. Would there be any change in the expenditure function? To the extent that the expenditure function maps out planned purchases of real goods and services at different levels of real income, it is not clear that the expenditure function would be affected. But recall that one of the components of total expenditure, investment, is affected by changes in interest rates. All other things equal, a rise in the price level would tend to increase the demand for money and, with an unchanged money supply, interest rates would have to rise to maintain equilibrium in the 'money market'. Hence, following a rise in the price level, we might expect that interest rates would rise and that the expenditure schedule

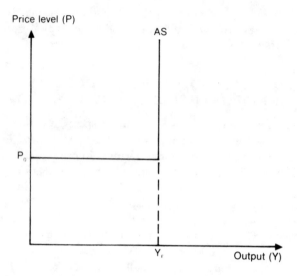

Figure 1.4 Aggregate supply and the 45-degree line diagram

(through the contraction of investment) would shift down slightly from E_0 to E_1.

In other words, at the higher price level P_1, the 45-degree line diagram suggests that the equilibrium level of income would be Y_1 rather than Y_0. By repeating the same exercise for different price levels, we can show that the aggregate demand schedule – which relates purchases of real goods and services to the price level – slopes downwards from left to right; that is, the higher the price level, the lower the aggregate demand for firms' output (see Figure 1.5b). Note that the aggregate demand curve in Figure 1.5b is drawn for particular values of the marginal propensities to consume and import and for given values for investment, the tax rate, government spending and exports. Any change that would shift the planned expenditure schedule in the 45-degree line model upwards (for a given price level) in Figure 1.5a will have the effect of moving the aggregate demand schedule to the right in Figure 1.5b.

Putting the aggregate supply and demand schedules together highlights the basic messages of the Keynesian approach to macroeconomic policy (see Figure 1.6). Because the aggregate supply schedule is perfectly elastic up to full employment, output in this range is demand-determined – 'equilibrium' could be consistent with 5

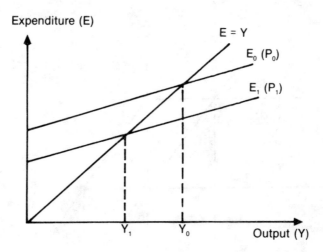

Figure 1.5a The effect of price changes on the 45-degree line diagram

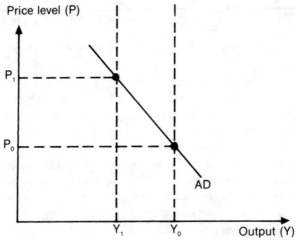

Figure 1.5b The derivation of aggregate demand

per cent, 10 per cent or even (as in the 1930s) 25 per cent unemployment. And if the private sector components of aggregate demand (notably, investment) are unstable, then output will tend to fluctuate over time. Thus, the role of government is to manage aggregate demand (stabilising it at AD_0) in order to neutralise

11

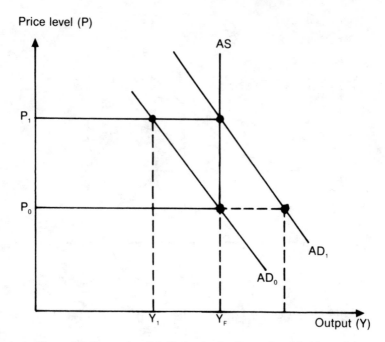

Figure 1.6 Demand-pull inflation in the Keynesian AS-AD model

changes in investment and keep the economy at full employment. Using this AS-AD version of the 45-degree line model also highlights the risks of allowing aggregate demand to get out of control. Suppose that aggregate demand were to increase from AD_0 to AD_1. The result would be demand-pull inflation, with prices (and wages) being dragged up from P_0 to P_1. As prices rise, the aggregate demand for real goods and services would be reduced back to Y_F by the rise in interest rates. Note that, because the price level has risen, the aggregate supply schedule shifts up in a ratchet-like fashion. If aggregate demand were now to fall to AD_0, rather than prices falling back to P_0, output would now fall to Y_1, with prices 'stuck' at their new, higher level, P_1.

We can also use the AS-AD diagram to incorporate cost-push inflation into the model. As we have seen, Keynesians advanced the concept of cost-push inflation during the 1960s in an attempt to explain the phenomenon of falling output and rising prices, arguing that monopolistic firms and trade unions would find it profitable to

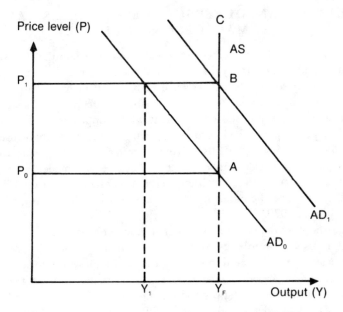

Figure 1.7 Cost-push inflation in the Keynesian AS-AD model

raise their prices even though this would reduce demand for their goods and services. The best-known examples of such exploitation of monopoly power were the two oil price rises in the 1970s, when a cartel of the world's main oil-producing nations first quadrupled (in 1973) and then doubled (in 1979) oil prices.

In Figure 1.7, cost-push inflation manifests itself as a vertical shift upwards in the aggregate supply schedule from P_0AC to P_1BC, which raises the price level from P_0 to P_1. With aggregate demand unchanged at AD_0, 'slumpflation' (inflation and falling output) would occur. To maintain full employment, the government would have to increase aggregate demand to AD_1, effectively 'validating' the price rises that firms and workers had awarded themselves by providing the extra demand to ensure that unemployment did not result. It was because many Keynesian economists feared that powerful corporations and unions might systematically exploit the government's commitment to full employment in this fashion – forcing through price and wage increases in the knowledge that the government would always 'bail them out' – that they argued so strongly for prices and incomes controls to check this tendency.

KEYNESIANISM VERSUS THE NEW CLASSICAL MACROECONOMICS

By translating the 45-degree line model into the familiar AS-AD framework, we can clarify the theoretical structures that underpinned the 'postwar consensus'. As we have seen, governments during this period used demand-side (i.e. demand-management) policy to achieve objectives for output and employment while supply-side policy (in the shape of prices and incomes controls) was increasingly used during the 1960s and 1970s to control inflation. By exposing the aggregate supply-side implicit in the 45-degree line model, we can also see the main differences between the Keynesian orthodoxy of the 1945–79 era and the monetarist/new classical theory that has guided policy since 1979.

Textbook accounts of the 'Keynesian-monetarist' controversy typically focus on the role of money in the economy. As we have seen, Keynesians regard fiscal policy as the more powerful means of influencing aggregate demand, arguing that the links between changes in the money supply and (via interest rates) investment and aggregate demand are weak and unstable. And monetarists, during the 1970s at least, certainly claimed that the impact of changes in the money supply on aggregate demand (and, in the longer term, inflation) was strong and predictable. But the fundamental difference between the two schools of thought related not to their views about the determination of aggregate demand, but to their theories of aggregate supply. It is developments in the theory of aggregate supply which have so radically reshaped the structure of macroeconomic policy in Britain, not arcane debate about whether fiscal or monetary policy has the greater influence on aggregate demand. Indeed, the use of monetary targets to control aggregate demand lasted only three years, yet the conduct of macroeconomic policy has continued to diverge steadily from the postwar consensus since their demise in 1982.

CLASSICAL ECONOMICS, MONETARISM AND THE NEW CLASSICAL MACROECONOMICS

The terms 'monetarism' and 'new classical' macroeconomics both apply to a school of thought which has a long tradition in mainstream economics. It goes back to the period before the Keynesian 'revolution' of the 1930s, when what Keynes dubbed the 'classical economics' held sway. The classical school held that market economies can be regarded as the sum of numerous, perfectly competitive markets which are co-ordinated by the 'invisible hand' of the price mechanism. Applying the principles of 'general equilibrium analysis' – the macroeconomic counterpart of the 'partial equilibrium analysis' used in microeconomics – classical economics argued that the economy would automatically tend to a full-employment equilibrium. While the prolonged recession of the interwar years eroded political faith in classical economics and promoted widespread acceptance of Keynes's ideas – which stressed the interdependence of markets at a highly aggregated level (e.g. the goods market and the money market) – academic interest in the classical tradition endured.

Its proponents staged their 'counter-revolution' during the early 1970s, when the apparent inability of Keynesian economists to provide convincing explanations for the acceleration in inflation and the inexorable rise in unemployment prompted academics and politicians to seek new answers. At first, most attention focused on the latter-day classical economists' proposition that governments should pay close attention to the growth of the money supply, hence the term 'monetarists' was coined to describe the growing band of economists rebelling against the Keynesian orthodoxy. But, as the differences between the two camps sharpened in the process of academic exchange, it became clear that the ideas being advanced were a modern version of the general equilibrium approach that had dominated the profession before 1930. Hence, the term 'new classical' macroeconomics has come to replace monetarism and is now generally used to refer to the theoretical framework that has underpinned macroeconomic policy since 1979.

THE NEW CLASSICAL LONG-RUN AGGREGATE SUPPLY SCHEDULE

Unlike the traditional Keynesian approach, which effectively ignores the complexities of the supply-side by assuming that the aggregate supply schedule is perfectly elastic up to full employment and perfectly inelastic thereafter, the new classical macroeconomics explicitly builds the labour market and the aggregate production function into the aggregate supply schedule. In deriving the new classical aggregate supply schedule, a useful point of departure is the short-run aggregate production function (APF). The theory assumes that, in the short run, all factors of production except labour are fixed;

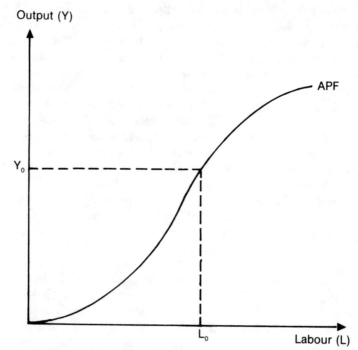

Figure 1.8 The relationship between output and employment

that is, there is a fixed quantity of land, capital and entrepreneurship. We also assume that the state of technology is given. On this basis, we can draw the short-run APF shown in Figure 1.8. It shows that the 'law of diminishing returns' applies. With all other factors of production fixed, as firms employ more and more labour, output rises, but at a diminishing rate. In other words, as firms expand employment, the marginal product of labour decreases.

How much labour will it be profitable for all firms to employ? To answer this question, we must move to the labour market itself. Basic microeconomics teaches us that profit-maximising firms hire labour up to the point where the last worker adds as much to total costs (i.e. the wage paid) as he or she adds to the firm's total revenue. The extra revenue generated is known as the 'marginal revenue product' (MRP). Assuming perfectly competitive goods markets, the MRP is simply the price of the product multiplied by marginal product (i.e. the increase in output contributed by the last worker). We know from our discussion of the shape of the short-run APF that marginal

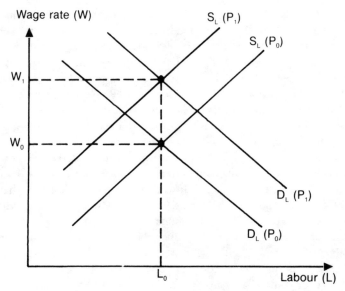

Figure 1.9 The operation of the labour market

product declines as employment increases. For a given set of product prices (with average price level, P_0), we can therefore derive the demand for labour schedule, $D_L(P_0)$, in Figure 1.9, which is simply the downward-sloping MRP schedule for the economy as a whole. It shows that as the (money) wage falls, firms in aggregate will find it profitable to employ more workers. What about the supply of labour? All other things equal (e.g. the price level, which here is P_0), the higher the wage, the greater the amount of labour offered. The labour supply schedule, $S_L(P_0)$ is thus upward-sloping in the normal way.

We can see that, assuming that the labour market is perfectly competitive, employment and wages will be determined in the normal way by the intersection of the labour supply and demand schedules. In other words, for a given set of product prices, a fixed stock of land and capital, and labour's relative preferences for work and leisure (which determine the shape and position of the supply schedule), we can work out the equilibrium wage rate, W_0, and level of employment, L_0. Moreover, by going back to the short-run APF in Figure 1.8, we can also read off the level of output consistent with equilibrium in the labour market.

To derive the long-run aggregate supply (LRAS) schedule, we must now examine what happens to employment and output if prices in

17

the economy rise. Let us suppose that the original price level is P_0 and that prices rise to P_1. How does this affect the labour market presented in Figure 1.9? First, the demand for labour schedule will shift to the right, from $D_L(P_0)$ to $D_L(P_1)$, because this is simply the marginal product of labour multiplied by the price level (i.e. the MRP). As the price level increases, so the MRP associated with each level of employment accordingly increases. But this is not the end of the story. Workers are primarily concerned about their 'real wages' (i.e. what their pay packets will buy in the shops), rather than money wages as such. The original labour supply schedule showed how workers would respond to changes in money wages at the original set of product prices, P_0. Provided that workers see the rise in prices that has taken place and the labour market functions smoothly, they will now demand accordingly higher money wages to supply any given amount of labour. In other words, when the price level rises to P_1, the labour supply schedule will also shift, this time to the left from $S_L(P_0)$ to $S_L(P_1)$. A moment's reflection will reveal that the size of the shifts in the labour demand and supply schedules is such that money wages must rise by the same amount as prices have risen, leaving employment and real wages (i.e. the purchasing power of money wages) unchanged.

We can now derive the LRAS schedule, which is shown in Figure 1.10. It shows that the level of output (Y_N) consistent with equilibrium in the labour market at P_0 is unchanged when prices rise to P_1 (note that Y_N is equal to Y_0 in Figure 1.8). The LRAS is therefore vertical. In the long run, an increase in aggregate demand will simply increase prices from P_0 to P_1 (and money wages from W_0 to W_1), without having any effect on either output or employment. In other words, provided that the product and labour markets are perfectly competitive and workers respond to the rise in prices by demanding compensating increases in money wages, in the long run changes in aggregate demand will have no lasting effect on the real economy.

THE NEW CLASSICAL SHORT-RUN AGGREGATE SUPPLY SCHEDULE

In the short run, however, workers may not react immediately to a rise in the price level by reducing the amount of labour supplied at any given wage rate. New classical economists argue that workers may temporarily suffer from 'money illusion', not realising that the price level has changed. Firms, in contrast, are unlikely to suffer

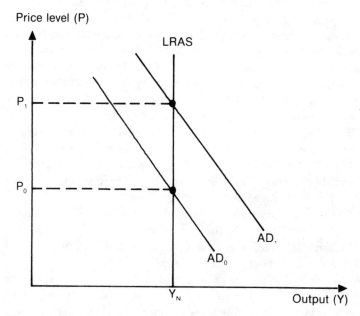

Figure 1.10 Changes in aggregate demand and the long-run aggregate supply
schedule

money illusion, adjusting their demand for labour by the full amount
of the price increase. The result is that, following a rise in the price
level, the supply of labour (relative to wages) is unchanged, while the
demand increases. Employment and output accordingly increase, so
that the short-run aggregate supply (SRAS) schedule is upward-
sloping.

This asymmetry in the reaction of workers and firms is worth
exploring further. As we have seen, firms profit-maximise by altering
employment until the money wage is equal to MRP. Each firm, in
turn, calculates its MRP by referring to the price of its own product,
which it knows day by day. Thus, a 10 per cent rise in the price level,
which increases all individual product prices by 10 per cent, increases
each firm's MRP at any given level of employment by 10 per cent.
Each firm can see the increase as soon as it takes place, and adjusts its
level of employment immediately. Now let us look at the situation
from the point of view of individual workers. We have seen that the
labour supply schedule (in terms of money wages) depends on the

19

price level. All other things equal, a 10 per cent rise in prices will cause workers to require 10 per cent higher money wages for any given number of hours' work. But the price with which workers are concerned is not the price of an individual product, but the price of all goods and services in the economy. This information is only available with a time lag and, as some prices (e.g. fruit and vegetables) fluctuate month by month due to seasonal effects, it may take some time before a clear change in average prices becomes apparent.

What this means is that while firms respond instantaneously to a change in average prices, it may be some time before workers fully appreciate what has happened to the price level. In the intervening period, they suffer money illusion, unable to appreciate that the value of money has changed and accordingly they sell their labour at too high or too low a money wage. Figure 1.11 illustrates the example of a price rise from P_0 to P_1. The demand for labour (MRP) schedule immediately shifts to the right to $D_L(P_1)$, for the reasons we have just explained. What about the labour supply schedule? In the short run, workers fail to appreciate that prices have risen. They therefore supply exactly the same amount of labour as before at any given money wage; i.e. the supply schedule remains at $S_L(P_0)$. The result is that, so long as money illusion persists, the effect of the rise in prices is to increase employment from L_0 to L_1 and, checking with our short-run APF, to increase output. (Notice that the initial excess demand for labour caused by the rightwards shift in the MRP schedule leads to a small rise in money wages to W', but one which still leaves real wages lower than before; i.e. W'/P_1 is lower than W_0/P_0.)

In the short run, therefore, while money illusion persists, workers are effectively 'tricked' into working harder for lower real wages. The SRAS is now upward-sloping (see Figure 1.12) along $SRAS(P_0)$. When prices rise from P_0 to P_1, output increases above its natural rate to Y_1. (Notice that because the process is completely symmetrical, when prices fall from P_0 to P_2, output falls below its natural rate to Y_2.) Gradually, however, workers come to realise that prices have changed, reducing the purchasing power of the wages they receive. Refer back to Figure 1.11. In the long run, the labour supply schedule moves to the left to $S_L(P_1)$, as workers demand compensating wage increases. Eventually money wages rise by the full amount of the price increase and the economy returns to its natural rate of output. In other words, in the long run, the economy always comes back to its LRAS.

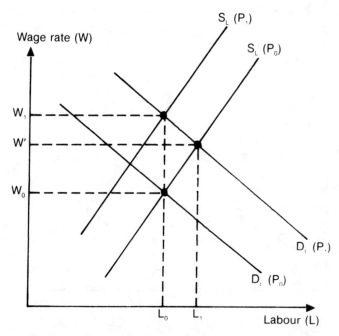

Figure 1.11 The effect of price changes on the labour market

ADAPTIVE EXPECTATIONS

The new classical theory of SRAS turns on the idea that workers' perceptions or 'expectations' of the price level may be incorrect in the short run, following a sudden change in prices. How do people form their expectations of the price level, or indeed, of any other economic variable? Some new classical economists argue that, in the main, expectations are formed 'adaptively' – that is, individuals adapt their earlier expectations in the light of experience. To take an example, suppose that inflation has always been 5 per cent. What would you expect inflation this year to be? Almost certainly, on the basis of past experience, you would expect inflation to remain at 5 per cent. Suppose, in fact, inflation picks up and you gradually come to realise that this year inflation is running at 7 per cent. Imagine it is now twelve months later. Once again, you are forming your expectation of inflation for the current year. What will it be? It is unlikely to be 5 per cent, since last year you underestimated the actual rate. The simplest solution would be to adapt your expectation upwards to 7 per cent.

21

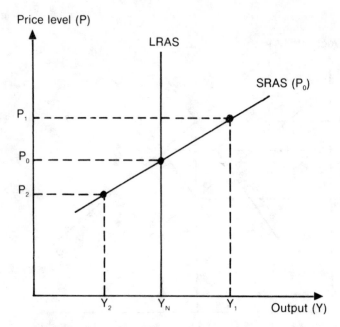

Figure 1.12 The short-run aggregate supply schedule

In other words, you would probably adapt your expectation in the light of your past error.

The key point about adaptive expectations is that people's expectations of, say, inflation always lags reality. When inflation is accelerating, people are always catching up with earlier mistakes caused by underestimating the actual rate. Conversely, when inflation is slowing down, people will tend to overestimate inflation in the short run.

RATIONAL EXPECTATIONS

During the 1970s, a group of new classical economists became increasingly dissatisfied with the notion of adaptive expectations. They argued that the concept of 'rationality' lies at the very heart of economics – that is, the principle that individuals act rationally to maximise utility, subject to the constraints they face. This principle, such economists felt, was being violated by the assumption that expectations are formed adaptively. It predicts, as we have seen, that during a period of accelerating inflation, people would persistently and systematically underestimate the actual rate of inflation, even though they would be continually punished (in the form of lower than expected real wages) for their errors. Surely such behaviour would be irrational? More fundamentally, it was claimed that adaptive expectations, since they are wholly backward-looking in the sense that they are formed only on the basis of past experience, downplay the critical role played by presently available information in formulating expectations.

To take an example, suppose that your weekly economics class is scheduled to start at 10.00, but your teacher or lecturer is habitually five minutes late. At the start of the academic year, you might not unreasonably expect her to turn up on time but, after a week or two of persistent lateness, you would probably adapt your expectation of the time at which the class would start to 10.05. This gradual modification of the time at which you think the class will begin is, of course, entirely consistent with the hypothesis of adaptive expectations. But now suppose that, one Saturday, you meet your teacher while shopping and she tells you that she will be out of town for the following week at a conference. Would you now expect the class to begin at 10.05? Of course not. In the light of this new information, your expectation is that the class will not run at all. You do not need to personally experience a 50-minute class without a teacher to modify your earlier, established expectation.

The essence of the so-called 'rational expectations' hypothesis is, therefore, that people will not just use past experience to form their expectations, but that they will additionally employ all available, relevant information in reaching a final judgement. The expectation is rational, because it is the outcome of rational, utility-maximising behaviour on the part of the individuals concerned. Moreover, if expectations are truly rational – in the sense that they are the best guesses people could make – then they should (on the average) be consistent with the predictions of macroeconomic theory based on the same set of information. This necessarily follows, since state-of-the-art theory should generate the most accurate forecasts in the long run. Note that the rational expectations hypothesis does not suggest that people actually use sophisticated models to produce their expectations. All it claims is that, on the average, people's subjective expectations will be broadly in line with forecasts based on the best economic theories. Nor does it imply that rational expectations are correct. Economic forecasters can, and do, make large errors, partly because their models do not perfectly describe the real world and

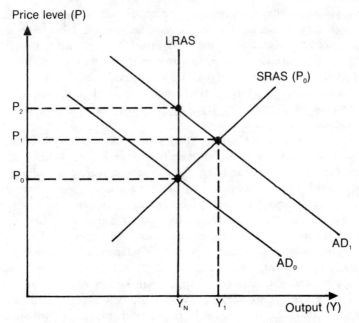

Figure 1.13 Rational expectations and the AS-AD model

partly because the information they have about present and future events is incomplete or inaccurate.

Nevertheless, the significance of the rational expectations hypothesis is enormous. Consider Figure 1.13. Suppose that after a period of stability, aggregate demand suddenly increases sharply from AD_0 to AD_1. If the government were to announce publicly that this expansion in aggregate demand were going to take place, what would happen? The answer is that people would immediately revise their expectations of the price level from P_0 to P_2, since this is the level to which the price will rise in the long run. By accordingly demanding higher wages to compensate, the result would be that the increase in aggregate demand would simply push the price level straight to P_2, with no effects on output or employment even in the short run.

ANTICIPATED VERSUS UNANTICIPATED CHANGES IN AGGREGATE DEMAND

What happens, however, if the increase in aggregate demand is not announced, so that people do not know that it will take place in advance? Since they believe that aggregate demand will continue to remain at its present value, the rational expectation (i.e. the one consistent with the predictions of Figure 1.13) is that the price level will stay at P_0. When the increase in aggregate demand actually takes place, it will therefore catch workers by surprise and the economy will slide up $SRAS(P_0)$ in the normal way to P_1, Y_1. To highlight the fact that the increase in aggregate demand must be unanticipated, new classical economists who subscribe to this view call the SRAS schedule the 'surprise function', since it only applies to circumstances in which people are surprised by an event which could not have been foreseen. One of the most important conclusions from the rational expectations hypothesis is that governments cannot systematically influence output and employment by changing aggregate demand. Even though the government may be able to surprise the private sector with sudden changes in demand-management policy to begin with, as people begin to work out what the government is doing, they will ignore its policy pronouncements and find other, more reliable ways to monitor the behaviour of the authorities. Once they are able to second-guess the government accurately, its policy actions will be rendered ineffective. This result is known as the 'policy ineffectiveness proposition'.

THE INEFFECTIVENESS OF DEMAND-MANAGEMENT POLICY

We can now summarise the implications of the new classical theory of aggregate supply for macroeconomic policymaking. As we have seen, if expectations are formed adaptively or – if expectations are formed rationally – increases in aggregate demand are unanticipated, then demand-management policy can cause money illusion and so temporary increases in output and employment.

Look at Figure 1.14, which shows the aggregate supply and demand diagram. Suppose that the government regards the level of unemployment consistent with the natural rate of output (Y_N) as unacceptably high, believing the 'full employment' level of output to be Y_F. The Keynesian approach suggests that to reduce unemployment, the government should increase aggregate demand (through a combination of spending increases, tax cuts and increases in the money supply) from AD_0 to AD_1. Because inflationary expectations are initially unchanged at P_0, the economy will slide up $SRAS(P_0)$, with workers increasing the quantity of labour supplied in response to the

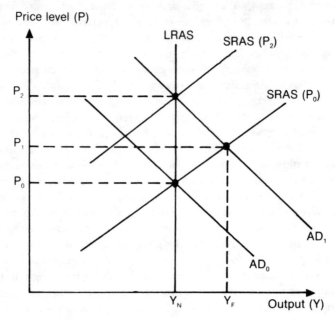

Figure 1.14 The effect of changes in aggregate demand in the AS-AD model

increase in money wages. As a result, output rises to Y_F while unemployment falls. The cost in terms of higher prices (which rise to P_1) appears relatively low. But as workers gradually come to realise that prices have risen, revising their expectations of price level upwards, they begin to withdraw their labour and to demand higher wages to compensate, causing the SRAS schedule to drift to the left to $SRAS(P_2)$, until long-run equilibrium is eventually re-established at P_2, Y_N. At this point, price expectations are again equal to the actual price level, P_2, and output and unemployment are back at their original values.

In other words, the adaptive-expectations version of the new classical theory of aggregate supply implies that, while attempts by the government to influence 'real' macroeconomic variables like output and employment may succeed in the short run (due to the existence of money illusion), such demand-management policies are ultimately ineffective, resulting only in inflation. This approach explains why, according to the new classical view, inflation rose steadily during the era of Keynesian demand-management policies between 1945 and 1979. Successive governments attempted to keep the level of output above its natural rate by repeatedly expanding aggregate demand each time the expansionary effects of the previous increase in aggregate demand began to wear off. Initially the strategy was successful, with money illusion persisting for a sufficient length of time to make the inflationary side-effects of pursuing full employment relatively modest. But as the private sector grew used to the new inflationary environment, two adverse developments combined to undermine demand-management policy. First, price expectations began to adjust more quickly, shortening the period during which the economy enjoyed an increase in output and employment following an expansion in aggregate demand. And second, as inflation became a daily fact of life, the nature of the private sector's expectations of the price level altered. Rather than expecting a particular price level, workers and employers gradually came to form their expectations in terms of the rate of change of the price level. For example, in a generally non-inflationary period, it would be reasonable for us to expect the price level to remain at its present value (say, P_0), only revising our expectation upwards to P_1 after the actual level had risen. But suppose, instead, that the price level has been rising for years at 5 per cent. Our expectation of the price level next year would not be P_0, but P_1 (P_0 x 105 per cent). Provided that the inflation rate were stable, money illusion would vanish even in the short run.

In other words, as inflation became embedded in the fabric of the economy, the private sector started to form its expectations in terms of inflation – a given rate of change of the price level – rather than the price level itself. Workers and employers increasingly built allowances for expected inflation into their wage agreements. The result was that, having created an inflationary psychology in the pursuit of its employment objectives, governments found that a steady expansion in aggregate demand was no longer enough to maintain full employment. To reap the output and employment benefits of an expansion in aggregate demand, governments had to accept not just an increase in prices, but an increase in inflation, so that actual inflation was always greater than expected inflation and money illusion was reintroduced into the economy.

This interpretation of the Keynesian years presents a stark picture of a fundamentally flawed macroeconomic policy which went increasing awry. It suggests, first and foremost, that governments cannot use systematic demand management to achieve objectives for output and employment in any lasting way. Second, it predicts that, if governments try to keep output above its natural rate, the result will be shorter and shorter periods of full employment and, in time, accelerating inflation. Sir Geoffrey Howe once likened this degenerative process to the experience of alcoholics. In the early years of addiction, drinkers enjoy the exhilarating effects of alcohol at fairly low levels of consumption. But, over time, they have to drink more and more, while the pleasurable effects steadily diminish.

AGGREGATE SUPPLY AND DEMAND VERSUS THE PHILLIPS CURVE

The role of inflationary expectations is conventionally analysed using the expectations-augmented Phillips Curve model. This framework is, however, just an alternative way of presenting the same relationships that we have been concerned with in our aggregate supply and demand model. Figure 1.15a reformulates the aggregate supply and demand diagram we have already used in terms of the rates of change of nominal magnitudes; that is, the vertical axis now measures the rate of change of prices (i.e. inflation) rather than the price level. The aggregate demand schedule, $\dot{A}D_0$, represents not a given level of aggregate demand, but a given rate of increase (e.g. 5 per cent per year). Similarly, the SRAS schedule, $SRAS(\dot{P}_0)$, is drawn for an expected rate of inflation, $\dot{P}_0$, rather than an expected price level. The horizontal axis remains in terms of the level of output and the LRAS is now the (natural) rate of output at which expected and actual inflation are equal.

Figure 1.15a shows that, if the government maintains a constant rate of increase of aggregate demand (AD_0), with inflationary expectations fully adjusted, the economy will settle at its natural rate of output (Y_N) and an inflation rate $\dot{P}_0$. If the government then increases the rate of growth of aggregate demand to AD_1, in the short run there is now money illusion, since the actual inflation rate, $\dot{P}_1$, jumps ahead of the expected rate, $\dot{P}_0$, and the economy slides up $SRAS(\dot{P}_0)$ to Y_1. But as inflationary expectations adjust and higher allowances for inflation are built into wage agreements, the SRAS schedule shifts steadily to $SRAS(\dot{P}_2)$, with the economy slowly returning to Y_N, but at a new, higher inflation rate, $\dot{P}_2$.

Figure 1.15b has the same vertical axis (the rate of inflation), but measures the rate of unemployment rather than output along the horizontal axis. As we have seen, all other things equal, the rate of unemployment is inversely related to the level of output – that is, an

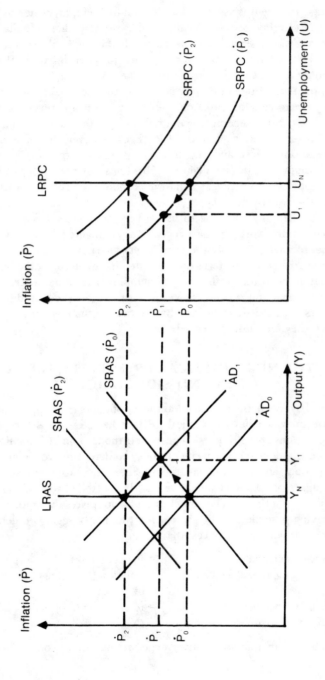

Figure 1.15a The dynamic version of the AS-AD model

Figure 1.15b The expectations-augmented Phillips Curve

increase in output is associated with a fall in unemployment and vice versa. Referring back to Figure 1.15a, we saw that initially the economy was in equilibrium at Y_N, $\dot{P}_0$. In Figure 1.15b, we can see that, with inflationary expectations equal to actual inflation, $\dot{P}_0$, the economy will be experiencing a rate of unemployment, U_N, consistent with the natural rate of output. Following the increase in the growth of aggregate demand, inflation rises to $\dot{P}_1$. With inflationary expectations fixed at P_0, unemployment falls to U_1 as the economy slides up its short-run Phillips Curve, $SRPC(\dot{P}_0)$. However, as inflationary expectations adjust and the inflation rate converges on its new equilibrium rate, $\dot{P}_2$ (see Figure 1.15b), the short-run Phillips Curve shifts upwards to $SRPC(\dot{P}_2)$ and the economy returns to its natural rate of unemployment, U_N.

It is, therefore, possible to use either the aggregate supply and demand framework or the expectations-augmented Phillips Curve model to analyse exactly the same phenomena. The only difference between the two is the focus on the trade-offs involved – inflation and output in the former, inflation and unemployment in the latter. In the chapters that follow, the choice of approach adopted by different authors is primarily influenced by the macroeconomic variable with which they are most concerned.

THE NEW CLASSICAL PRESCRIPTION FOR DEMAND-SIDE POLICY

As we have seen, the new classical theory of aggregate supply – at the centre of which lies the vertical LRAS schedule – turns the policy prescriptions of the Keynesian postwar orthodoxy on its head. Rather than using demand-management policy to determine real objectives like output and unemployment, this alternative approach suggests that aggregate demand should be strictly controlled with the aim of eliminating inflation. The new classical theory places the emphasis on achieving a stable rate of growth for (nominal) aggregate demand consistent with stable prices; that is,

aggregate demand	= the price level (P) x output (Y)
growth of aggregate demand	= inflation (P) x rate of growth of output (Y)
non-inflationary growth rate of aggregate demand in the long-run	= rate of growth of natural output (Y_N)

To the extent that inflationary expectations can be conditioned by current events, as well as by the past behaviour of inflation, new classical economists also argue the need for clear policy 'rules'. If governments commit themselves to pursuing a course of action which guarantees a non-inflationary rate of growth of aggregate demand, the argument runs, the costs of securing and maintaining price stability in terms of unemployment will be reduced. If the private sector is convinced that the government will stick to a non-inflationary demand-management policy (i.e. if it regards the government's policy announcements as 'credible'), then even if inflation temporarily jumps (e.g. due to a rise in oil prices or an unexpected increase in consumer spending), inflationary expectations and so wage increases will be unaffected, allowing prices to restabilise without causing a temporary rise in unemployment.

In the 1970s, new classical economists believed that the link between monetary growth and the growth of aggregate demand was very strong. The nature of this relationship is summarised in the famous quantity theory equation:

money supply x velocity of   = price level (P) x output (Y)
circulation

where P x Y = aggregate demand. Recasting this simple relationship in terms of rates of change and rearranging it slightly gives us:

rate of growth of money   = inflation plus rate of growth of
                                   output minus rate of change of
                                   velocity of circulation

non-inflationary rate of growth   = rate of growth of natural output
of money supply in the long run (Y_N) minus rate of change of
                                   velocity of circulation

Empirical studies in the 1970s indicated that the velocity of circulation (the average number of times each pound changes hands each year) was growing at a steady rate each year, suggesting that to ensure stable prices, the money supply should be allowed to grow somewhat slower than the underlying rate of growth of natural output. Encouraged by such findings, the Thatcher government laid great stress on the importance of achieving preannounced monetary targets in the period 1979–82. However, the stability exhibited by the velocity of circulation in the 1970s broke down in the early 1980s. The deregulation of the banking system in Britain, which the government had introduced as part of its supply-side programme, caused enormous upheavals in the financial markets, as banks began to compete with other financial institutions (notably building societies) by offering a range of new products and services. As bank deposits (which were included in the official definition of the money supply) began to acquire many of the characteristics of building society deposits (which were excluded), the proportion of total bank deposits held primarily for savings, rather than transactions, purposes rose sharply. The velocity of circulation (which reflects the link between money and spending) accordingly fell sharply, reversing the steady upward trend of the 1970s. For a period, demand-management policy was in disarray.

EXCHANGE RATE TARGETS VERSUS MONETARY TARGETS

During the mid-1980s, the government began to search for an alternative 'rule' to guide domestic demand-management policy and eventually settled on the exchange rate. Between 1985 and 1990, the government pegged the exchange rate at an adjustable, undisclosed target value, finally entering the EMS in October 1990 at a central rate of DM2.95. Under circumstances in which sterling is pegged against the currency of a country (e.g. Germany) which is pursuing a firm, anti-inflationary policy, an exchange rate target performs the same basic function as (assuming a predictable velocity of circulation) a monetary target. To illustrate the links between exchange rate management and domestic monetary policy, consider the familiar exchange rate diagram in Figure 1.16, which shows the supply of, and demand for, sterling against the deutschmark. Suppose that, as is presently the case, the British government pegs its exchange rate at a central target rate of £1 = DM2.95 ±6 per cent. This commitment obliges the Bank of England to ensure that sterling rises to no more than £1 = DM3.13 (DM2.95 x 106 per cent) and falls to no less than £1 = DM2.77 (DM2.95 x 94 per cent). Maintaining the pound within such narrow bands requires both 'open-market operations' in the foreign exchange market – official sales and purchases of sterling by the Bank of England – and adjustments in interest rates as necessary.

Provided that the market rate remains within its target band of DM2.77–3.13, such exchange rate intervention is unnecessary. But suppose, for the purpose of illustration, that the money supply in

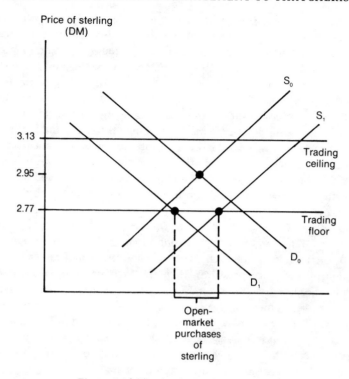

Figure 1.16 The foreign exchange market

Germany is constant, while in Britain the money supply begins to increase. All other things equal, an increase in the British money supply tends to reduce interest rates and boost aggregate demand – including the demand for imports. As a result, the demand for sterling (e.g. from Germans wanting to deposit money with British banks) falls, while the supply of sterling (e.g. from British residents wanting to switch their sterling into deutschmark deposits with German banks or buy imports from Germany) increases. In terms of Figure 1.16, these developments manifest themselves as a leftward shift in the demand (from D_0 to D_1) for, and a rightward shift in the supply (from S_0 to S_1) of, sterling, pushing the pound towards the bottom of its target band against the deutschmark.

Once sterling falls to DM2.77, the Bank of England is required to undertake open-market purchases of sterling, using deutschmarks from its foreign exchange reserves to buy up the excess supply of sterling, while at the same time raising interest rates to boost the demand for sterling. What does this mean for monetary policy in Britain? By maintaining sterling within such narrow target bands against the deutschmark, Britain is forced to adopt the same monetary policy as Germany. This is because the Bank of England's sales of its deutschmark reserves reduce the British money supply (in the same way as open-market sales of government bonds), while the increase in interest rates slows the underlying rate at which the British money supply is growing, by choking off the demand for bank lending. Assuming that Germany continues with an unchanged monetary policy throughout, the contractionary pressure on the British money supply persists until monetary policy – and so the growth of aggregate demand – in Britain comes into line with that in Germany.

In other words, if the British government adheres to a firm exchange rate target against a non-inflationary partner country (refusing to devalue the exchange rate when the pound comes under sustained downward pressure), then the exchange rate target performs the same basic function as a monetary target – that is, it sets demand management on a medium-term, non-inflationary path (see Healey, 1992b). Like monetary targets, exchange rate targets can also help to condition inflationary expectations, by making it clear to the private sector that the government is committed to ensuring a non-inflationary rate of growth of aggregate demand.

THE NEW CLASSICAL LONG-RUN AGGREGATE SUPPLY SCHEDULE REVISITED

As we have seen, new classical economists argue:

1 that the economy automatically tends to a natural rate of output and unemployment, with the speed of adjustment depending on how quickly inflationary expectations react to changes in the actual rate of inflation; and
2 that these natural rates are independent of the level of aggregate demand and hence of government's demand-management policy.

This leaves unanswered two fundamental questions. First, what determines the natural rate of output (and the natural rate of unemployment)? And second, if the government cannot influence these real variables through demand-management policy, how can it achieve its policy objectives for output and unemployment?

We have already outlined the derivation of the LRAS schedule, which identifies the natural rate of output. Figure 1.17c shows an LRAS schedule, $LRAS_0$, which is vertical at Y_0. Recall that to derive this schedule, we need first to establish the equilibrium rate of employment (from which we can, if we choose, work out the natural rate of unemployment) in the labour market (see Figure 1.17a) and then read off from the short-run APF the level of output consistent with this amount of employment (see Figure 1.17b).

What does economic growth mean in terms of Figure 1.17c? Surely what it means is a rightward shift in the LRAS – for example, from $LRAS_0$ to $LRAS_1$. At $LRAS_1$, the economy can enjoy more goods and services at any given price level, P. How could such an increase in the underlying or long-run level of output come about? First, consider the labour market in Figure 1.17a. If the labour supply were to increase – either because there was an increase in the number of workers available for employment or because the existing workforce offered more hours' labour at any given money wage – shifting the supply schedule to the right, then the level of output consistent with equilibrium in the labour market would increase from Y_0 to Y_1, shifting the LRAS schedule from $LRAS_0$ to $LRAS_1$.

Second, look at Figure 1.17b. If the short-run APF were to shift upwards from APF_0 to APF_1, this would mean that at every level of employment, a greater amount of output could be produced than before. With equilibrium employment unchanged at L_0, the level of output would increase, as before, from Y_0 to Y_1. The short-run APF could shift upwards if:

1 the productivity of labour were to rise, because the 'quality' of labour increased through better training and education (note that this might also increase the marginal productivity of labour, shifting the MRP – that is, the labour demand curve – to the right, but for simplicity we shall ignore this possibility in what follows);
2 the capital stock were to rise, allowing each employee to produce more output for a given number of hours worked; or
3 technological advances were to improve the 'quality' of the capital stock, enabling each worker to produce more output from a given amount of machinery.

To summarise, the natural level of output, Y_N, will increase if the labour supply schedule shifts to the right, or if the APF function shifts upwards. There is, however, a fundamental difference between these two routes to higher output. The gains that can be achieved from the former are necessarily finite (i.e. they are inherently 'exhaustible').

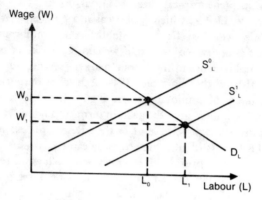

Figure 1.17a The labour market

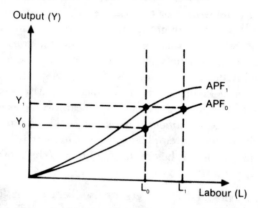

Figure 1.17b The short-run aggregate production function

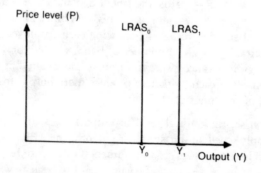

Figure 1.17c The long-run aggregate supply schedule

While the economy can produce more output by using its existing labour force more intensively – for example, by people working longer hours, by fewer mothers staying home to look after children, by old people retiring later, etc. – we cannot achieve higher and higher output, year after year, in this way. At some point, when the entire adult population is fully employed, the rightwards shift in the labour supply schedule must come to a halt. Nevertheless, in many capitalist economies, in which a very high proportion of adults are either not working (e.g. students, stay-at-home mothers, retired people, etc.), working part-time or unemployed through choice, the short-run gains in output may be substantial and continue to accrue for an extended period.

In contrast, the increases in output that can be obtained by shifts in the APF function – whether via training and education to improve the workforce, investment in plant and equipment or research and development (R&D) into new processes – can continue indefinitely over time (i.e. they are 'sustainable'). Indeed, a moment's reflection should confirm that it is shifts in the APF function which are the source of enduring economic growth. During the last century, output has grown at a year-on-year rate of 2 to 3 per cent. Over this time, the average number of hours worked each week has fallen steadily, while more and more young people have stayed on in school and older workers have retired earlier. Although there have been trends in the opposite direction, most notably an increase in the proportion of married women working, on balance the labour supply schedule has almost certainly shifted leftwards – rather than rightwards – over the last one hundred years. Hence, the source of the increase in our living standards has been better training and education, capital investment and R&D, rather than ever-harder work.

THE NEW CLASSICAL PRESCRIPTION FOR SUPPLY-SIDE POLICY

Our review of the sources of economic growth highlight the key areas new classical economists regard as essential if the performance of the supply-side is to be improved. They argue that government policy should concentrate on increasing the supply of, and demand for, labour (which increases the equilibrium level of employment), while at the same time promoting R&D, investment in physical and human capital, and encouraging the more efficient allocation of resources.

New classical economists assign primary importance to reducing the disincentive effects of taxation, claiming that penal rates of tax reduce both the supply of labour (by reducing the amount that workers actually take home at any given wage rate) and the demand for labour (by inflating the amount over and above the actual wage – for example, through the addition of social security contributions – that firms have to pay to employ workers). It is also argued that high rates of corporation and capital gains tax blunt the incentive to invest in R&D, new plant and equipment and training and education (see Chapter 8). For this reason, new classical economists argue that reducing marginal tax rates must lie at the heart of a successful supply-side strategy.

More generally, new classical economists claim that government intervention and bureaucratic red-tape obstruct the smooth operation of the 'invisible hand' and thereby prevent the optimal allocation of resources. The spread of nationalisation during the 'Keynesian' era and the growth of legally protected trade unions are normally identified as key causes. Accordingly, 'rolling back the frontiers of the state', by the privatisation of nationalised industries, the contracting-out of public services, and the deregulation of the private sector – including the financial system, the labour market and the goods market – are also keys to a revitalised supply-side.

CONCLUSIONS

This chapter has examined the theoretical foundations of the Keynesian demand-management policies which characterised the period 1945–79. We have seen how the essentials of this approach to macroeconomic policymaking are contained within the 45-degree line diagram. By deriving the aggregate supply and demand schedules implicit in this simple model, we have highlighted the weaknesses identified by the new classical economists and shown that the fundamental difference between the two schools of thought lies less in their theories of aggregate demand (i.e. whether fiscal or monetary policy has the greater affect on aggregate demand) and more in their theories of aggregate supply. If the aggregate supply curve is perfectly elastic and wages and prices set in monopolistic markets, as Keynesians traditionally argued, then governments should use fiscal and monetary policy to fine-tune aggregate demand to achieve full employment, while using prices and incomes policies to suppress inflation at source. If, on the other hand, the aggregate supply schedule is perfectly inelastic in the long run, sloping upwards in the short run only as a result of money illusion as the new classical economists claim, then governments should set demand-management policy on a non-inflationary path and use supply-side policies to accelerate economic growth and reduce the natural rate of unemployment.

Since 1979, the traditional Keynesian approach to macroeconomic policy has fallen from political favour, to be replaced by policies in the new classical mould. While early attempts to guide demand-management policy by the use of monetary targets proved unsuccessful, membership of the EMS has provided an alternative, external rule by which governments will continue to be bound into the 1990s. New classical supply-side policies have left a similarly dramatic mark on the British economy. Successive waves of privatisation, deregulation and market liberalisation have altered the face of supply-side policy in Britain. It is now time to examine the effects of this sea-change in economic policy on the performance of the British economy. It is to this question that we now turn in Chapters 2 to 13.

Part I

COMPETING PERSPECTIVES ON THE MACROECONOMY

2

THE ECONOMY IN THE 1980s

A review of the decade

Andrew Britton

INTRODUCTION

Four times a year, we publish in the *National Institute Economic Review* a brief account of recent economic developments, together with our forecasts for a few years ahead. To do this, we use a mathematical model of the economy, developed at the National Institute as part of a continuing research programme designed to explain how the economy works. Looking back over a decade of Conservative government macroeconomic policy, it is interesting to stand back from the detail of events month by month and year by year and to take stock of how the British economy is performing in the longer term. In this chapter, I use the same methods of explanation and more or less the same format as we use in our quarterly analysis, but I shall try to paint on a much broader canvas.

In the *Review*, we always try to keep the description and explanation of events separate from assessment and policy recommendations. I shall do the same here. The sections that follow are intended as a detached commentary on the figures in the tables that go with them. What might be called the 'editorial matter' (which would be called an 'appraisal' in the *Review*), comes separately at the end of the chapter.

TOTAL OUTPUT AND EXPENDITURE

Table 2.1 illustrates the performance of the British economy over the 1980s. The average growth rate of gross domestic product (GDP) for the decade as a whole was a little over 2 per cent a year. This was about the same as the growth rate in the 1970s and well below the rates achieved in earlier postwar years. The decade began with a severe recession, in which the economy suffered two years of falling

Table 2.1 Total output and expenditure at constant prices (£bn, 1985 prices)

Year	Income (GDP)[1]	Consumer spending	Government spending[2]	Investment	Exports	Imports
1979	92.9	195	70	56	89	84
1980	90.3	195	71	53	89	81
1981	89.0	195	71	48	88	79
1982	90.1	197	72	51	89	83
1983	94.0	205	73	53	91	88
1984	96.6	209	74	58	97	97
1985	100.0	217	74	60	103	99
1986	103.0	229	75	61	107	106
1987	108.1	241	76	67	112	114
1988	113.1	258	77	76	113	128
1989	115.7	268	77	79	119	140
1990	116.4	273	79	80	123	139
1991	113.9	271	81	71	125	135

Growth rates (%)

Year	Income (GDP)[1]	Consumer spending	Government spending[2]	Investment	Exports	Imports
1980	−2.8	0.1	1.6	−5.4	0.0	−3.4
1981	−1.4	0.1	0.3	−9.6	−0.7	−2.8
1982	2.1	1.0	0.8	5.4	0.8	4.9
1983	3.4	4.3	2.0	5.0	2.2	6.5
1984	2.7	1.8	1.0	8.6	6.5	9.8
1985	3.6	3.7	0.0	3.9	5.9	2.5
1986	3.0	5.6	2.1	1.9	4.2	6.7
1987	5.0	5.4	1.2	8.8	5.1	7.6
1988	4.7	6.9	0.4	13.1	0.7	12.2
1989	2.3	3.8	0.3	4.9	5.1	9.7
1990	0.6	1.7	2.6	1.3	3.4	−0.7
1991	−2.1	−0.7	2.5	−11.3	1.6	−2.9

Source: National Institute Economic Review
Notes: [1] 1985 = 100
[2] current spending

output between 1979 and 1981. This was followed by a long recovery in the middle years of the decade, building up to the boom of 1987–9, before the economy was once again struck by recession in 1990–2.

By definition, the total volume of output is equal to the total of the expenditure that paid for it. Spending by consumers is the largest component and it was the buoyancy of consumer demand that led the recovery and fuelled the subsequent boom. Public spending on goods and services was deliberately held back throughout most of the decade, although there was no year in which it actually fell. It grew fairly steadily at about 1 per cent a year. Investment fell sharply in the

1979–81 recession, because firms revised down the level of output they expected to produce in the future, or simply because firms were short of finance, if not actually going out of business. It recovered well in the mid-1980s (the timing being distorted a little by the reform of company taxation in 1986); even so, the stock of capital equipment remained low, especially in manufacturing industry. New technology, or forced closures, resulted in an exceptionally high rate of scrapping. By the end of the decade, investment growth was slowing and turned strongly negative during the recession of 1990–2.

At the beginning of the decade, the volume of exports was larger than the volume of imports (at 1985 prices). For a few years the balance improved, partly because output of oil in the North Sea was still increasing. (The sharp rise of imports in 1984 resulted from the coal miners' strike.) In the later years of the decade, as output in this country approached the limits of capacity, imports raced ahead. Most of the time, however, exports held up well, keeping their share of world markets better than they had done in any comparable postwar period. By the end of the decade, output growth had slowed down again, turning negative in 1990–1. As the British economy had been growing faster than the economies of most other advanced industrial countries, it suffered from 'overheating' and a growing deficit on the balance of payments. Against this background, the recession of 1990–2 – which can be seen as a period of 'cooling off' – was inevitable.

PERSONAL INCOME AND EXPENDITURE

To explain the path of consumer spending during the 1980s, the first step is to explain the growth of personal sector incomes (see Table 2.2). The largest component consists of wages and salaries, which rose at a fairly steady pace for most of the decade after their big step up in 1980. In the period 1987–9, there was a dramatic, if temporary, acceleration, due mainly to the buoyancy of employment and to overtime working during the boom. Not surprisingly, this growth slowed sharply in 1990–2, as the economy moved into recession.

'Government Grants' to the personal sector consist largely of national insurance benefits and income support. Payments of grants rose very fast between 1979 and 1982 because unemployment more than doubled at that time. During the late 1980s, grants hardly rose at all, as unemployment was falling and the uprating of benefits was meagre. As the decade ended, however, 'Government Grants' again jumped as recession began to bite. 'Other Personal Incomes' includes

Table 2.2 Personal income and expenditure (£bn)

Year	Wages & salaries	Gov'ment grants	Other pers. income	Pers. disp. income (current prices)	(1985 prices)	Savings ratio (%)
1979	98	21	34	136	222	12.2
1980	117	26	38	161	226	13.1
1981	125	31	43	177	224	12.5
1982	133	37	48	192	223	11.4
1983	142	40	52	206	228	9.8
1984	152	43	57	221	233	10.5
1985	165	47	61	240	240	9.8
1986	179	51	67	259	248	8.5
1987	194	53	74	279	257	6.9
1988	215	54	86	307	270	5.4
1989	237	56	95	334	279	7.1
1990	276	62	114	385	301	9.2
Growth Rates (%)						
1980	18.4	22.0	14.5	18.1	1.6	
1981	7.4	22.4	10.6	10.3	–0.8	
1982	6.5	17.1	12.0	8.3	–0.4	
1983	6.8	8.9	9.2	7.3	2.3	
1984	6.7	8.0	8.7	7.4	2.2	
1985	8.7	8.7	8.4	8.2	2.8	
1986	8.4	8.6	9.8	7.6	3.7	
1987	8.4	3.4	10.2	7.3	3.6	
1988	10.9	3.1	15.5	10.1	4.9	
1989	10.3	2.9	10.3	8.8	3.3	
1990	16.4	10.7	20.0	15.3	7.8	

Source: National Institute Economic Review

several categories which increased very fast in the 1980s. Self-employment became much more widespread: perhaps a sign of the 'enterprise culture'. Dividend receipts rose fast as companies prospered in the later years of the decade. On the other hand, interest receipts were offset by growing interest payments, as households borrowed more heavily from banks and building societies.

'Personal Disposable Income' (i.e. the post-tax income of the personal sector, after taking into account grants) rose at around 7 to 8 per cent a year for most of the decade – faster at the beginning and again at the end. But in real terms (that is, after deducting the rate of price inflation), the story is different, with a strong acceleration in the second half of the 1980s. In 1988, the real rate of increase peaked at 5 per cent, far above the long-term trend. This goes a long way to account for the growth of consumer spending during the 1987–9 boom, but it is not the whole explanation.

One of the most striking changes in behaviour during the 1980s was the fall in the ratio of savings to personal income (the 'Savings Ratio'), from 13.1 per cent in 1980 down to 5.4 per cent in 1988. Several reasons for this can be suggested (Pearce, 1991). Savings are measured net of borrowing and the deregulation of banks and building societies and the ending of restrictions on hire purchase terms made it easier for households to borrow. The rise in the value of household wealth, as a result of much higher house prices, may have persuaded many consumers that they could afford to borrow more or to save less. The fact that inflation was lower may also have reduced savings, because some part of savings normally goes just to make good the loss in the real value of assets with fixed money values, like bank and building society deposits.

Towards the end of the decade, the consumer boom got out of hand and interest rates were raised abruptly between 1988 and 1990 in an attempt to arrest it (O'Doherty and Flegg, 1991). The effect of tighter monetary policy became evident during 1989, with the growth of spending slowing sharply. Reflecting this slowdown was a rapid recovery in the savings ratio. Many of the forces that contributed to its decline during the mid-1980s reversed as the decade ended: house prices peaked in 1988, falling sharply thereafter (see also Chapter 13); inflation temporarily soared, exceeding 10 per cent in 1990, thereby reducing the real value of household wealth and encouraging extra saving; finally, it may also be that the increase in unemployment, which took place after 1989, also curbed both households' appetite for taking on debt and the willingness of institutional lenders to extend credit to individuals who risked being made redundant.

OUTPUT AND EMPLOYMENT

Until 1986, oil output in the North Sea was rising strongly and making a very useful contribution to the British economy, especially by improving the balance of payments and increasing government revenue. In the last few years, oil output has levelled off, actually falling in 1988 and 1989 because of production difficulties – in particular the Piper Alpha disaster. The level of oil production recovered somewhat in the early 1990s, but the long-term outlook is for a slow decline as reserves become exhausted.

The composition of non-oil output changed significantly over the 1980s. The share of manufacturing declined, whilst that of the non-manufacturing private sector, especially private sector services, increased. Manufacturing industry was hit particularly hard by the recession at the beginning of the decade and did not regain its 1979 level of output until 1987. Some parts of the country, especially the West and East Midlands which were particularly dependent on manufacturing, suffered a decline relative to the more prosperous South and South-East (see Chapter 13). The activities which have shown most growth tend to be those that use new technology, for example, services such as banking and telecommunications. Services that are mainly provided by the public sector, however, like health and education, have grown at a much slower pace.

Total employment was about the same at the beginning and end of the decade. Within the total, however, there were important changes: increases in the numbers working part-time, for example; increases in the numbers retiring early; and a fall in the ratio of men to women in the labour force. Productivity, or output per head, rose very fast in the latter half of the decade and seemed to be making good some of the ground lost in the 1970s relative to levels of productivity in the rest of Europe or in America. This was best documented in the case of manufacturing industry, where employment fell especially fast in the recession, and hardly rose at all even in the 1988 boom (see Chapter 6).

It is difficult to be sure how fundamental a change these improvements in productivity involved. There have been reorganisations and rationalisations in many industries which were long overdue, putting an end to overmanning and outdated working practices. New technology also played an important part, although Britain continues to fall behind in many areas of industrial research and development (R&D). But a continuing concern must be the quantity and the quality of vocational training in this country: for example, the number of apprentices in engineering have actually declined (Ashton *et al.*, 1989). Skill shortages may limit production in the future and hold back the further growth of productivity.

Part of the productivity increase in the 1980s consisted of laying off workers who were underemployed. This tougher attitude to manning levels has probably raised the national level of unemployment

Table 2.3 Output and employment

	Oil output	Non-oil output	(1985 = 100) Manu- facturing output	Total employ- ment	Employ- ment in manu- facturing	Unem- ployment (millions)
1979	65	94.1	105.9	107.9	134.8	1.1
1980	66	91.3	96.7	106.0	127.0	1.4
1981	73	89.7	90.9	101.5	115.4	2.2
1982	83	91.3	91.1	99.1	108.4	2.5
1983	91	94.1	93.7	98.0	102.7	2.8
1984	97	96.6	97.6	98.9	100.8	2.9
1985	100	100	100	100	100	3.0
1986	101	103.0	101.0	100.4	97.5	3.1
1987	99	108.5	106.6	102.2	96.5	2.8
1988	90	114.2	114.0	105.1	97.8	2.3
1989	75	117.6	118.7	106.6	97.0	1.8
1990	73	119.2	118.4	106.7	96.0	1.7
1991	75	116.1	112.5	103.6	91.7	2.4
Growth rates (%)						
1980	1.4	–3.0	–8.8	–1.6	–5.8	
1981	10.3	–1.7	–6.0	–4.2	–9.1	
1982	13.9	1.6	0.2	–2.3	–6.1	
1983	9.5	3.1	2.9	–1.1	–5.2	
1984	6.9	2.5	4.2	0.9	–1.9	
1985	2.7	3.7	2.5	1.1	–0.8	
1986	1.2	3.1	1.0	0.4	–2.5	
1987	–2.6	5.3	5.6	1.8	–1.0	
1988	–8.7	5.2	6.9	2.7	1.2	
1989	–17.1	3.0	4.1	1.2	–0.5	
1990	–2.7	1.4	–0.3	0.1	–1.0	
1991	2.7	–2.6	–5.0	–2.9	–4.5	

Source: National Institute Economic Review

permanently. At the end of the decade and despite the boom, the number of unemployed was still much higher than it was in 1979. A particular problem arose with the longer-term unemployed, who lost their jobs in the 1979–81 recession, but whose experience of unemployment made firms less likely to recruit them. As output growth has slumped in the early 1990s, unemployment has inevitably begun to rise once again, further worsening the position of the long-term unemployed, many of whom are in danger of joining a new, social 'underclass'.

Table 2.4 Wages and prices (% increase)

	Average earnings	Import prices	Export prices	Wholesale prices	Retail prices
1979	15.6	8.9	11.4	12.0	13.4
1980	20.4	10.0	14.4	15.4	18.0
1981	12.1	8.0	8.5	7.4	11.9
1982	9.0	6.9	6.9	6.9	8.6
1983	7.9	7.4	7.8	5.4	4.6
1984	5.7	8.8	7.7	5.1	5.0
1985	7.5	4.0	5.2	5.7	6.0
1986	8.0	−4.0	−7.9	4.1	3.5
1987	6.8	2.7	3.5	4.4	4.1
1988	8.0	−0.7	0.6	4.8	4.9
1989	9.0	5.4	8.5	5.5	7.7
1990	11.3	2.1	n/a	6.1	9.5

Source: National Institute Economic Review

WAGES AND PRICES

The average rate of inflation in the 1980s was about 7.5 per cent, compared with 12.5 per cent in the 1970s. The rate fell as low as 3.5 per cent in 1986. At that point it seemed as if the problem of inflation had been virtually overcome, but the rate rose again in the boom at the end of the decade, touching over 10 per cent at its peak in October 1990 (see especially Chapter 7).

Inflation had earlier reached 18 per cent in 1980, partly because incomes policy, which had held back both wages and prices in the late 1970s, broke down and partly because the pressure of demand was high and some kinds of goods and labour were in short supply. World prices were accelerating, following the oil price increase of 1979, so that import prices were rising relatively fast, even though the exchange rate was appreciating. Moreover, an increase in taxes on expenditure (Value Added Tax) and cuts in government subsidies added to prices at a time when inflation was already speeding up.

After 1980, the reduction in inflation came sooner than was expected. The depth of the recession seems to be the main explanation, slowing down the growth of costs and causing firms to cut their profit margins. From 1983 to 1988, the rate of inflation stayed in the range 3.5–6 per cent, the variation year to year being explained partly by exchange rate changes and partly by the fall in world oil prices in 1986.

Initially the boom of 1988 seemed to have little effect on prices, perhaps because its effect was masked by a rise in the exchange rate and a surge in productivity growth (which suppressed the impact of rapid wage inflation on retail prices). Only in 1989 did inflation again become a major problem and even then it was sometimes argued that the retail price index (RPI) exaggerated its scale. (The housing component of the RPI shows a large but temporary increase every time interest rates are raised.) However, by 1990 the full extent of the inflationary surge was evident.

From 1982 to 1989, the growth of average earnings was steady at around 7 to 9 per cent a year (the figure for 1984 being depressed by the miners' strike). It was almost as if a constant 'going rate' of increase had been established which responded very little to variation in the rate of inflation or the state of the labour market. These steady and rather rapid increases did not raise unit costs as much as might have been expected because, as we have seen, productivity was accelerating in most sectors. Right at the end of the decade there are signs of an acceleration in earnings, as tends to happen in the late stages of a boom. Earnings growth eventually peaked in 1990 at over 12 per cent.

Historically, it has been very difficult to forecast the rate of inflation more than a year ahead at the most. Much depends on the way in which the exchange rate behaves. But now that Britain has joined the European Monetary System (EMS) as a full member (as of October 1990), thereby relinquishing control of demand-management policy to the German Bundesbank (see Chapters 1 and 7), our model leads us to predict a rate of inflation in this country close to the European average, which could be as low as 2 per cent a year by the mid-1990s.

FINANCIAL INDICATORS

The path actually followed by the exchange rate over the 1980s was erratic and unpredictable. In 1979 and 1980 it rose sharply, despite the high rate of inflation, perhaps because monetary policy was being tightened, and perhaps because the increase in the value of North Sea oil production was improving the outlook for the balance of payments.

Between 1981 and 1987 (when the government first attempted to 'peg' the exchange rate against the deutschmark – see Chapter 7), the trend of the exchange rate was downwards, but there was never a

Table 2.5 Financial indicators

	Interest rates (%)	Change in the exchange rate (%)	Balance of payments on current account (£ bn)	Public sector borrowing requirement (£ bn)
1979	13.4	7.2	-0.6	12.7
1980	15.7	10.1	2.8	11.8
1981	13.5	-1.2	6.6	10.6
1982	12.0	-4.7	4.6	5.0
1983	9.8	-8.0	3.8	11.9
1984	9.6	-5.5	1.9	10.2
1985	11.9	-0.7	3.2	7.3
1986	10.6	-8.2	0.1	2.4
1987	9.5	-1.6	-3.7	-1.4
1988	10.0	6.0	-14.6	-11.6
1989	13.5	-2.9	-21.0	-12.7
1990	14.8	-1.4	-14.3	-0.4
1991	11.7	0.3	-6.3	10.6

Source: National Institute Economic Review

dramatic sterling crisis of the kind experienced in 1976. In terms of levels, the exchange rate (measured by an index of rates against all other major currencies) was about 15 per cent lower by 1989 than in 1979. This fall roughly compensated for relative rates of inflation at home and abroad. Thus, the ratio between the prices of UK exports and manufactures and those of their main competitors (in any common currency) was about the same at the beginning and the end of the decade. The same relationship did not hold for shorter periods. Thus, when sterling rose rapidly at the beginning of the 1980s, British goods became uncompetitive in world and domestic markets and the resulting loss of market share contributed to the depth of the recession.

Until Britain entered the EMS in 1990, interest rates were set by the monetary authorities (the Treasury and the Bank of England) and constituted the principal instrument of monetary policy, quantitative controls of the banking system having been abandoned in the early 1980s. The average level of nominal interest rates in the 1980s was much the same as it was in the 1970s, but the real rate of interest (the nominal rate minus the rate of inflation) was considerably higher, because inflation was so much lower. In fact, the real return to such assets as building society deposits, which was substantially negative in the 1970s, has now been positive for many years. During the last decade, the authorities did not respond anything like one for one to inflation when they were setting interest rates; year by year the influences on the rate of interest varied, as the concern of the authorities shifted between the exchange rate, the growth of the money supply, the rate of output growth and the rate of inflation (see Chapter 7). Taking one year with another, the state of the exchange market and the level of interest rate abroad seem to have been the most consistent influences over the 1980s.

One of the reasons for the rise in interest rates in the late 1980s was the government's concern over the balance of payments and its fear of a resulting fall in the exchange rate. The current account had been in surplus for most of the decade, thanks to the low level of demand and activity at home and to North Sea oil. The surplus peaked in 1981 and was slowly eroded in the years that followed. In 1988–9 it moved, quite dramatically, into large deficit as a result of the surge in domestic demand. Since the abolition of exchange controls in 1979, the flows of borrowing and lending which make up the capital account of the balance of payments have grown much larger. They are far larger than the flows associated with trade or current transactions. Thus, even a current account deficit of the scale experienced in 1989 does not present a problem of finance, provided that confidence in sterling is maintained (Healey and Levine, 1990; Healey, 1991a). But confidence itself is influenced by the trade figures, so that an improvement in the current account must be brought about sooner or later. This is one reason why the growth of the economy had to be relatively slow in the early 1990s.

Usually when a country has a deficit on its balance of payments, the government sector has a deficit on its accounts as well. In the late 1980s, Britain was exceptional, in the sense that the whole of the public sector was temporarily in large surplus, repaying some of its accumulated debts. The counterpart was a large deficit for the personal sector, financed as we have seen by borrowing from the banks and other financial intermediaries. In the late 1970s, the size of the public sector borrowing requirement (PSBR) was a major cause of concern and the methods of controlling public spending were reformed in order to correct it. During the 1980s, public spending was held back wherever possible. At the same time, government revenue rose rapidly as the economy recovered from the 1979–81 recession and especially during the consumer boom of 1987–9. Taxes were cut in the budget most years in the 1980s, but not cut by enough to prevent a large surplus from emerging. Budgets were cautious in this respect, because the government was concerned to keep inflation low and would have liked to see interest rates fall. In the event, even a large surplus on the public finances did not correspond to a tight enough policy to keep demand in check.

Looking ahead to the mid-1990s, the prospects for taxes and public spending depend, of course, on the policies of the governments of the day. One way or another, however, it will be necessary to keep the growth of demand in check. As a full member of the EMS, British interest rates are likely to fall quite rapidly towards the rates ruling in Germany. But there would be all the more need to keep the domestic economy under control by, if not 'fine-tuning', then 'coarse-tuning' taxation and public spending. It seems very likely, therefore, that (abstracting from the effects of the economic cycle) the public sector will stay in broad balance for the next few years at least.

CONCLUSIONS

In the late 1980s, the behaviour of the British economy seemed so much improved that there was talk of an economic 'miracle' (see, for example, Walters, 1986). As the decade ended and overheating turned into recession, assessments became less euphoric. Nevertheless, many supporters of the Conservative government continue to argue that once the recession has run its course, the British economy will emerge fundamentally stronger than it was in the 1970s.

Compared with the 1970s, some things undoubtedly have improved. During the 1980s, inflation was lower and Britain's comparative productivity performance improved. Unemployment on the other hand was much higher, but that was partly because the extent of unused labour in the 1970s was masked by overmanning. Living standards continued to rise, although this did relatively little to reduce the problem of poverty (see Chapter 12). It is still possible to look back, with something like nostalgia, to the 1950s and 1960s, when the behaviour of the economy was better than in either the 1970s or the 1980s. From 1953 until 1967, for example, the growth rate of output was 3 per cent, well above the average of the 1980s; the rate of inflation was also 3 per cent, well below recent experience. With all this, full employment was maintained continuously, with unemployment averaging less than 0.4 million. This longer-term comparison helps to put the 'improvements' of the 1980s into perspective.

It is never easy to judge what contribution has been made by a government's economic policies to the strength or weakness of economic performance. Typically, governments get an unfair share of the blame when things go wrong and take an unfair share of the credit in good times. I would prefer to emphasise the change in social attitudes which took place around the end of the 1970s. Wholehearted concentration on efficiency and profit became, as it never had been before, the style of management in Britain. The attitudes of workers and trade unions changed as well, becoming more concerned about the living standards of their members, less concerned with politics or solidarity. This change of mood was encouraged by the rhetoric of economic policy and fostered by some specific policy changes. One reason why Britain became more productive in the 1980s may have been simply that the British became harder working and gave a higher priority to economic achievement than they had in the past.

The specific contribution of policy changes is best seen by looking at particular industries. Output per head was raised substantially in the steel industry and in coal mining, for example, largely by closing uneconomic units of production. The deregulation of banking and other financial services made possible the important contributions made by these sectors to the growth of the economy as a whole. It is much more difficult to identify the effects of more general policy changes – for example, the reform of trade union law, or the reduction in marginal rates of tax. They may have made an important contribution to economic performance, but it cannot be proved that they did.

For the future, British industry needs to concentrate more on the underlying causes of economic growth and innovation, on research and development (R&D) and particularly on the training of the workforce. As the economy becomes more closely integrated with the rest of Europe, Britain's prosperity will depend more and more on the advantage of this country as a place for industry to locate itself. And that choice must depend on a comparison of workforce skills.

Full membership of the EMS should also make it possible to get British interest rates down to something more like the European average. Lower real interest rates will stimulate fixed capital investment and, more generally, encourage industry to look to the long-term future, rather than concentrating on short-term solutions to its problems. But a greater reliance on fiscal rather than monetary policy to guide the path of aggregate demand may mean delaying for a considerable time the further cuts in taxation, or the increases in public spending, which in different circumstances would be viable and popular measures.

3

BRITAIN'S ECONOMIC RECOVERY

Geoffrey Maynard

INTRODUCTION

The Conservative government which came to power under the leadership of Mrs Thatcher in 1979 was determined to make a complete break with the past in its management of the British economy. The new strategy effectively abandoned Keynesian short-run demand management aimed at full or high employment. Instead, emphasis was placed on improving the long-run, supply-side performance of the economy. Deregulation, the abandonment of controls over prices, incomes and capital movements, the return of state-owned industries to private ownership and management and, as urgent as anything, the reduction in the power of trade unions and the reform of labour laws, were all seen to be necessary (see also Chapter 10).

An urgent priority was to reduce inflation and to establish an environment of price stability, since without this the supply-side performance of the economy could not be improved. The proposed method of doing this was by monetary control, incomes policy being rejected partly on grounds of its demonstrable ineffectiveness and partly because control over incomes was incompatible with improved supply-side performance. With the abandonment of short-run demand management, fiscal policy became a matter of reducing both government expenditure and taxation as a proportion of gross domestic product (GDP), as a means of increasing incentives and resources for the private sector. Although it was clearly unrealistic to think of balancing the fiscal budget in any quick period of time, this seemed to constitute a long-term aim.

At the centre of macroeconomic policy lay the Medium-Term Financial Strategy (MTFS), which incorporated declining targets for monetary growth and budgetary deficits over an initial four-year period (see also Chapter 7). With modifications made in the light of outturns and experience, the MTFS was extended throughout the life of the Conservative government, although by 1987 targets relating to broad money supply had been virtually abandoned and membership of the European Monetary System (EMS) in 1990 finally rendered monetary targets meaningless – see Chapter 1.

Initially, with the abandonment of short-term demand management, the new Conservative government had no explicit policy for employment (see also Robins, 1985). The government subscribed to the view that a weakening, through legislation, of the monopoly power of the trade unions would produce a more competitive labour market, and consequently the greater flexibility of money and real wages that was necessary if full employment was to be restored and maintained. However, the failure of the labour market to behave in the expected way forced the government to undertake a series of microeconomic measures to alleviate the unemployment problem.

The government was also committed to increasing work and saving incentives through structural reform of the tax system and cuts in the burden of tax (see Chapter 8 for details), but the scale of the changes that were introduced in its first budget surprised many of its own supporters, let alone opponents, and had macroeconomic effects that were probably not fully expected at the time.

In brief, the policies pursued by Mrs Thatcher's first administration (1979–83) represented a substantial change from those pursued in the postwar period. The new approach seemed to represent a return to the classical macroeconomics which had preceded Keynes: ideas of balanced budgets, of the quantity theory of money, of equilibrating labour markets and of supply determining demand rather than demand determining supply returned to the centre of the stage. Naturally, it did not work out quite like this, but none the less there was a significant change of philosophy which might be summarised as the substitution of an attitude of 'non-accommodation' of wage and other cost-push pressures for an attitude of 'accommodation' to them. Critics of this change in attitude saw it, of course, as the replacement of 'conciliation' with 'confrontation'. Few can deny, however, that the change has had a significant impact on the performance of the British economy (Maynard, 1988).

THATCHERISM IN OPERATION

The early results of this new strategy appeared catastrophic. By 1981, the country's GDP had fallen by 4 per cent, industrial production by even more (with manufacturing production being particularly affected), and unemployment had more than doubled. Only the government's policy with respect to inflation appeared to have been a success. Such was the scale of the apparent catastrophe that, in an unprecedented (for economists) show of agreement, 364 of the country's leading economists, including many of its most distinguished and influential academics, put their signatures to a letter to *The Times* newspaper in March 1981 deploring the policies being pursued and predicting dire consequences if they were continued. Somewhat ironically, although the government remained unimpressed and broadly continued with its strategy, the publication of this letter coincided with the trough of the downturn in output. While employment continued to fall and unemployment to rise for the next year or two, output began to rise strongly; and this was broadly sustained over the next seven years, accelerating in pace towards the end of the decade. Between 1987 and 1990, even unemployment temporarily fell, reaching a low of under 6 per cent.

The impressive performance of the economy over the 1980s is summarised in Table 3.1. GDP growth averaged over 3 per cent per annum including oil and 3.5 per cent per annum excluding it (compared with barely 2 per cent in the previous decade). Manufacturing output, having been pulled down sharply in 1979–81, rose by 28 per cent, at an annual average rate of 3.6 per cent. Between 1987–9, it rose by almost 13 per cent. Unemployment fell from the peak level of 1986 for the remainder of the decade and the inflation rate was modest for most of the period, only picking up again after 1988.

PRODUCTIVITY IMPROVEMENTS

The most significant feature recorded by Table 3.1 is the substantial increase in labour productivity that took place in manufacturing industry. This rose by over 4.5 per cent per annum between 1979 and 1989 and by 6 per cent per annum between 1981 and 1989. Indeed, as the boom gathered pace between 1987 and 1989, productivity growth accelerated to over 7 per cent per annum. This performance was

Table 3.1 UK macroeconomic performance 1979–88

	GDP Incl. oil	GDP Excl. oil	Manu-facturing output	Employment Total	Employment Manu-facturing	Productivity Whole economy	Productivity Manu-facturing
			% change over the period				
1979–88	+20.0	+25.2	+9.9	−4.5	−30.0	+21.7	+51.0
1979–81	−3.6	−2.0	−14.2	−5.5	−13.3	−0.1	−0.5
1981–8	+24.5	+27.6	+28.0	+1.0	−18.3	+22.2	+52.0
			(% per annum)				
1979–88	2.0	2.5	1.0			2.2	4.2
1981–8	3.2	3.5	3.6			2.9	6.0

	Unemployment % labour force	Inflation %	Companies' real rate of return (%)	Share of world trade in manufactures (%)
1979	4.7	13.5	5.0	8.5
1981	9.4	12.0	3.0	7.0
1988	8.2	4.5	11.0	6.6

Source: Central Statistical Office

Table 3.2 Labour productivity trends in UK manufacturing industry (% p.a. growth in cyclically adjusted measures)

Period	Capital intensity effect[1]	Other effects[2]	Total productivity trend
1956–72	1.5	2.5	4.0
1972–80	1.3	0.3	1.6
1980–8 (Spencer)	1.7	3.2	4.9
1980–8 (Muellbauer)	1.4	3.6	5.6

Source: Calculated from Muellbauer (1986) and Spencer (1988)
Notes: [1] Due to capital per worker
[2] Due to technological progress, education, more efficient use of capital stock

superior to that experienced in the 1950s and 1960s and, of course, far better than in the 1970s (Table 3.2).

According to Muellbauer (1986) and Spencer (1987, 1988), only 0.5 per cent of the increase since 1980 can be attributed to the cyclical effect of expanding output, the remainder being due to increased capital intensity (i.e. capital per worker) and other effects – i.e. those due to technological progress, education and more efficient use of the capital stock.

Muellbauer attributes about 1.7 per cent per annum of the cyclically adjusted productivity rise to the exceptional labour shedding of 1979–81, which raised the capital intensity of production. He believes that this labour shedding was a once-and-for-all phenomenon – thus suggesting that the underlying trend rate of growth of productivity lies in the region of 3.5 per cent per annum rather than 5 per cent. However, Spencer takes the view that the capital intensity effect is likely to be more permanent. Whilst agreeing that capital intensity was raised by the exceptional labour shake-out of the early 1980s, he suggests that it will continue to be important as long as further investment in manufacturing industry takes place.

Spencer's view is supported by the steep rise in capital productivity which took place in the 1980s, the result of more efficient labour and capital use against a background of declining union power and more effective shop-floor management (Spencer, 1987). Thus, total factor productivity (i.e. changes in output that cannot be explained by labour hours worked, employment levels and changes in the measured capital stock) rose by more than 3 per cent per annum, a faster rate than at any time during the postwar period. Because of this, and the contemporaneous increase in the share of profits in income, the rate of profit on capital employed in manufacturing industry rose strikingly in the late 1980s, from the abysmally low level of barely 3 per cent in 1979 to approximately 12 per cent in 1987 (Bank of England, 1988).

Equally striking was the improved British productivity performance relative to other major industrialised countries (Table 3.3). In the fifteen years prior to 1979, Britain's productivity performance in both manufacturing and the whole economy was stuck at the bottom or next to bottom of the international league table, well below the average performance of the group as a whole. During the last decade, however, output per head in manufacturing industry increased at a faster rate than in any other major industrial country and the whole economy grew at a rate inferior only to that of Japan. Thus, there is some evidence that a sea-change took place in the British economy, even though the relative improvement as compared with the 1970s is somewhat exaggerated – since Britain's performance in this decade was, as for all other countries, adversely affected by oil price shocks which not only checked output growth, but also led to the

Table 3.3 Output per person employed in the major seven industrialised countries (average annual % change)

	Manufacturing[1]			Whole economy[2]		
	1960–70	1970–80	1980–8	1960–70	1970–80	1980–8
UK	3.0	1.6	5.2	2.4	1.3	2.5
US	3.5	3.0	4.0	2.0	0.4	1.2
Japan	8.8	5.3	3.1	8.9	3.8	2.9
Germany	4.1	2.9	2.2	4.4	2.8	1.8
France	5.4	3.2	3.1	4.6	2.8	2.0
Italy	5.4	3.0	3.5	6.3	2.6	2.0
Canada	3.4	3.0	3.6	2.4	1.5	1.4
G7 average	4.5	3.3	3.6	3.5	1.7	1.8

Sources: [1] UK data from Central Statistical Office. Other countries' data from OECD, except France and Italy which use IMF employment data. 1988 data for France and Italy cover first three-quarters only

[2] UK data from Central Statistical Office. Other countries' data from OECD, except 1988 which are calculated from national GNP or GDP figures and OECD employment estimates

substitution of labour and capital for energy and consequently to a decline in productivity.

It seems clear that an improvement in productivity which was sustained for so long must be explained in terms of at least some of the longer-term, fundamental factors typically underlying productivity growth – improved management, better working practices, better directed investment and greater readiness to change. The improved performance seems to be spread over most sectors of British manufacturing industry, being particularly marked in the metals, motor-car manufacturing and electrical engineering sectors of the economy (see Chapter 6).

Indeed, the improvements in some key sectors of the economy were dramatic. For example, British Steel, which in the 1970s was the most inefficient steel producer in Europe with labour productivity 40 per cent below that in comparable German plants, achieved a rate of production which was on a par with that in Germany by the end of the last decade. Whereas each tonne of steel took an average of 14.5 hours to produce in 1980, as early as 1986 it was taking only 5.6 hours. British Steel's enormous financial losses of the 1970s were turned into profits. The British auto industry, virtually destroyed in the 1970s by anarchic industrial relations and frequent strike action, enjoyed a growing vitality over the 1980s. Productivity in some plants more than doubled, bringing it up to continental standards.

Table 3.4 Output, jobs, productivity in the UK 1979–86: % change (+ or –)

| | Since first half of 1979 | | | Since first quarter of 1981 | | |
	Output	Jobs	Output per head	Output	Jobs	Output per head
Metals	–11.1	–56.0	+120.0	+16.8	–39.2	+90.8
Motors, parts	–30.2	–47.9	+34.0	+11.9	–33.8	+69.0
Electrical engineering	+29.6	–21.0	+64.1	+44.7	–13.9	+68.1
Mechanical engineering	–16.6	–30.8	+20.5	+5.1	–23.3	+37.0
Chemicals	+13.9	–14.9	+33.8	+27.0	–4.7	+33.3
Textiles	–19.2	–38.6	+31.6	+11.3	–16.4	+33.1
Paper, print	–3.1	–6.6	+3.7	+9.1	–1.9	+11.2
All manufacturing	–3.9	–28.0	+33.5	+13.9	–17.9	+38.7

Source: Economic Progress Report, HM Treasury

Table 3.5 Labour productivity in manufacturing (output per hour: UK = 100)

	1980	1984	1986
United States	273	262	267
Japan	196	177	176
France	193	179	184
Germany	255	232	178
Italy	173	156	155
Belgium	207	200	154
Netherlands	269	267	205

Source: G.F. Ray, 'Labour Costs in Manufacturing', NIESR, May 1987

Undoubtedly, although the dramatic fall in strikes, both official and unofficial, and in work stoppages was a major factor in the auto industry's greater productivity, improved technology, made possible by better industrial relations, was at least as important. However, despite the relative improvement since 1980, labour productivity in Britain still lags well behind that in its major competitor countries, showing that much remains to be achieved.

THE CONTRIBUTION OF MACROECONOMIC POLICY

Can the undoubted absolute and relative improvement in Britain's productivity performance which took place in the 1980s be ascribed in any specific way to the economic policy pursued by the Conservative government? There would probably be general agreement that the government's legislative attack on trade union power and privilege and its willingness to stand up against crucial strikes (such as that of the coal miners in 1984), or to provide explicit or implicit support for others who have done so (for example, during the Wapping dispute of 1986–7), played a significant role in reducing trade union opposition to the introduction of new technology and to changes in working practices. But there is perhaps less agreement on the precise part played by macroeconomic policy *per se*, except perhaps that the government's willingness to accept or (as some would say) deliberately create massive unemployment through its fiscal and monetary policies may be given credit for weakening the power of labour and strengthening the power of management.

On the surface, a macroeconomic policy which – with the notable exception of the 1986–8 period – appears to have excessively constrained aggregate demand for both goods and labour, which produced high nominal and real interest rates and (at times) an overvalued exchange rate, and which by the abolition of exchange control diverted British savings and North Sea oil revenue away from investment in Britain to investment overseas, would seem to have been calculated to weaken manufacturing industry and the British economy generally rather than to strengthen it. This has certainly been the view of the Conservative government's critics (e.g. Godley, 1989).

There is no doubt that policy pursued by the government during the 1980s ran greatly counter to that advocated by many influential economists (e.g. Lord Kaldor) in the 1960s and 1970s. This held that the way out for the British economy was export-led growth based on an undervalued exchange rate and (perhaps) subsidised labour costs, emulating, so it was thought, the example set by other highly successful countries such as Germany and Japan.

Of course, the parallel drawn with Germany and Japan (by the proponents of export-led growth) was always highly misleading: it failed to note that although Germany's and Japan's export success was related to the depreciation of their real exchange rates, their nominal exchange rates remained strong throughout. The bases of success, in fact, lay in these countries' superior productivity performance, which enabled competitiveness to be combined with a strong nominal exchange rate, low inflation and rising real wages, rather than the reverse. Advocates of the undervalued exchange rate approach often seem to overlook the fact that they are, in effect, advocating a low real-wage strategy that would keep Britain competing in low value-added product areas; these are the very areas in which competition from Third World countries is already acute and likely to intensify in the 1990s. In fact, UK export performance has been poorest in those high-tech and high-quality product areas where price competition is less important than non-price competitiveness and where world demand has been increasing fastest. A policy of exchange rate depreciation to maintain price competitiveness discourages, rather than encourages, British industry from changing its pattern of output in a direction that is necessary if Britain is to join the high productivity, high-real wage league.

It is in this context – namely, the central role of the exchange rate – that macroeconomic policy under the Conservative government must be judged. Admittedly, partly because the commercial exploitation of North Sea oil coincided with a rise in world oil prices and partly because of the intended tightness of monetary policy, the real exchange rate initially appreciated too severely in 1979–80. Also, in the early stages of its strategy, the government undoubtedly saw the key role of a strong exchange rate as the major instrument for pulling inflation down, rather than as a key element in long-term industrial strategy, and it was happy to see the exchange rate later fall from the excessively high level of 1979–80.

Even so, it rightly stood up to pressure from political opponents, academics and industrialists to embark on a policy of exchange rate depreciation to increase short-run competitiveness. By refusing to 'accommodate' rising costs and poor productivity with exchange rate depreciation, macroeconomic policy imposed pressure on industry to raise productivity, to lower costs and generally to move its products up-market (the same argument was later used by the government to justify its decision to join the EMS in 1990, at a time when British inflation was twice the European Community average). It is significant that many firms whose management was often vociferous in its criticism of the government's policy with respect to the exchange rate in the early years of the strategy subsequently achieved productivity improvements and product upgrading to a degree that was almost revolutionary.

NORTH SEA OIL

It is obvious that a policy of maintaining a strong ('overvalued') exchange rate in the interest of encouraging a change in industrial structure and a rise in labour and capital productivity – which is necessary if international competitiveness is to be combined with high real wages – would be difficult, if not impossible, without some short-run support to the balance of payments. Fortunately for the Conservative government and the country, the balance of payments had that support in the shape of North Sea oil.

The government has been attacked for wasting North Sea oil in a consumption splurge. In fact, by the end of 1986, between a third and a half of the 'economic rent' from the North Sea had been invested in overseas assets, yielding a substantial return in the form of dividends and interest to the British economy. Perhaps more importantly, North Sea oil revenue enabled the country's real income to be maintained at a reasonably high level whilst necessary structural changes in the economy were taking place. As a result of this income support, the country's willingness to accept change was probably greater than would otherwise have been the case (Maynard, 1988).

The years 1979–81 are generally viewed as a disaster for British manufacturing, but future historians may well judge them less as a period that pulled the Conservative government's record down than as one in which the essential basis for sustained long-run improvement in economic performance was laid down. It is hard to overstate the significance of the economic shock of 1979–81, whether one takes the view that in these years UK manufacturing industry was virtually destroyed or, on the contrary, that it was forced to accept changes in its management and work practices which now give it a serious chance to survive. Indeed, although it seems unlikely that the government did in fact favour 'shock' treatment as against 'gradualism' when it first came into office in 1979 (see also Chapter 4), it can well be argued that the intractable nature of Britain's problems at the end of the 1970s necessitated shock treatment if the country was to escape from them. Given this view, the government's apparent overdoing of monetary restriction in 1979–81 may have been a blessing in disguise, despite its high cost in terms of unemployment; and the steep fall in UK manufacturing output (16 per cent) which occurred in those years is, on a long-term view, irrelevant. The real test of policy is perhaps still to come, in the performance of British industry as North Sea oil runs out.

While the evidence of the 1980s suggests that UK manufacturing does have a future, one better than could conceivably have been expected in the traumas of the 1970s, doubts as to the sustainability of the improved economic trends in the British economy certainly cannot be dismissed (e.g. Healey, 1992a). One such doubt arises from the low level of capital formation in UK industry in the 1980s; and indeed the government is accused of pursuing monetary and exchange rates policies that have discouraged investment. Also, the following questions might well be asked. If the underlying supply-side performance of the British economy has improved so markedly, why did the overseas trade balance deteriorate so badly in the late 1980s? Why did Britain end a decade of supply-side policy facing a balance of payments crisis, despite the continuing benefits of North Sea oil?

As to the first point, it is certainly the case that capital formation in British industry was at a low level in the 1980s. The fixed investment to GDP ratio averaged around 19 per cent in the years 1980–7 and only about 38 per cent of this took place in industry. However, as noted above, capital productivity and the rate of profit on capital were at abysmally low levels in 1979, making further investment unattractive. It might be argued that the priority in the early 1980s was to raise the productivity of the existing capital stock, rather than to increase its size. Against a background of declining trade union power and more effective shop-floor management, this was largely achieved by the mid-1980s and the rate of profit on capital employed in manufacturing industry returned closer to the levels of the 1960s. It is not surprising, therefore, that it was not until the late 1980s that Britain actually enjoyed a substantial investment boom; indeed, this investment boom contributed significantly to the deterioration in Britain's balance of payments in 1988–9.

THE RETURN OF A BALANCE OF PAYMENTS PROBLEM?

Table 3.6 illustrates the scale of the deterioration in Britain's balance of payments which took place in the late 1980s. In the period 1979–85, current account surpluses averaged almost £3bn a year; 1986 saw a rough balance and 1987 a deficit of £2.5bn. In 1988, however, the deficit approached £15bn, exceeding £20bn in 1989 (over 4 per cent of GDP). While these deficits did not represent a crisis situation for Britain, since the country has sizeable overseas assets and foreign exchange reserves, it is evident that deficits of this size could not

Table 3.6 UK balance of payments

	Non-oil balance	Oil balance	Goods and services balance	IPD balance	Current balance
1985	−4.5	8.1	3.6	−0.3	3.3
1986	−7.2	4.1	−3.1	2.9	−0.2
1987	−8.7	4.2	−4.5	2.2	−2.5
1988	−18.7	2.5	−16.2	2.0	−14.2
1989	−25.6	1.0	−21.7	1.6	−20.1

Source: CSO Economic Trends

continue without eventually creating serious problems for Britain (Healey, 1991a).

A deficit on the current account of the balance of payments indicates that a country is attempting to consume more than it is producing; and a deterioration in the balance would indicate either (i) that aggregate demand has risen relative to aggregate supply or (ii) that supply has fallen relative to demand. Even when a country is not running a trade deficit, supply-side deficiencies can still exist if aggregate demand and employment have to be restrained by deliberate policy measures in order to keep overseas payments and receipts in balance.

The worsening trade situation in the late 1980s does not seem to have been connected with a worsening in Britain's supply-side performance, at least in a short-run sense: on the contrary, GDP rose by more than 4 per cent per annum in the course of 1987–8, a significantly faster rate than in the preceding five years, and employment rose quite strongly. The output of manufacturing industry, which is the source of the greater part of Britain's 'tradables' (exports and import-substitutes) also rose at an exceptionally rapid rate – by more than 6 per cent per annum in 1987–8. Thus a failure of the supply-side of the economy in 1987–8 does not, *per se*, provide the answer, and we must look to demand.

Table 3.7 summarises the behaviour of domestic demand and its major components in the late 1980s, as well as that of GDP and exports and imports. The acceleration of domestic demand, particularly in 1988, stands out, as do the rapid rise in imports in 1987 and 1988 and the sharp fall in export growth in 1988. Evidently, during the late 1980s, imports were sucked in by the strength of demand in the economy and exports sidetracked from meeting foreign demand to satisfying home consumers.

The alternative view that the problem lies in a loss of competitiveness of British tradable goods and services – although supported by the International Monetary Fund's index of normalised unit labour costs which indicates a loss of competitiveness by some 20 per cent between 1986 and 1988 – is not borne out by other, perhaps more telling, developments. First, despite high earnings growth of 9 per cent per annum, unit labour costs in manufacturing were virtually flat through 1987–8 when the trade balance worsened so markedly. Second, the profitability of British exports relative to home production, which increased significantly over the 1980s, showed no deterioration in 1987–8. Third, the British share of world manufactured exports, which had steadily fallen for over 100 years, stabilised in the 1980s and may actually have risen as the decade drew to a close. It is significant that 40 per cent of the increase in domestic demand in 1988 represented fixed investment (see p. 67), a large part of which took place in industry (gross capital formation rose from 19.5 per cent of GDP in 1987 to 21.5 per cent in 1988); indeed, the increase in fixed investment between 1987 and 1988 may have approached almost two-thirds of the increase of net imports of goods and services between those two years.

CONCLUSIONS

Although Britain's foreign trade problem in the late 1980s does not bear witness to the failure of the government's supply-side strategy, the government cannot be exculpated from allowing domestic demand to increase too fast (see also Cook and Healey, 1990; Healey and Levine, 1990). The failure of policy lay mainly in the explosion of credit and money between 1986 and 1988, which fuelled a substantial boom in house prices and, through an associated withdrawal of equity from house ownership, led to a boom in consumer spending (see Chapter 2). The substantial cut in taxes in the 1988 budget also contributed.

Unfortunately, the government's failure to adhere to its own monetary policies and targets (via the MTFS) put at risk some of the gains of its long-term strategy. Although labour cost inflation was dissipated harmlessly through 1988 by exceptionally rapid productivity growth, as the economy slowed down in 1989 and 1990, so too did productivity growth, with money wage increases increasingly

Table 3.7 Domestic demand and GDP (1985–8) (1985 prices)

	Domestic demand	Consumers' expenditure	Fixed investment	Government consumption	Exports	Imports	GDP average measure
1985	300.7	215.3	60.3	74.0	102.8	99.2	304.7
1986	311.8	226.8	60.8	75.4	106.6	105.6	314.0
1987	324.8	238.5	64.2	76.0	112.5	113.3	327.1
1988	345.0	251.4	72.9	76.3	114.4	126.6	345.1
			Annual % change:				
1985	2.9	3.5	3.8	0.0	5.9	2.6	3.8
1986	3.7	5.4	0.9	1.9	3.8	6.5	3.1
1987	4.2	5.1	5.5	0.9	5.5	7.3	4.2
1988	6.2	5.4	13.6	0.4	1.7	11.7	4.4

Source: Shearson Lehman Hutton
Note: Stock building and factor cost adjustment are omitted from this table

feeding through into price rises which eventually pushed inflation to a peak of over 10 per cent in 1990. A period of relatively slow growth and rising unemployment then became necessary to pull inflation back to a more acceptable level, stopping the investment boom in its tracks.

Moreover, although the deterioration in Britain's balance of payments at the end of the last decade does not prove that the Conservative government's supply-side policies have failed, it is too soon to claim overwhelming success for them. While the government can claim that the stance of macroeconomic policy – i.e. the abandonment of short-run demand management and a determination not to accommodate price and cost pressures by deliberate exchange rate depreciation – has been consistent with the need to bring about urgently needed changes in the structure and efficiency of Britain's industry, it can hardly claim that its actions so far have been sufficient to bring about long-term industrial rejuvenation. Much remains to be done, particularly in the area of education and training. Indeed, the government is much more vulnerable to attack for things it did not do than for the things it did do. Convincing evidence of the success of the government's strategy is not likely to be seen before the mid-1990s and, given the deep-rooted nature of Britain's educational and training problem, perhaps not even then.

4

BRITAIN'S ECONOMIC RENAISSANCE

Kent Matthews

INTRODUCTION

Has Britain undergone an economic renaissance? To answer this question, we need to compare Britain's economic performance and policies pre-1979 with what followed during the 1980s. If the improvement in economic performance over the last decade proves to have been a uniquely British phenomenon – linked to the policies of the Conservative government and not just the result of a cyclical upswing in world economic activity – then we can conclude that Britain's position has improved significantly relative to other countries. Although the British economy temporarily moved into recession during the early 1990s, this downturn was essentially a correction following the years of rapid economic growth during the late 1980s. This chapter is concerned less with the 'Lawson boom' and its aftermath than with the preceding period, during which Mrs Thatcher's administration laid the foundations for Britain's improved long-term performance.

Accordingly, this chapter concentrates on the Thatcher years. It begins with a narrative of the period, assessing the main strands of the Conservative government's programme and its effects. Second, it outlines the implications of supply-side policy and its effects on unemployment and productivity. The third section outlines the structure of the Liverpool (University) macroeconomic model which is used in simulation analysis to decompose the effects of various shocks to the economy over the period 1980–7. This exercise in 'counterfactual' analysis is used to diagnose the causes of the recession of 1980–1, the subsequent recovery and the productivity revival of the mid-1980s. The final section draws the analysis together to restate and reconfirm the conclusions of an earlier article by Matthews and Minford (1987).

THE THATCHER PROGRAMME

Any diagnosis of the British economy in the 1970s would have identified four main problems: chronic inflation, low productivity growth, poor industrial relations and rising unemployment. The causes were, in turn, a lack of fiscal and monetary control, an excess of trade union power, government intervention and taxation, and a lack of incentive to take up low-paid jobs because of the operation of unemployment benefit support. The historical roots of these causes predate the 1970s. The mass unemployment of the 1930s provided the political pressure to switch unemployment support away from the principle of 'insurance' to that of 'need' and laid the foundations for the postwar policy on unemployment support. The Second World War was a watershed in the role of the government because, according to Peacock and Wiseman (1961), it generated a threshold of governmental organisation and finance that led to the gradual expansion of the state sector, the experiment with demand management and the 'stop–go' cycle (see also Chapter 5). The financial implications of growing state expenditure programmes in the form of higher taxation resulted in weakening incentives, higher labour costs and higher unemployment during the 1960s and 1970s.

The Thatcher programme envisaged action on all fronts. However, the approach was step-by-step rather than a grand assault. The reason for this was that a grand reforming approach would, in all likelihood, have failed by crossing too many vested interests too soon without producing sufficiently rapid results to impress a sceptical electorate. By tackling problems one at a time and by showing success in each area, Mrs Thatcher demonstrated considerable political entrepreneurship. Walters (1986) identified four areas of economic reform, which were to be carried out in stages according to priority. The immediate priority was the control of inflation, which had reached 18 per cent in 1980 after the breakdown of the previous Labour government's 'Social Contract' (whereby the trade unions were to deliver an incomes policy in return for favourable legislation). The second area of urgent reform was the deregulation of the economy. The third field entailed the privatisation of state-owned industries (see especially Chapter 9), and the fourth area was the reform of the trade unions (see Chapter 10).

Initially, all other policies were subordinated to the aim of reducing inflation. This meant that medium-term control of the budget deficit was used as a means of underpinning the long-term 'credibility' (see Chapter 1) of monetary policy. The medium-term strategy announced by the Conservative government originally envisaged a gradualist approach to the reduction in the rate of growth of the money supply (see Chapter 7). Paradoxically, the success of the anti-inflation policy was due entirely to the accidental over-tightening of monetary policy in 1980. In terms of the rate of growth of M0, monetary growth fell from over 12 per cent in 1979 to 5.7 per cent by the end of 1980. The over-tightness of monetary policy over 1980–1 was fortuitous, in that it had considerable impact on expectations by squeezing out the 'inevitable U-turn factor' (Minford, 1979) associated with past governments' economic policy.

By inadvertently going for immediacy rather than gradualism, the Thatcher government was able to bring down inflation more rapidly than otherwise, thereby circumventing the forces of opposition that would have built up to force a 'U-turn'. By 1982, inflation had come down to single figures and the battle had been won. The cost in terms of lost output and higher unemployment is an open question, which can only partially be answered within a specific macroeconomic model framework. Matthews and Minford (1987) estimate that the effect of the tightening in monetary policy contributed 0.8 million to the jobless figures by 1985. Yet despite the cost, the success of the policy had strengthened the hand of the government.

The main strands of the supply-side programme, launched in earnest in 1982, were: curbing the power of the unions; privatisation; deregulation; and the cutting back of taxes and social security benefits. Trade union power in this country has historically been based on immunity from civil actions in tort for breach of employment contract. This was tackled by making union assets liable for civil damages if primary industrial action is not agreed by a majority of union members in a secret ballot or if the action is secondary. Also, the legal recognition of the closed shop was restricted. The effect of legislation on the power of the unions has been significant. Its main impact has been to increase greatly the efficiency of employers in the use of resources, but not to affect the trade-union mark-up on wages (see also Chapter 10). A secondary consideration has been the change in the attitude of the general public as regards trade unions in general.

The second strand of the Conservative government's supply-side strategy was the deregulation of markets and the privatisation of nationalised industries (see Chapter 9). The aim of this programme was to increase the power of the consumer and to free producers from restrictive legislation such as employment protection laws, limits on nationalised industry borrowing, and interference with management decisions. Deregulation, or even the threat of it, has produced results as diverse as more competitive financial trading and more competitive bus services, but it has been the programme of privatisation that has captured the imagination of the public. Although privatisation has been attacked by free-market economists for not introducing stronger competition by breaking up the various industries (e.g. British Telecom, British Gas), the gains in efficiency have come from the liberation of managers from government interference. These gains have shown up in higher profits.

The threat of privatisation has also produced greater efficiency gains in other nationalised industries (e.g. British Coal), but it must be recognised that as a long-term model to promote efficiency, the privatisation of regulated monopolies has its drawbacks. The short-term attractiveness of the exercise is that:

1 it 'buys' the co-operation of the managers in the swift transfer of the industry to the private sector;
2 it produces almost immediate and perceived gains in efficiency; and
3 it maximises the revenue from asset sales, thereby increasing the likelihood of tax cuts.

What is certainly remarkable about the whole privatisation programme has been its popularity with the public at large.

The third strand of the programme was the reform of taxation and benefits. The greatest disincentives from marginal rates of tax were faced by both high-income and low-income groups. The former faced implicit rates, sometimes over 100 per cent, in the form of the 'poverty trap' (see also Chapter 12). Evidence from the New Earnings Survey married with migration statistics suggests that the cuts in the top tax rate (first to 60 per cent and later to 40 per cent) and the rise in tax thresholds have changed the net emigration of managerial and professional talent to net immigration (see Ashton and Minford, 1987). It should also be noted that the earned income of top UK taxpayers has risen sharply, almost entirely because of performance-related pay.

Concerning low incomes, the government instituted a reform of the benefit system, along the lines of the Fowler/Lawson proposals for tax-benefit reform. The standard rate of income tax was cut to 25 per cent, and there is the presumption that this will fall further under a Conservative government to 20 per cent in due course. Similarly, thresholds were raised by 26 per cent in real terms over the 1980s.

Although this has had some effect on the 'unemployment trap', further reforms are needed.

Thus, we can conclude this brief examination of the Thatcher programme by recapping its aims and successes. During her eleven years as Prime Minister, Mrs Thatcher may not have turned the clock back to a Golden Age of economic freedom and self-reliance, but her gradualist programme of reform nevertheless succeeded in injecting a new enthusiasm for market-based rules into British life. We would argue that the change in attitudes has been influenced by the success of the step-by-step strategy adopted by the Conservative government, with the aim of recording recognisable gains to the consuming and tax-paying public. We would argue further that the greater acceptance of a market-orientated philosophy by the public has been conditioned by the success of the programme.

UNEMPLOYMENT AND THE PRODUCTIVITY STORY

The ultimate objective of supply-side policy is to raise the level of productivity of the labour force and the capital stock and eventually to reduce unemployment. The economy has shown progress on this front. Output per person in the production industries grew at an average of 4.5 per cent per annum between 1979 and 1987, while productivity in manufacturing grew at an average rate of 4.2 per cent (see Figure 4.1). Independent research puts the underlying rate of growth of productivity at between 3.5 per cent and 4.5 per cent (e.g. Muellbauer, 1986; Spencer, 1987, 1988). Unemployment fell from a peak of 3.1 million at the beginning of 1987 to under 2 million by 1989 and, while the early 1990s have seen a recession-induced increase in unemployment, there are signs that the equilibrium, or natural, rate of unemployment is now lower.

Such facts, of course, beg the question: how much does the productivity performance of the 1980s depend on the strong cyclical recovery following the labour shedding of 1980–1 and how much does it depend on fundamental structural change? Attempts to differentiate between cyclical effects and capital-labour substitution by Muellbauer (1986) reveal a trend growth of total factor productivity of 2.8 per cent between 1980 and 1985 against a trend of 0.6 per cent per annum from 1973–9. Adding the total factor productivity trend to the productivity effect of capital-labour substitution produces an underlying trend in labour productivity of 4.4 per cent.

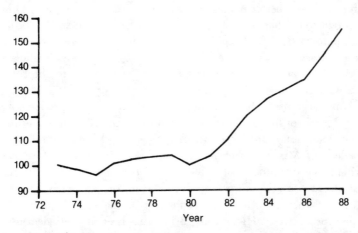

Figure 4.1 Manufacturing industries: output per person employed
(1980 = 100)

These estimates have been updated recently by Spencer (1987), who
finds that the growth trend in total factor productivity in the period
1980–5 is 3.2 per cent and total labour productivity growth is 4.8 per
cent. Further updating these results to include the years 1986–8,
Spencer (1988) suggests that the cyclical effects, accounting for the
business cycle plus the effect of labour shedding (capital intensity),
account for only 2 per cent of a growth in total labour productivity of
5.6 per cent. The implied underlying rate of growth of productivity is
calculated to be around 3.5 per cent over the period to 1988. Extending
his analysis to the manufacturing sector, Spencer (1988) puts the
underlying rate of growth of productivity in manufacturing at 5 per
cent between 1980 and 1988. Additionally, the index of percentage
utilisation of labour (see Smith-Gavine and Bennett, 1988) shows that
while output per operative hour had risen at an average of 0.7 per cent
from 1973 to early 1980, from 1980–7 it 'took off' to an average of 4.3
per cent per year.

It is clear that several strands of research show that the cyclical
effect of labour shedding, while being important, was not the main
reason for the productivity improvement of the 1980s. The shedding
of below-average workers, management and machinery – suggested
by Buiter and Miller (1983) as being the main reason for the
productivity upturn – has been tested and rejected by Oulton (1987).
The conclusion must be that the productivity improvement was, by

and large, determined by fundamental factors. Undoubtedly, technical innovation and better management contributed to the improvement in productivity, but such factors would not have found such a fertile environment but for the programme of union reform and tax cuts. Other measures such as the privatisation programme and liberalisation of markets contributed by enhancing and adding to the competitive environment.

This argument has greater force when the productivity performance of Britain during the 1980s is compared with that of the major industrial countries, particularly those which have not followed the lead of Mrs Thatcher in her supply-side revolution. Whereas Britain lagged behind most European countries during the 1970s, the last decade saw a sharp improvement in the country's relative position. What is particularly striking from Table 4.1 is the upturn in capital productivity. Historically, Britain has been an inefficient user of capital, exhibiting an excessive capital-output ratio compared with the other major economies. The decline in the capital-output ratio during the 1980s owes something to the cyclical upturn, but not all.

Capital productivity improved against virtually all other countries, as did total factor productivity, indicating a more efficient use of factor inputs. The corollary of improved relative productivity was the improvement in relative profit rates. During the 1980s, gross operating surplus as a proportion of gross value added increased significantly in relation to the major industrial economies (see Table 4.2). Higher profit performance undoubtedly occurred as a result of increased efficiency. In this, the recession of 1980–1 and the following labour shake-out played its part in improving the bargaining position of management, but union reform, a more deregulated environment and, importantly, the cut in top taxes resulted in a renaissance in management. McWilliams (1988) argues that the increased sophistication and globalisation of financial markets has pressurised British managers into coming into line with internationally given positions of profitability.

To this we can add the evidence of the effects of tax cuts, particularly at the top end, on work effort and tax yields. Ashton and Minford (1988) estimate, using General Household Survey (GHS) data, that the elasticity of substitution between marginal income and leisure for the top 30 per cent of earners, is around 0.5 per cent. The implication of this is that the cut in top tax rates from 60 per cent to 40 per cent, given that on average the top 5 per cent of earners work 5

Table 4.1 Productivity trends in the business sector in selected OECD countries

	OECD	USA	Japan	Germany	France	UK	Italy
Total factor productivity							
Pre-1973	2.8	1.5	6.3	2.6	3.9	1.9	4.8
1974–9	0.7	–0.1	1.8	1.8	1.8	0.2	1.6
1980–6	0.6	0.1	1.7	0.8	1.2	1.0	0.7
1987–90	1.2	0.8	2.2	1.3	1.8	1.8	1.6
Labour productivity							
Pre-1973	4.2	2.2	8.8	4.7	5.6	3.3	6.6
1974–9	1.6	0.3	3.2	3.4	3.2	1.3	2.4
1980–6	1.4	0.7	2.8	2.0	2.4	1.9	1.3
1987–90	1.9	1.3	3.5	2.3	2.7	2.2	2.4
Capital productivity							
Pre-1973	–0.4	0.3	–2.0	–1.2	0.3	–0.9	0.6
1974–9	–1.4	–0.8	–2.9	–1.0	–1.4	–2.0	–0.3
1980–6	–1.3	–1.0	–2.0	–1.3	–1.3	–0.8	–0.6
1987–90	–0.6	–0.1	–2.2	–0.5	–0.1	0.9	–0.4

Source: OECD Economic Outlook
Notes: Total factor productivity = real gross value added (at factor cost)/total factor inputs (1985 weights)
Labour productivity = real gross value added/private sector employment, including self-employed
Capital productivity = real gross value added/gross capital stock (constant prices)

Table 4.2 Profit shares: gross operating surplus as a % of gross value added

Country	1973	1975	1980	1981	1982	1983	1984	1985	1986	1987
United States	30.2	32.7	32.1	33.0	32.6	34.6	35.9	35.6	35.5	35.6
United Kingdom	31.2	23.9	31.8	33.5	36.6	39.5	41.0	41.9	39.5	42.5
Japan	46.7	39.6	42.0	41.1	40.1	38.8	40.2	40.4	40.6	40.8
Germany	32.7	31.0	30.2	29.3	30.4	32.8	33.3	34.1	35.1	35.4
France	35.1	31.2	32.4	31.5	30.9	31.3	32.2	32.9	34.4	35.3
Italy	34.1	30.6	39.0	37.4	37.5	36.5	40.2	40.6	42.1	42.2

Source: Gerald Holtham, 'The UK "revolution": an international perspective', *Shearson Lehman Hutton*, 8 December 1988

per cent harder and that their marginal product is six times that of the average earner, increased gross domestic product (GDP) by around 1 per cent.

It can be argued that, since high-income earners are more productive in the sense of having higher marginal products, tax cuts at the top end yield proportionately more benefits to society than at the bottom end, but here too tax cuts can be expected to yield benefits through increased incentives. The conventional finding of researchers is that the wage elasticity of supply for the average earner is small or effectively zero – see, for instance, Brown *et al.* (1987). However, unpublished research has come up with significant elasticities, once individuals in the GHS sample are split up by union and non-union membership (e.g. Walker of Keele University and Minford and Ashton at Liverpool). Incentives work not only by altering the marginal rate of substitution between work and leisure for the employed, but also for the unemployed.

To illustrate this point, consider the changes to tax and social security benefits introduced in the 1988 budget, which improved the poverty trap. Figure 4.2 depicts the changes in marginal tax and benefit withdrawal rates, taken from Ashton (1988). Under the old system, a couple on £110 per week who increased their earnings by £10 faced a reduction in net income by £7. In the new system, their net income would have risen by £2 – still a high marginal rate of tax, but better than the 176 per cent previously faced. The 'unemployment trap' was also improved for all those on gross earnings above £80 per week.

If tax cuts represent the 'carrot' which increases the incentive to work or work harder, the 'Restart' programme is the 'stick' designed to drive more off the dole and into jobs. The more stringent application of the 'Worker Test' (UB671) condition had the effect of reducing the replacement rate for the long-term unemployed. Expected benefits are now less than actual benefits because the probability of obtaining benefit is now less than one (see Ashton, 1987).

Other effects of tax cuts are to shift the balance between risk and return at the margin of operating in the black economy. Estimates of the size of this sector vary substantially. The semi-official estimate is that it lies between 6 and 8 per cent of GDP, a figure supported by Matthews and Stoney (1987) who, using survey data for Merseyside, come up with a figure of 7 per cent of GDP. Other estimates, however, suggest that the official figure may be an underestimation of the true size. Matthews and Rastogi (1986), for example, estimate that the black economy may be as large as 14 per cent of GDP. As the balance between risk and return shifts away from return, more

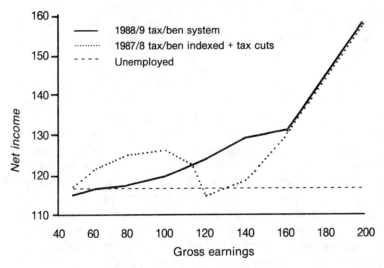

Figure 4.2 Poverty trap: couple with two children

activity, once supplied in the black economy, can be expected to find its way back into the regular economy.

The supply-side reforms initiated by the Conservative government during the 1980s created a 'wind of change' in attitudes. One indicator of this is the greater willingness to accept more risk on the part of management: for example, a greater reliance on performance-related pay; another is the growth in self-employment as a proportion of the labour force. In 1979, it was only 7.5 per cent, while in 1988 it was 11.6 per cent.

A MODEL-BASED ANALYSIS

The previous two sections have examined the evidence in favour of the economic renaissance by outlining the development of the Conservative government's economic and political strategy over the last decade and by linking the supply-side strategy to the productivity boom of the 1980s. While such an approach is useful in highlighting the priorities of the government and the order in which policy has been implemented (plus its potential impacts), a more formal empirical analysis is necessary to support what is still a matter of interpretation. An interpretation of the 1980s requires a clear framework of analysis. To understand the framework of analysis in which the period is interpreted, the main features of the Liverpool macroeconomic model are briefly outlined. The following section describes the use of the model in tracking and explaining the period 1980–7.

The Liverpool model has been in operation for both forecasting and policy analysis since March 1980. It differs from other models in terms of its size, structure and treatment of expectations. The model is small and aggregative (eight behavioural equations) and is new classical in spirit (see Chapter 1). A comprehensive description of the model can be found in Minford *et al.* (1984). The structure consists of a fairly orthodox demand-side, which can be interpreted in the familiar IS-LM framework. It incorporates powerful wealth effects on private sector spending, which respond strongly to real and capital valuation effects. That is, changes in the price level or interest rates will have powerful indirect effects on spending via the wealth effect.

Portfolio balance, in combination with the government's balance sheet constraint, implies that in the long run the public sector borrowing requirement (PSBR) must be financed by an equi-proportionate growth in money and bonds. In other words, in the long run, the government must issue money and bonds to finance a deficit, according to the private sector's portfolio balance. The model is concerned with the long run because of its treatment of expectations, which are rational or 'model-consistent'; that is, expectations of the future are precisely the predictions from the model. The effect of incorporating forward-looking rational or consistent expectations is that the long run is telescoped into short-run behaviour. Thus a PSBR to GDP ratio raises expectations of future inflation because of its long-run financing implication, irrespective of whether current monetary growth is rising or not.

The supply-side of the model is based very much on classical theory. Output depends, through a production function, on capital, labour and imported raw materials. This yields the open economy aggregate supply curve which relates the real exchange rate to output. The real exchange rate is the relative price of domestic goods to foreign goods, converted to a common currency. An appreciation (rise) in the effective exchange rate, *ceteris paribus*, raises the real exchange rate (lowers competitiveness). Similarly, a rise in the domestic price level, *ceteris paribus*, (i.e. without an offsetting reduction in the effective exchange rate) also raises the real exchange rate. The real exchange rate, in turn, is determined by unit wage costs, and wages and unemployment are determined in the labour market.

The labour supply responds to social variables such as income taxes and unemployment benefits, and to trade union strength measured by the rate of unionisation. Adjustment costs provide the underpinning for sluggishness in real wages, but money wage sluggishness is introduced in the form of nominal wage contracts so that unanticipated inflation reduces the real wage in the short run. In this way, a short-term trade-off is produced between employment and unanticipated inflation along the lines of the conventional expectations-augmented Phillips Curve (Friedman, 1968).

The full model can be represented in the stylised form of the textbooks' IS-LM and an open economy aggregate supply schedule, illustrated in Figure 4.3. The IS curve is of the standard textbook variety, except that it is drawn in terms of the real exchange rate rather than the real interest rate. The PP schedule is the open economy aggregate supply curve. A rise in the real exchange rate (caused, say, by a rise in domestic prices or a rise in the effective exchange rate) raises the unit return (profitability) to domestic firms. Output is expanded as firms move up their marginal cost curves to the point where the unit marginal profit is zero.

An increase in government spending, world trade or wealth shifts the IS curve up to the right. An increase in trade union power, benefits or taxes shifts the PP schedule up to the left, because these factors raise wage costs and so, for every given level of output, causes a rise in the real exchange rate. An unexpected decrease in inflation temporarily raises real wages and temporarily shifts the PP schedule to the left. The LM schedule is defined in price-output space rather than in the familiar nominal interest rate-output space. A decrease in the money supply, for a given level of output, reduces the price level – LM shifts back. The description of the properties of the model in terms of the stylised representation is a useful means of understanding the following analysis of the decomposition of the shocks in 1980–7.

The shocks are identified on the following lines. A base run of the model is the projection of all variables forecast by the model for predictions of exogenous variables based on the previous period's information. Exogenous variables such as world trade and unionisation rate are projected at past trend growth rates, whereas taxes, benefits and the PSBR/GDP ratio are projected as a 'random walk'. The PSBR/GDP ratio in the previous year is taken as indicative of the long-run growth in the money supply, which also determines long-run inflation expectations.

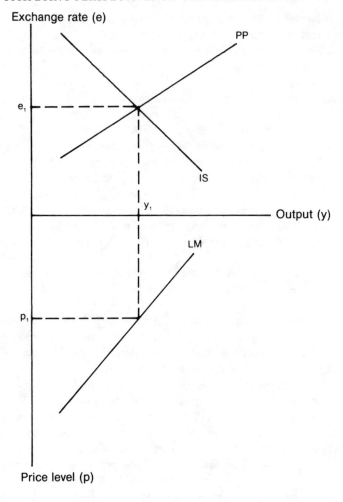

Figure 4.3 The Liverpool model

It is assumed that the MTFS is not credible and therefore policy announcements do not influence expectations (see Chapter 1). However, expectations are affected through the successful application of the MTFS. Thus reductions in the PSBR/GDP ratio influence long-run expectations by adding to the government's 'stock' of credibility. Hence, a series of base runs are constructed for 1980–7, which provide the expected outcome based on the previous year's information. The individual shocks are obtained by simulating the model for the difference between the actual and expected outcomes of the relevant exogenous variable.

We separate out the shocks into domestic demand shocks, external shocks and supply shocks. Domestic demand shocks are the sum effects of unexpected changes to monetary and fiscal policy; external shocks are the sum effects of unexpected changes to world trade and world real interest rates; and supply shocks are the sum effects of unexpected changes to taxes, benefits, VAT, unionisation rates and employers' National Insurance contributions. A full decomposition of the shocks, their sources and effects are presented in Matthews and Minford (1987) for 1980–5. This has been updated to include 1986 and 1987, but we present here only the trend projections and implications for the fight against inflation, the recession and recovery in output, the outcome for unemployment and the productivity renaissance. The model-fitted values from the sum effect of all the shocks are charted against the actual values for inflation, growth, unemployment and the real exchange rate in Figures 4.4a–d. The model clearly captures the trend and major turning points of these variables, although there is some tendency to overpredict growth and unemployment.

However, the model's success story is inflation, which is captured with impressive accuracy. The trend effects of shocks and their decomposition is shown in Table 4.3. The model suggests that inflation was brought down by repeated negative fiscal and monetary shocks. Each negative shock reduced expected inflation in the next period. Thus, the improvement in expected inflation was brought about by the costly process of shocking the economy with a series of unexpected deflationary shocks. The failure of expectations to respond to anything other than unexpected deflation can be explained, initially, by a lack of credibility. However, this argument loses force after two elections and a continued adherence by the government to its anti-inflationary policy. One argument is that the inflationary 'risk premium' increases as inflation falls. In other words, the temptation to renege on the anti-inflationary policy increases as inflation expectations decrease (as in, for instance, Barro and Gordon, 1983). Consequently, credibility is enhanced only by the continuation of unanticipated deflationary shocks. What Table 4.3 shows is that the strength of deflationary monetary and fiscal policy was greatest at the beginning of the period. Towards the end of the period, positive supply shocks were also contributing to the process of disinflation.

According to the model, the recession was caused not by an unexpected tightening of fiscal and monetary policy, but by an

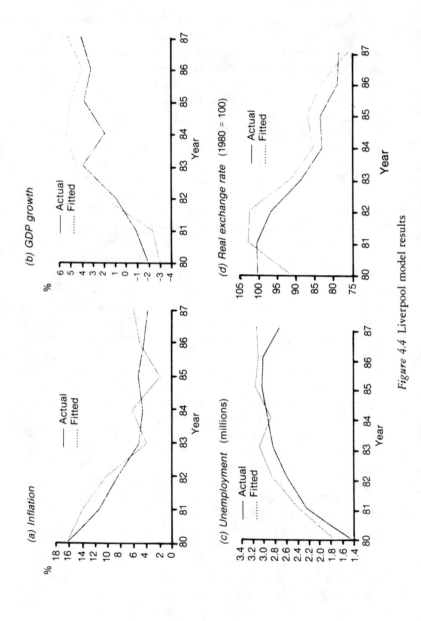

Figure 4.4 Liverpool model results

Table 4.3 Inflation analysis (annual rates %)

	1980	1986–7	Average 1980–7
Base run (expectations)	18.0	6.9	9.3
Domestic monetary/fiscal shocks	–6.6	–1.1	–3.3
External shocks	2.1	0.6	1.5
Supply shocks	1.5	–1.0	–0.3
Fitted model values	16.4	5.5	8.0
Actual	16.4	4.1	7.5

Table 4.4 Recession and recovery: real output growth (annual average %)

	1980–1	1986–7	1982–7
Base run (expectations)	1.8	–3.7	3.7
Domestic monetary/fiscal shocks	–0.5	0.1	0.1
External shocks	–2.9	–0.4	–0.9
Supply shocks	–1.4	1.3	1.4
Fitted model values	–2.8	4.6	4.3
Actual	–1.6	3.6	2.9

unexpected decline in world activity, the rise in world real interest rates and by a combination of adverse supply shocks (see Table 4.4). Unlike the Buiter and Miller (1983) case, in which tight monetary policy causes the reduction in activity, the Liverpool model suggests that this would only have a marginal impact on activity. The reasoning can be made clearer by reference to Figure 4.3 again. Tight monetary policy shifts the LM curve to the left and tight fiscal policy initially shifts the IS schedule back to the left. The fall in the price level (disinflation) raises the real value of wealth which offsets the contractionary effect on aggregate demand. The IS schedule therefore moves to the right; meanwhile the unexpected fall in inflation causes the PP schedule to move up to the left, temporarily. The overall effect is that the real exchange rate appreciates (as in Dornbusch, 1976), but the effect on output is ambiguous. A fall in world trade and adverse supply shocks will shift the IS schedule down to the left permanently. This has the unambiguous effect of reducing output.

For the rest of the period, monetary and fiscal policies had

Table 4.5 Productivity growth[1] 1979–87 (annual average %)

Underlying	4.4
external shocks and trend	2.7
supply shocks	1.8
Equilibrium	3.6
external shocks and trend	2.1
supply shocks	1.6
Fitted actual	2.8
fiscal/monetary	0.2
external and supply shocks and trend	2.6
Actual	2.1

Note: [1] Real GDP per person employed

negligible effects on output, while supply shocks offset the negative effects of external shocks. The recovery was therefore caused by the ending of temporarily adverse shocks, some supply effects and robust growth projected in the base run. The base run is governed principally by the state of inflation expectations and the long-run or steady state level of output (capacity output). Lower inflation expectations boost demand through the wealth effect, and positive supply shocks increase steady state output. Projected output, in the Liverpool model, converges on its steady state value, therefore a rise in the latter produces a rise in the former.

We can now use the model to address the question posed at the beginning of this paper. To what extent was the productivity boom of the 1980s caused by fundamental supply factors? Table 4.5 provides a breakdown of the factors contributing to the rise in productivity (real GDP per person employed). The actual rate of growth of productivity over 1979–87 was 2.1 per cent. The model provides three alternative measures of productivity. Underlying productivity is equilibrium output per head of working population and therefore represents potential output per head when the potential labour force is fully employed. Equilibrium productivity is measured as equilibrium output per head of equilibrium employment and thus measures the potential effectiveness of those who will eventually be employed. Fitted productivity is fitted output divided by fitted employment.

According to the model, all measures of productivity grew substantially over the period. Underlying productivity grew by 4.4 per cent, with a substantial increase occurring in 1986–7 as a result of a sharp downturn in union membership and tax cuts. The trend or base projection explains most of the rise in underlying productivity; external shocks had little effect; as such, there is little external shocks had little effect; as such, there is little the model can say about the overall rise, except to note that 40 per cent of the rise was generated by supply innovations (i.e. shocks). The rest is put down to technological, organisational and managerial factors, in part born out of the new entrepreneurial spirit kindled by supply-side reforms. Even when the model's projection for actual productivity is examined, it can be seen that fiscal and monetary shocks have had a negligible effect. It can therefore be concluded that, in so far as the determinants of the productivity boom can be identified, nearly half is explained by supply innovations, the rest, we can speculate, is associated with the supply-side programme. The government's supply-side reforms therefore contributed significantly to the productivity boom.

CONCLUSIONS

There are several conclusions that can be drawn from this exercise. First, the lesson for the government is that credibility for an anti-inflation policy is won only through a continuous series of contractionary shocks to fiscal and monetary policy. Any relaxation of the basic aim could damage credibility seriously. This message is particularly significant in the light of developments at the end of the 1980s, when inflation was allowed to slip out of control. While a negative PSBR in the late 1980s implied zero inflationary pressure in the long run, the consistent breach of the narrow money targets created an inconsistency between fiscal and monetary policy, which added to the inflation 'risk premium'.

The second lesson is in the area of political economy and the strategy of implementing the supply-side programme. The so-called 'Thatcher revolution' was successful because it rolled back the boundaries of the state in a cautious, piecemeal way. In carrying through each step, the former Prime Minister exhibited unusual political judgement in tackling those areas that yielded the most immediate results. The supply-side programme succeeded by altering the structure of the economy and the attitude of the workforce. Further reforms are being carried through (e.g. National Health Service, education) and the privatisation programme is being extended further (e.g. British Rail, British Coal). Despite the success of the programme to date, each step has taken the Conservative government into a potential political minefield, which has required astuteness as well as political will.

The third lesson is for the professional economist. Before Mrs Thatcher embarked upon her programme, there was little support for the MTFS or for the new classical rational expectations theory that underpinned it. The success of the programme may not have occurred in the way theory predicted, but few macroeconomists today would deny the force of the new classical revolution. Consistent or rational expectations, once the preserve of the Liverpool model only, are now a feature of the London Business School (LBS), National Institute (see Chapter 2) and Treasury models.

The economic forecaster has also had to eat humble pie as conventional models failed to predict both the inflationary downturn and the economic recovery (Liverpool excepted). In the field of applied economics, the consensus view has been challenged. Conventional empirical regularities have been challenged, overturned or simply ignored if they failed to persuade. Examples of this are the so-called 'zero wage elasticity of demand for labour', the zero effect of taxes and benefits on labour supply, the unimportance of supply and the all-importance of demand.

Monetary economists have also been forced to recognise the importance of the narrow money supply (M0) for the determination of inflation, which has received theoretical support from the 'new monetary economics'. On the whole, economists have come to accept the case that the world is much closer to the description given to it by their predecessors – the 'classical economists' like Adam Smith and David Ricardo – than they once believed. One no longer hears of the famous 364 economists who once signed a declaration (in March 1981) that there was no theoretical or empirical basis for the Conservative government's policy. As to whether the economy has fundamentally altered and climbed on to a higher productive plane, only time will tell. The speculation of this chapter, backed up with the pseudo-econometric analysis of the Liverpool macroeconomic model, is that Britain has undergone an economic renaissance.

5

THE ECONOMY AFTER TEN YEARS

Stronger or weaker?

John Wells

INTRODUCTION

The Conservative government's claim to economic success rests on a number of genuine achievements. Before Mrs Thatcher became Prime Minister in 1979, Britain had for many years been at the bottom of the international league table in terms of rates of growth in gross domestic product (GDP), but during her time in office it was operating much closer to the top. The same can be said about the rate of growth of labour productivity (i.e. output per person employed) in manufacturing industry (but see Healey, 1992a).

Moreover, between 1982 and 1989, the country chalked up seven consecutive years of continuous output growth. As a result, total employment – which fell by 1.8 million during the years 1979–83 and then increased by 2.6 million over 1983–8 – peaked in 1989 at a level which (including those on official government training programmes) was 0.8 million higher than in 1979. Unemployment, which reached 11.1 per cent of the labour force in 1986, dropped below 6 per cent during 1990. Although Britain entered the 1990s in recession, with unemployment once again rising rapidly, the performance of the economy between the peak of the late 1970s boom in 1979 and the peak of the last boom in 1990 was undoubtedly impressive. By the end of the decade, real national income was some 23 per cent – nearly one-quarter – higher than it was in 1979, and the increase in total domestic absorption (the sum of consumption and investment, both public and private) was 26.2 per cent higher in real terms.

It is claimed that such success is due to a new spirit of enterprise abroad in the country, unleashed by the Conservative government's unconditional commitment to competition and the operation of market forces; and that it has been reinforced by the major reduction in the role of the state in economic life and by the government's incentive and supply-side policies of tax cuts, deregulation and privatisation.

The other main factor contributing to success has been the new industrial relations scenario – as evidenced by the big fall in the number of days lost through strikes and the greater spirit of co-operation and conciliation on the shop floor. This change has been the product, the government argues, of its trade union legislation (see Chapter 10) and of its courage in tackling head-on the exercise of overweening and irresponsible trade union power.

A REAL 'ECONOMIC MIRACLE'?

Yet doubts concerning whether the government really has delivered an economic miracle remain. If such is the case, then why did Britain suffer a trade deficit as large as any in her history at the end of the 1980s? (See also Chapter 3.) The only other modern parallel in 1974 was in the wake of the OPEC oil price rise, when Britain was a substantial net importer of oil. Why did inflation, previously thought to have been brought under control, rapidly accelerate at the end of the decade to peak at over 10 per cent? Furthermore, why was the government forced to deflate the economy in the early 1990s, even though the country was still far from full employment?

It looks as though, now that North Sea oil is beginning to run out, Britain under the Conservative government has, in fact, failed to escape from the so-called 'stop–go' cycle which bedevilled economic life in the 1960s and 1970s. The 1986–8 episode looks similar to the 1972–3 'go' phase of massive injections of domestic spending, which came to grief amid mounting balance of payments and inflation crises. Will the early 1990s repeat the pattern of the past, with a subsequent 'stop' phase of slower growth and rising unemployment?

THE PHASES OF THE THATCHER DECADE

In trying to determine whether an economic miracle has in fact taken place, the most obvious indicator to start with is the rate of GDP growth, which measures the change in the total output of goods and services in the economy as a whole. In doing so, it is worth dividing the Thatcher decade into three phases, so far as macroeconomic policy and performance are concerned.

Phase I, which lasted from 1979 to 1982, was presided over by Sir Geoffrey Howe as Chancellor of the Exchequer. During this period, the defeat of inflation was elevated to become the overriding objective of economic policy – to which all other goals, in particular the achievement of a reasonably high level of employment and a satisfactory rate of output growth, were completely subordinated.

Deliberately eschewing the prices and incomes policies of the previous social democratic era, the Thatcherites turned Britain into the test-bed for a laboratory experiment in reducing inflation via the adoption of so-called 'monetarist' policies (Healey, 1987b). Based upon a diagnosis of inflation as simply the result of excess demand, such policies sought to squeeze inflation out of the system by reducing demand. To this end, the government adopted very restrictive monetary policies (high interest rates and a tough credit squeeze), together with a tight fiscal stance (increased taxes and severe restrictions on the growth of public expenditure). These policies were undoubtedly extremely successful in bringing about big reductions in domestic expenditure, especially investment spending. In addition, the fact that Thatcherite monetarist policies came on stream at the same time as North Sea oil resulted in a considerable appreciation of the real value of sterling. This, in turn, had strongly negative effects on the international competitive position of domestic producers, in both home and overseas markets. The high value of the pound had particularly pronounced, adverse effects on the sector most exposed to international competition, namely manufacturing industry.

The policies of Phase I (deflation of domestic spending and exchange appreciation) undoubtedly succeeded, together with disinflationary pressures worldwide, in dampening down inflation. But, set against this achievement, a very high price was paid in the form of the most severe output recession since the Second World War, with two consecutive years of substantial reductions in GDP, whilst unemployment shot up to well over 3 million. British manufacturing industry suffered even more than during the Great Depression of the 1930s: manufacturing output fell by as much as 19.6 per cent from peak (June 1979) to trough (January 1981); between one-fifth and one-quarter of the sector's equipment and capacity were destroyed and 1.7 million jobs (or 23 per cent of the 1979 manufacturing labour force) were lost.

Phase I of Thatcherism gradually gave way, particularly following the General Election of 1983, to Phase II, which lasted until 1988. This period, presided over by Nigel Lawson as Chancellor, saw much more expansionary policies being followed. In fact, Phase II was characterised by an almost complete 'U-turn', as regards some of the principal aspects of macroeconomic policy.

Monetary restraint was, in practice, completely abandoned, and there ensued a period of exceptionally rapid monetary expansion, fuelled by deregulation and increased competition within the financial sector, together with the willingness of those in the personal sector to get themselves into debt on a quite unparalleled scale. The consequential rapid growth of private consumption was also stimulated by rapid increases in real earnings, personal tax cuts and asset (especially house) price inflation – with all these factors reinforcing and feeding on one other.

A further change in policy during Phase II was the substantial depreciation of sterling from the unsustainable heights of 1981, which had the effect of improving the international competitiveness of British producers. Even fiscal policy was relaxed slightly during Phase II, although mainly as a result of income tax cuts and not because of any significant relaxation of the restrictions on the growth of government spending. The rapid growth in private consumers' expenditure unleashed during the recovery phase was also accompanied by a gradual recovery in investment from the exceptionally low levels of 1981–2. The rapid growth of these two important elements of domestic expenditure resulted in a strong recovery in domestic output and employment during Phase II.

Phase II gave way, during the course of 1988, to Phase III, in which the government, amidst mounting trade deficits and accelerating inflation, used high interest rates to dampen down growth. For the rest of the decade the authorities battled against the explosion in demand which had been unleashed by the earlier credit boom of 1986–8. By 1990, the tide had turned and inflation fell swiftly, but at the cost of a sharp rise in unemployment.

EVALUATING THE GROWTH PHASE

It is the rapid output and employment growth of Phase II which the Thatcherites point to as evidence of having achieved an economic miracle. And it is the evaluation of this experience with which this chapter is primarily concerned, rather than the recessions which preceded and succeeded Phase II. In assessing the 'miracle' claim, a number of points needs to be borne in mind. First, the rates of output growth achieved during the 1980s were not, in any sense, particularly spectacular. They were certainly no higher than the growth rates attained during the decades prior to the oil crises of the early 1970s.

Second, Britain's growth performance in the international league table of the 1980s looks good for two reasons:

1 the selective exclusion from the calculations of the disastrous years 1979–81;
2 the fact that large parts of continental Western Europe, but particularly Germany and France, are still wedded to the restrictive 'monetarist' policies of Phase I Thatcherism.

They failed to adopt expansionary policies, not on account of any underlying weakness in their economies, but because of an obsessive and almost certainly exaggerated fear of the adverse consequences of expansion for inflation. Third, it is not at all remarkable that massive increases in domestic spending should have given rise to substantial increases in output and employment.

The reasons for this last point are easy to appreciate. As total domestic spending rises, there is an increase in expenditure on each of its two component parts: non-traded goods and services (i.e. commodities that are relatively sheltered from the forces of international competition) and traded goods and services (i.e. those exposed to international competition). The non-traded sector incorporates the output of construction, public utilities, and a large proportion of the output of the service sector (including both private and publicly provided services). Within the traded categories, on the other hand, there is North Sea oil, most of manufacturing, and the internationally traded component of the services.

Obviously, given the high level of unemployment after the recession of Phase I, it was relatively easy for the non-traded sectors of the British economy to respond to an increase in the demand for their output. Employment creation, especially in the services, was also facilitated by the comparatively low capital requirements per job created and by the comparatively high elasticity of employment growth relative to output growth – a consequence of the sector's comparatively low level and rate of growth of labour productivity.

When it came to satisfying that part of the rapidly growing total of domestic expenditure which was devoted to traded goods and services – and it should be remembered that British demand for some traded goods and services, such as consumer durables and foreign holidays, is highly income-elastic – then the British economy benefited from two favourable developments during Phase II (1983–8). First, the depreciation of the real exchange rate of the 1980–1 period, resulted in at least some improvement in the international competitiveness of traded production, thereby enabling the sector to respond more effectively to the increase in domestic demand for traded goods and services.

Second, the economy's ability to satisfy the increase in domestic demand for traded goods and services was facilitated by the rapid build-up of North Sea oil and gas output at a time of high energy prices, which contributed directly to the increase in traded output. For a while at least, therefore, improvements in the oil balance of trade enabled the country to satisfy, from overseas suppliers, part of the increase in domestic spending on traded goods and services (especially of manufactures) via increased net imports. Put another way, the rapid build-up of North Sea oil and foreign exchange earnings permitted (at least up until 1986–7) a very considerable relaxation of the balance of payments constraint which, during the 1950s and 1960s, had brought earlier attempts at economic expansion, fuelled by rapid increases in domestic spending, to a painful end amidst mounting balance of payments crises.

Finally, the fact that the output boom of the late 1980s was sustained for so long was the result of dramatically changed conditions (at least compared with the 1950s and 1960s) in international financial markets. The increased availability of a massive volume of internationally foot-loose funds enabled Britain to attract sufficient finance to sustain a current account deficit in 1989 of over £20bn (or 4 per cent of GDP). Such massive resort to foreign savings kept the domestic boom going for longer, and with an intensity which was greater, than would otherwise have been possible, for the simple reason that it enabled the economy to sustain a level of domestic expenditure (on traded goods and services, as well as on non-traded goods and services) far higher than the level of domestic output (see Healey and Levine, 1990).

Of course, the non-traded component of that higher level of domestic expenditure gave rise to further increases in output and employment. However, the fact that the current account was gradually sliding into deficit shows that the economy was failing to match the increase in domestic spending on traded goods and services with a corresponding increase in domestic output.

THE TRADED SECTOR AND THE CURRENT ACCOUNT DEFICIT

The external developments of the late 1980s revealed the full predicament of the British economy. Massive increases in domestic expenditure certainly succeeded in bringing about substantial increases in output and employment in the non-traded sector. However, the failure of British traded sector output to grow as fast as domestic spending on traded goods and services gave rise to an unsustainable current account deficit.

Faced with mounting inflation and balance of payments pressures, the government was forced to moderate the growth of domestic spending – thereby seeking to depress the growth of output and employment in the economy, especially in its non-traded sectors – at a time when, at least according to the old method of counting, there are probably still well over 2 million unemployed (Southworth, 1987). Thus, whereas, as the former Chancellor, Nigel Lawson, put it 'we have been having a little bit too much of a good thing' (i.e. the rate of growth of domestic spending was excessive relative to the productive capacity of the economy, especially its traded sector), the level of domestic expenditure still fell short of what is necessary to achieve anything remotely approaching full employment.

The principal lesson of all this is as follows: any country can generate substantial increases in output and employment – especially in the non-traded sector of its economy – on the basis of rapid increases in domestic expenditure. However, such a process clearly has its limits, particularly in a situation where a primary product bonanza, such as North Sea oil, is of diminishing importance. Unless the expansion of expenditure and output of traded goods and services proceed at the same pace, then the trade balance will deteriorate – posing a threat to continued increases in domestic output and employment (especially in the non-traded sector). Thus, the performance of the traded sector is absolutely crucial to an economy's ability to attain employment and external balance targets – in other words, to its ability to reconcile internal balance (full employment and price stability) with external balance.

To understand why the performance of the internationally exposed or traded sector of the British economy was inadequate during the Thatcher decade, it is convenient to start with the manufacturing sector. For one thing, manufacturing accounts for by far the largest share of total traded output (taking both exports and import-

97

Table 5.1 The rate of growth of output per person employed in manufacturing

	1960–70	1970–80	1980–8
UK	3.0	1.6	5.2
US	3.5	3.0	4.0
Japan	8.8	5.3	3.1
Germany	4.1	2.9	2.2
France	5.4	3.2	3.1
Italy	5.4	3.0	3.5
Canada	3.4	3.0	3.6
G7 average	4.5	3.3	3.6

Source: HM Treasury, *Economic Progress Report*
Note: UK data from Central Statistical Office. Other countries' data from OECD, except France and Italy which use IMF employment data. 1988 data for France and Italy cover first three-quarters only

competing production together). In addition, whilst the share of trade in total output is far from insignificant in the case of services, it is much higher in the case of manufacturing.

MANUFACTURING PRODUCTIVITY AND PROFITABILITY

Two of the indicators most favourable to the miracle hypothesis are to be found in the manufacturing sector during the Phase II period: a pronounced acceleration in the rate of growth of labour productivity (output per person employed); and a greatly enhanced profitability of manufacturing enterprises. There is no doubt that manufacturing labour productivity growth did accelerate – both in relation to Britain's own past performance and in comparison to its international competitors (see Table 5.1). Previously bottom of the league table in terms of manufacturing labour productivity growth, Britain was at the top in the 1980s. Profitability in manufacturing also improved, as rapid productivity growth helped to keep labour costs down.

However – and this was one of the central failures of economic performance during the Thatcher decade – these manufacturing productivity gains were not reflected in a corresponding increase in output and world market share. How can this be demonstrated? The conventional approach to assessing manufacturing performance is to examine the sector's share of world manufactured exports. Following several decades of virtually uninterrupted decline (see Figure 5.1),

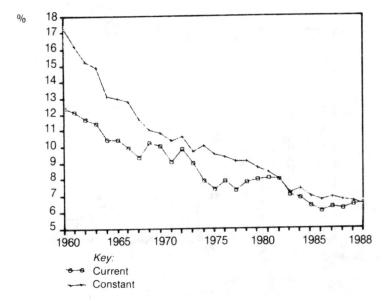

Figure 5.1 UK's share of world manufactured exports, 1960–88 at current
US$ and constant 1980 US$
Source: UN, *Yearbook of International Trade Statistics*

Britain's share of world manufactured exports fell by a further 2 per
cent during the early 1980s. However, during the latter half of the
1980s, Britain's share stabilised – and may well have increased
slightly. This is certainly a remarkable development – and one which
the Conservative government, perhaps rather surprisingly, has
almost entirely ignored in its litany of 'miraculous' economic events.

However, in the internationally integrated markets in which
manufacturing enterprises operate today, performance in world
export markets is only part of the story – and hence does not provide
a comprehensive and unambiguous measure of manufacturing
performance. When there exists, as there does today, virtually a
single, unified, global market in manufactures, encompassing all of the
developed, as well as many developing, countries, what counts is
performance across all markets. It is not only a country's (or a firm's)
ability to hold on to overseas market share that matters, but also its
capacity to fend off imports and foreign penetration of its domestic
market. And, here, on the import-penetration side, manufacturing's
performance during the Thatcher decade was simply abysmal: the

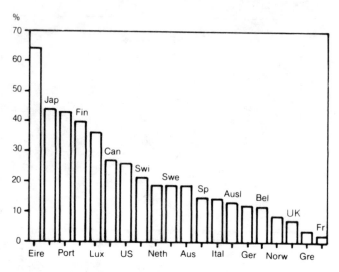

Figure 5.2 Percentage increase in manufacturing output: twenty OECD countries, 1979–88
Source: OECD, *Main Economic Indicators*

ratio of imports to total manufacturing output increased by 31.2 per cent between 1979 and 1988, reflecting a rise in manufactured imports of 98.7 per cent.

In fact, there is just one measure that summarises satisfactorily manufacturing's performance in global markets and that is the growth of total output (whether for home or for overseas markets) relative to that of its competitors. And in this respect, the precise extent of the weakness of British manufacturing's performance during the Thatcher decade is not very widely appreciated. Comparing the growth in manufacturing output among the G7 most advanced industrial countries (1979–88), Britain stands sixth – with only France showing a weaker performance. In a group of twenty OECD countries, Britain stands eighteenth – with only France and Greece doing worse (see Figure 5.2).

The problem with British manufacturing output growth during the Thatcher decade was that, whereas growth was rapid during the post-1982 recovery phase (at least as rapid as in services and in the economy as a whole), the sector failed to make good the massive output losses (relative to GDP) of 1980–1. The reason for this appears to lie in the failure of British manufacturing as a whole to translate increases in labour productivity and profitability into higher levels of investment. Estimates of manufacturing investment (including leased assets) show that it was only during 1988 that gross fixed investment in manufacturing, at constant prices, managed to rise above the levels attained at the end of the 1970s – and then by only a very small margin.

The reasons why manufacturing investment in sectors such as mechanical engineering and clothing was not stronger – even during Phase II – are worth reflecting upon. One explanation must lie in the lingering effects that the policies of Phase I (a squeeze on domestic absorption plus real exchange appreciation) had on investors' confidence – effects that led investors to adopt a 'wait-and-see' attitude to the recovery, despite improved prospects in Britain. Doubts probably also existed about the permanence of the Thatcher political revolution. There is also the question of corporate strategy to consider: there is a growing body of evidence that many British manufacturers have decided to opt for 'niche' strategies. Having conceded certain mass markets for standardised commodities, both at home and abroad, to their competitors, they have decided to concentrate on smaller, more specialised, possibly high-profit activities – a strategy that guarantees a company a quite viable and profitable existence, but does not result in the recapturing of mass markets at home or abroad.

PERFORMANCE IN THE SERVICE INDUSTRIES

Surely the answer will come back: in today's world, we no longer need to worry if the country's manufacturing performance is relatively weak. After all, in Britain today, manufacturing now accounts for only 24 per cent of total output and just 22 per cent of total employment. Surely, it is argued, in the 'post-industrial' society into which we are moving, in which spending and employment are shifting away from manufactures and towards the services, it is performance in the services that counts – not manufacturing.

In responding to this point, it certainly has to be accepted that the services were the really bright spot in the British economy during the 1980s. Whilst manufacturing output grew to no more than 11.5 per cent above its 1979 level by the end of the decade, with manufacturing employment 2 million lower, service output jumped by 29 per cent and nearly all of the jobs that have been created since 1983 have been in the services (see Figure 5.3).

However, this imbalance or unevenness between manufactures and

101

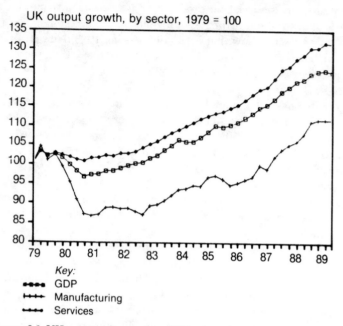

Figure 5.3 UK output by sector: GDP, manufacturing and services, at constant 1985 £m, reference base 1979 = 100
Source: UK official statistics

services, and the weak manufacturing performance that underlies it, does remain a grave cause for concern (see also Chapter 13), for the following reason. In employment terms, it is certainly true that Britain is becoming more of a 'post-industrial' society, as employment in the services increases both absolutely and relatively. However, in addition to the recent, more rapid growth of service output relative to manufactures, this simply reflects the much slower rate of growth of labour productivity in services, compared with manufacturing, as a result of which the scope for employment creation in services is much greater compared with manufacturing.

However, when we look at the pattern of domestic spending, there is no sign that Britain is becoming a post-industrial society, in the sense of experiencing a shift in the pattern of spending away from manufactures towards services. Taking the Thatcher decade as a whole, total domestic expenditure rose in real terms by 26.2 per cent. But, within that total, spending on manufactures and services rose by roughly the same amount. It is here that we find the reason why the poor manufacturing output record is such a cause for concern. Whilst the increase in domestic demand for services in 1979–88 (of roughly 26 per cent) was associated with a roughly equal increase in the domestic output of services (27.4 per cent), the increase in domestic spending on manufactures (of roughly 26 per cent) contrasts with an increase in manufacturing output of just 7.8 per cent.

The fact that the growth of domestic demand for manufactures outstripped the growth of domestic output of manufactures resulted, of course, in a steady deterioration of the manufacturing trade balance – from the onset of economic recovery (in 1982–3) onwards up until recession once again struck in 1990. Initially, the manufacturing trade balance went from surplus into deficit. But, then, as the decade drew to a close, those deficits grew larger and larger (see Figure 5.4) to the point where, by 1988, the deficit in British manufacturing trade amounted to £14.9bn. What this means is that roughly 15 per cent of Britain's total domestic spending on manufactures was being supplied, net, by overseas producers during the late 1980s.

But, surely, the response will be: in this post-industrial society into which we are moving, is Britain not becoming increasingly specialised as a net exporter of services, especially of financial services? Consequently, surely the country can afford to offset any deterioration in its manufacturing trade balance with growing surpluses in service trade? In other words, there are other areas of traded output that can compensate for the unsatisfactory rate of growth of manufacturing output.

It is certainly true that, in the early 1980s, the adverse effect on Britain's overall trade balance (taking manufactures and non-manufactures together) of the deterioration of manufacturing trade was obscured by large and growing surpluses in non-manufacturing trade (i.e. food, raw materials, fuel and services: see Figure 5.4). And the non-manufacturing balance was greatly strengthened by improvements in fuel trade, resulting from the build-up in North Sea production, as well as the large surpluses being earned in service trade.

However, in recent years, Britain's export surplus in oil trade has almost completely disappeared as a result of falling oil prices and depressed production (due, partly, to the Piper Alpha disaster). Meanwhile, Britain's balance in service trade, though it is still in surplus, deteriorated sharply in the latter half of the 1980s, partly as a result of the rapid growth of British tourist spending abroad. The effect of these developments was that, by the end of the decade,

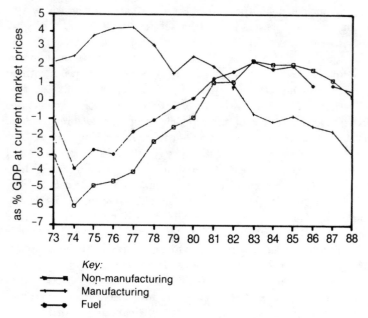

Figure 5.4 UK external balances as percentage of GDP at current market prices 1973–88
Source: UK official statistics

Britain's non-manufacturing trade was no longer in surplus and was actually recording small deficits (see Figure 5.4). As a result, there was nothing to set off against the huge manufacturing trade deficit, which coincided almost exactly with the deficit on current account as a whole (the sum of trade in manufactures and non-manufactures taken together).

Current account deficits of this size are quite unprecedented in British history – except, briefly, in 1974, in the immediate aftermath of OPEC's first oil price increase, when Britain was a net oil importer: a very different situation from today. At the same time as Britain is running a huge deficit on current account, it is also investing, on a massive scale and, long-term, abroad – to a far greater degree than foreigners are investing, long-term, in Britain (see Healey and Levine, 1990). As a result, the long-term capital account registered a deficit of £31bn in 1989. The sum total of these twin deficits (the so-called 'basic balance') in 1989 was £52bn (or 10 per cent of GDP), a total of quite unprecedented proportions, requiring massive short-term capital inflows (hot money inflows) to balance the books.

INTERNAL AND EXTERNAL BALANCE

At the most general level, the fundamental cause of Britain's inability to reconcile internal and external balance lies, as argued earlier, in the inadequate volume of traded output as a whole (including not only manufactures but also primary products and internationally traded services). However, if we examine possible scenarios for the 1980s, then the most reasonable conclusion to reach is that the inadequate rate of growth in manufacturing output bears the lion's share of responsibility for the inadequate level of traded output overall. So far as primary production is concerned, it is difficult to imagine that the rate of oil depletion could have been any higher; whilst there simply would not have existed any additional international market outlets for Britain's relatively high-cost agricultural output.

On the other hand, the output of internationally traded services could certainly have been higher (and, in the case of tourism, was undoubtedly depressed by the high real exchange rate of the early 1980s). However, in some of the principal areas of internationally traded services – in particular, financial, consultancy and engineering services – output and export growth were already exceptionally rapid during the 1980s. Moreover, in many services, Britain's world market share is considerably higher than in the case of manufactures. Thus, it is difficult to believe that the growth of internationally traded service output could have been much faster than it actually was.

The British manufacturing sector that survived the Thatcher decade is certainly leaner and fitter, employing a vastly reduced labour force more productively and much more profitably. However, given the likely potential of the other traded sectors of the British economy, it can be argued that the manufacturing sector has become too small. Britain simply does not have a large enough manufacturing sector to sustain the level of total domestic expenditure on traded and non-traded goods and services alike that would be associated with full employment.

THE BALANCE OF PAYMENTS DEFICIT

But, surely, people will argue: why worry about running such large trade deficits and engaging in foreign borrowing on such a scale? Is this not just a sign of buoyancy of the economy and of the investment boom that is underway? If increased investment cannot be financed from domestic savings, what is wrong with resorting to foreign savings? If the developing countries can be encouraged to borrow abroad to build up their economies, why should a developed economy, such as Britain, not engage in foreign borrowing to renovate its economic fabric?

In itself, this is a perfectly acceptable argument – with quite a long pedigree to it (see Healey, 1991a). However, when engaging in foreign borrowing, developing countries are typically encouraged to ensure that, simultaneously, every effort is made to promote domestic savings and to ensure that the foreign savings, which are being absorbed, are used productively. With these points in mind, a number of doubts inevitably arise concerning Britain's resort to foreign savings during the 1980s.

For one thing, it was only in 1988 that gross investment as a percentage of GDP rose above the levels seen at the end of the 1970s: in every intervening year it was lower. Moreover, the 1988 investment boom was already running out of steam within twelve months. Thus, Britain's long-standing underinvestment problem was actually accentuated during the Thatcher decade. Another anxiety concerns composition of the investment that took place. Too much of it, almost certainly, was in sheltered activities, not exposed to international competition (such as shopping centres, hypermarkets, inner-city redevelopments, etc.), whereas an insufficient proportion went into internationally exposed activities, such as manufacturing. The problem with this will surface as Britain is forced to close its current trade gap during the 1990s, via a combination of increased exports and import-substitutes. As this happens, the deficiencies of the recent investment composition will come to light.

Moreover, the increase in investment share (1979–88) amounted to 1.7 per cent of GDP against a deterioration in the current account balance of -3.8 per cent of GDP. Thus, the increased resort to foreign savings can only partly be justified on the basis of the strength of domestic investment; the rapid growth of British consumption and the corresponding reduction in domestic savings were equally responsible. Certainly, any developing country that engaged in a rapid expansion of private consumption, whilst resorting to foreign savings, would be severely castigated.

Finally, it is to be regretted that all of the potential for increased domestic savings, which accrued from the squeeze on public consumption spending, was lost in a private consumption boom. The result was that, when the recovery in investment eventually occurred, domestic resources had already been pre-empted by the rapid growth

Table 5.2 Internal–external balance trade-off for the UK (1979 and 1988 compared)

	Unemployment (as % of total working pop.)	Inflation (RPI % increase on year earlier)	Current A/C balance (as % of GDP)
1979	4.0	13.3	−0.3
1988	8.0	4.9	−3.2

of private consumption – so that, in order to keep the investment boom going, the country had to gain access to overseas resources via a growing current account deficit and increasing resort to foreign savings. The main point here is that private consumption was allowed to become too great and domestic savings too low.

CONCLUSIONS

Is there a simple way of summarising Britain's overall economic performance since 1979? And of answering the question: is the economy in a stronger or weaker position now than it was at the end of the 1970s? One way of doing this is to answer the question: to what extent, comparing 1979 with the present, is Britain capable of achieving what are normally taken to be the conventional goals of economic policy? Namely, being in a position to reconcile the achievement of internal balance (i.e. full employment and a stable price level) with external balance (i.e. balance on current plus long-term capital account).

The data presented in Table 5.2 help us to answer this question. In fact, we find that there was both a higher rate of unemployment and a weaker external position in 1988 than in 1979. Only with respect to inflation was the position better in 1988 than in 1979 – though not by a great deal: the retail price index (RPI) was rising at 8.3 per cent per annum, in May 1989; in May 1979 it was 10.3 per cent per annum.

The information in Table 5.2 would seem to constitute quite strong *a priori* evidence against an economic miracle and in favour of the view that the economy is now almost certainly in a weaker position with respect to achieving internal and external balance than in the late 1970s. This is particularly unfortunate given the enormous opportunity for modernising the economy, represented by North Sea oil wealth. Thus, to be in a position where, with still well over 2 million unemployed, the government was forced to deflate the economy (as it did from mid-1988 onwards with its high interest rate policy), in order to stem inflationary pressures and limit the extent of the trade balance deterioration represents a severe condemnation of the economic record of the three Conservative administrations.

For those who remain unconvinced by this argument, the next few years will see an exceptionally demanding test of the record. The principal medium-term aim of economic policy must be to bring about a reduction in the size of the trade deficit, although the speed at which this will happen is impossible to predict, depending, as it does, on the willingness of international capital markets to keep on lending us money.

If the Thatcher decade had produced an economic miracle – in other words, a fundamental improvement in competitiveness in the internationally exposed sectors of the economy – then, in response to the recent cutbacks in domestic expenditure, British producers should have had no difficulty in switching output from home to overseas markets and building up import-competing areas of production. Had they been able to do this, then the early 1990s might have seen a 'soft landing' – a recession-free improvement in the trade balance. In fact, the economy has suffered a very definite 'hard landing', with improvements in the trade balance requiring quite savage cuts in domestic expenditure. It is hard to escape the conclusion that there has been no economic miracle in Britain.

6

AN ASSESSMENT OF BRITAIN'S PRODUCTIVITY RECORD IN THE 1980s

Has there been a miracle?

David H. Blackaby and Leslie C. Hunt

INTRODUCTION

After more than ten years of Conservative government, there has been much analysis of the performance of the British economy over this period. See, for example, articles by Godley (1989); Layard and Nickell (1989), (1990); and Matthews and Stoney (1990). These tend to discuss a wide range of issues, such as unemployment, inflation, trade performance, income distribution and productivity. This chapter, however, focuses on one issue for which the government has claimed particular success, namely, productivity.

Growth in productivity is a major contributor to a nation's prosperity. Higher living standards can normally only be obtained through higher productivity, which, in turn, is an important determinant of international competitiveness. A country's competitive position in international markets improves when its productivity increases faster than that of its international competitors, unless there are offsetting adjustments in exchange rates or real labour costs.

Given the importance of productivity, it is not surprising that it attracts much political and media attention. Nigel Lawson, the former Chancellor of the Exchequer, often claimed a productivity 'miracle' for the Thatcher era:

> The plain fact is that the British economy has been transformed. Prudent financial policies have given business and industry the confidence to expand, while supply-side reforms have progressively removed the barriers to enterprise.
>
> Nowhere has this transformation been more marked than in manufacturing where output rose by 5.5 per cent during the 1980s. This outstanding performance was founded on a further

Table 6.1 UK output per head (average annual % changes)

	1964–73	1973–9	1979–88
Manufacturing	3.8	0.7	4.2
Non-manufacturing	3.0	0.5	1.75
Whole economy	2.7	1.1	2.1

Source: Central Statistical Office (CSO) data bank at the University of Bath
Notes: Manufacturing and whole economy figures calculated from the output per head index. Non-manufacturing are HM Treasury figures which exclude public services and North Sea oil and gas extraction

big improvement in productivity. In the 1980s, output per head in manufacturing went up faster in Britain than in any other major industrial country. This was in stark contrast to the 1960s and the 1970s, when in the growth of manufacturing productivity, as in so much else, we were at the bottom of the league.[1]

The 'miracle' hypothesis has been questioned, however. With manufacturing output and investment only returning to 1979 levels at the very end of the decade, and manufacturing employment failing to regain its 1979 level, some commentators argue that the long-standing problems of British industry have yet to be tackled. This chapter attempts to answer the following two questions:

1 Has there been a productivity 'miracle' (or at least a significant breakthrough)?
2 If the answer is yes (with or without qualifications), can the productivity performance of the 1980s be sustained into the 1990s?

THE FACTS ABOUT BRITAIN'S PRODUCTIVITY PERFORMANCE

Before looking at the evidence, it is necessary to clarify exactly what is meant by 'productivity'. Strictly speaking, productivity refers to the average amount of output produced by all inputs. The debate, however, has largely centred around output per unit of labour or 'labour productivity', in particular 'output per person employed' (usually referred to as 'output per head'). This is by no means the only measure of labour productivity. It may also be measured by 'output per person hour', involving adjustment for changes in the utilisation of labour over time (due to changes in the length of the working day, week or year). In addition, there is 'capital productivity', measured by output per unit of capital. Another useful measure is the more comprehensive 'total factor productivity'. This is output per unit of 'average input', where average input is a weighted average of the factors of production. The weights in this average are the shares of the factors of production, labour and capital, in gross domestic product – roughly 70 per cent for labour and 30 per cent for capital – see Whitmarsh (1982) and Venables (1989) for more discussion of these issues.

The growth in British output per head for the manufacturing and non-manufacturing sectors and for the whole economy is shown in Table 6.1. Both broad sectors of the economy suffered a marked slowdown in the growth of output per head during the 1970s after the first OPEC oil crisis of 1973–4. Since 1979, however, there has been a considerable improvement, with manufacturing output per head rising much faster than during the 1973–9 period. Moreover, manufacturing output per head has grown faster in the 1980s than in the period before 1973–4, leading the Conservative government to claim in 1988 that:

> Underlying growth in labour productivity in manufacturing now appears to be higher than the rate experienced in the 1960s.[2]

However, it appears that no underlying improvement has taken place in non-manufacturing and 'whole-economy' output per head growth. While some improvements took place in the 1980s compared to the 1973–9 period, non-manufacturing and whole-economy output per head growth in the 1980s is still below that achieved between 1964 and 1973. Indeed, non-manufacturing productivity growth in the 1980s is barely half that achieved in the earlier period. There has been, though, a large increase in part-time employment in the service sector in the 1980s which has depressed the growth in output per head. During the last decade the gap in output per head growth between manufacturing and non-manufacturing increased owing to the 'acceleration' in growth in manufacturing output per head.

Most analyses of productivity concentrate on the manufacturing sector, justified on the grounds that it is the key to the growth and transformation of the whole economy. The idea is that a country will not achieve strong total output growth without a corresponding manufacturing output growth which, in turn, is unlikely to occur without strong manufacturing productivity growth. It is of some

Table 6.2 UK manufacturing output per head (average annual % changes)

1980 SIC	Sector name	1973-9	1979-88
21-4	Metals, Other Minerals and Mineral Products	-0.2	7.9
25-6	Chemicals and Man-Made Fibres	1.6	5.7
31	Metal Goods n.e.s.	-0.9	3.6
32	Mechanical Engineering	-0.8	2.3
33-4, 37	Office Machinery, Electrical Engineering and Instruments	2.0	7.6
35	Motor Vehicles and Parts	-1.3	5.1
36	Other Transport Equipment	-0.6	5.9
41-2	Food, Drink and Tobacco	1.8	3.6
43	Textiles	0.8	3.3
44-5	Clothing, Footwear and Leather	3.2	2.6
47	Paper, Printing and Publishing	0.1	3.0
46, 48-9	All Other Manufacturing (including Timber, Furniture, Rubber and Plastics)	0.9	2.7
2-4	TOTAL MANUFACTURING	0.6	4.6

Source: CSO data bank at the University of Bath and the Department of Employment
Notes: Calculated from the index of output for each year and employees in employment as of June of each year. The CSO does produce an output per head index for these sub-sectors which includes self-employment in the denominator. However, the revised index only goes back to 1978 and the actual self-employment data are not published at a disaggregated level. Thus the average annual growth for total manufacturing differs from that in Table 6.1. (Although self-employment has grown significantly in the 1980s it is still a small proportion of total manufacturing employment, about 4 per cent in 1986.)

interest, therefore, to look at the growth in output per head of the sub-sectors of manufacturing. Table 6.2 shows that most sub-sectors experienced an improvement in the growth of output per head in the period 1979-88 compared with 1973-9. These improvements, however, are by no means evenly distributed. Output per head growth in the 'Clothing, Footwear and Leather' sector was actually less in the period 1979-88 than the period 1973-9 (when it had well above average growth), while 'Food, Drink and Tobacco', and 'All Other Manufacturing' improved by less than 2 per cent per year on average. 'Metals, Other Minerals and Mineral Products', 'Motor Vehicles and Parts' and 'Other Transport Equipment', on the other hand, showed improvements of over 6 per cent per annum on average.

Table 6.3 gives similar figures for sub-sectors of non-manufacturing. The change in the growth of output per head for services is smaller and more evenly distributed than that of manufacturing.

Table 6.3 UK non-manufacturing output per head (average annual % changes)

1980 SIC	Sector name	1973-9	1979-88
0	Agriculture, Forestry and Fishing	3.2	5.3
1	Energy and Water Supply	10.4	6.6
5	Construction	-0.9	4.6
6	Distribution, Hotels and Catering, and Repairs	-1.0	2.3
7	Transport and Communication	1.8	4.3
8	Banking, Finance, Insurance, Business Services and Leasing	1.5	1.0
91	Public Administration and Defence	-0.5	0.8
93, 95	Education and Health Services	0.8	0.4
92, 94, 96–9	Other Services	-0.4	0.5
6–9	TOTAL SERVICES	0.2	1.5
0–1, 5–9	TOTAL NON-MANUFACTURING	0.9	2.1

Source: CSO data bank at the University of Bath and the Department of Employment

Notes: Calculated from the index of output for each year and employees in employment as of June of each year, thus as in Table 6.1 self-employment is ignored due to the lack of data at the disaggregated level. In addition, total non-manufacuturing includes public services and North Sea oil and gas extraction, so consequently the average annual growth differs from the HM Treasury figures in Table 6.1. (See footnote 1 in Table 6.1 for reference concerning the problems with the measurement of output in the service sector.)

'Total Services' improved by about 1.25 per cent per year on average in the period 1979–88 compared with the period 1973–9, with 'Distribution, Hotels and Catering, and Repairs' showing the largest improvement of just over 3 per cent and 'Education and Health Services', and 'Banking, Finance, Insurance, Business Services and Leasing' showing falls of about 0.5 per cent. The remaining sectors of non-manufacturing show a larger variation, with the growth in output per head in 'Agriculture, Forestry and Fishing' improving by about 2 per cent, 'Construction' improving by about 5.5 per cent, and 'Energy and Water Supply' falling by about 3.75 per cent. Overall, therefore, non-manufacturing growth in output per head improved by about 1.25 per cent per annum on average in the period 1979–88, compared to the period 1973–9.

It is possible that some or all the improvements in the growth of output per head could have come about by the more efficient use of the workforce, by working shorter days, weeks and years. Table 6.4,

Table 6.4 UK manufacturing output per hour (average annual % changes)

1973–9	1.1
1979–88	4.2

Source: CSO data bank at the University of Bath
Notes: Calculated from the output per hour index for each year. (The CSO do not produce non-manufacturing and whole economy output per hour figures for the UK.)

Table 6.5 UK capital productivity (average annual % changes)

	1964–73	1973–9	1979–88
Manufacturing	–0.5	–3.1	0.1
Whole economy	–1.0	–2.1	–0.0

Source: CSO data bank at the University of Bath
Note: Calculated using the index of output and gross capital stock at 1985 replacement cost for each year

therefore, gives the growth in British manufacturing output per hour. The figures show that this is not the major reason: this measure of labour productivity, although not so large, still shows a marked improvement compared with the previous period.

Table 6.5 gives estimates for the growth in British capital productivity for manufacturing and the whole economy. There is a marked improvement in the growth of manufacturing capital productivity in the 1980s compared with the 1973–9 period and even an improvement over the 1964–73 period. The figures for the whole economy show similar improvements although to a lesser extent.

As Venables (1989) illustrates, increases in both labour and capital productivity may arise not only through an increase in efficiency, but also by means of the substitution of one factor for another. However, given that both labour and capital productivity showed a marked improvement in the 1980s, this would not appear to be the major source of such improvement. This is supported by Table 6.6, which gives the growth in total factor productivity for British manufacturing and for the whole economy. Again, a similar pattern emerges: the growth in total factor productivity increased considerably in the 1980s compared to the 1973–9 period and shows a modest improvement on the 1964–73 period. Similarly, 'whole-economy' total factor pro-

Table 6.6 UK total factor productivity (average annual % changes)

	1964–73	1973–9	1979–88
Manufacturing	2.5	–0.5	3.0
Whole economy	1.6	0.1	1.5

Source: CSO data bank at the University of Bath
Notes: Calculated using the index of output, the index of output per head and gross capital stock at 1985 replacement cost for each year, assuming weights of 70 per cent and 30 per cent for capital and labour respectively

ductivity growth shows some improvement in the 1980s over the 1973–9 period, but still remains slightly less than the preceding period.

It is clear that a consistent pattern emerges from all the measures of productivity analysed; that is, manufacturing productivity growth in the 1980s was markedly greater than the 1973–9 period and on at least a par with the 1964–73 period. 'Whole-economy' (which, of course, incorporates the non-manufacturing sector) productivity growth also shows improvement in the latter period, but only capital productivity shows any improvement over the 1964–73 period. It is Britain's position *vis-à-vis* its international competitors, however, that is of major importance. Table 6.7 gives official Treasury estimates for the growth in output per head for British manufacturing and for the whole economy, along with those of the other six major industrialised countries, while Table 6.8 gives OECD figures for the 'Business Sector' for the same group of countries.

Britain's recent productivity growth performance has out-performed that of the other countries cited. During the 1960s, when many countries experienced strong productivity growth, Britain lagged well behind. During the 1970s all countries experienced a slowdown in productivity growth, but Britain was again near the bottom of the international league table. In the 1980s, however, manufacturing labour productivity growth in Britain outstripped that of all major OECD countries, with labour productivity growth in the economy as a whole second only to Japan. The business sector shows similar gains relative to competitors: Britain was the only country experiencing positive growth in capital productivity in the 1980s and the growth in labour productivity and total factor productivity was second only to Japan. This is what has led many commentators to talk of the British or Thatcher productivity 'miracle' in the late 1980s.

Table 6.7 International comparison of output per head (average annual % changes)

	1960–70	1970–80	1980–8
WHOLE ECONOMY[1]			
UK	2.4	1.3	2.5
US	2.0	0.4	1.2
Japan	8.9	3.8	2.9
Germany	4.4	2.8	1.8
France	4.6	2.8	2.0
Italy	6.3	2.6	2.0
Canada	2.4	1.5	1.4
G7 average	3.5	1.7	1.8
MANUFACTURING INDUSTRY[2]			
UK	3.0	1.6	5.2
US	3.5	3.0	4.0
Japan	8.8	5.3	3.1
Germany	4.1	2.9	2.2
France	5.4	3.2	3.1
Italy	5.4	3.0	3.5
Canada	3.4	3.0	3.6
G7 average	4.5	3.3	3.6

Source: HM Treasury, Autumn Statement, November 1988, HMSO
Notes: [1] UK data from CSO. Other countries' data from OECD except 1988 which are calculated from national GNP or GDP figures and OECD employment estimates
[2] UK data from CSO. Other countries' data from OECD, except France and Italy which use IMF employment data. 1988 data for France and Italy cover first three-quarters only

It would appear from the data, therefore, that there was some kind of productivity growth breakthrough in the 1980s. But this is only half of the story. As well as the growth in productivity, Britain's relative position in terms of the level of productivity is also important. Unfortunately, the productivity gap in relation to competitor countries is still considerable. After many decades of slow productivity growth, Britain's relative level of productivity lagged well behind many other industrialised countries at the beginning of the 1980s. Thus, although Britain's productivity has grown faster than most of these other countries during the 1980s, this was only making up for lost ground in terms of productivity levels, and Britain still remains far behind its major competitors. The Confederation of British

Industry (CBI) estimates that labour productivity is 22 per cent higher in Germany than Britain, 27 per cent higher in France, 16 per cent higher in Japan and over 30 per cent higher in the United States. Moreover, if Britain and its main competitors continue with the productivity growth rates achieved in the mid-1980s, it should be another seven or eight years before Britain catches up with Germany and France, some twenty years to match Japan and longer, if at all, before Britain matches the United States (see CBI, 1988; Williams, 1988).

POSSIBLE REASONS FOR IMPROVEMENT IN THE 1980s

A number of academic studies have attempted to analyse the reasons for the Thatcher productivity 'miracle', but have typically concentrated on British manufacturing. Probably the most influential has been the work by Muellbauer: see, for example, Mendis and Muellbauer (1984); Muellbauer (1984); and Muellbauer (1986). He has put forward five main hypotheses to explain the productivity gains of the 1980s:

1 'micro-chip';
2 'capital scrapping and utilisation';
3 'shedding of the below-average';
4 'labour utilisation';
5 'industrial relations'.

The surge of innovation and the growth of new technology in the 1980s through the spread of computer-controlled machines and computer-aided design (CAD) gives rise to the 'micro-chip' hypothesis. This new technology, however, is generally available to other industrialised countries. Thus, this may not necessarily explain the relative improvement in Britain's position, unless Britain has been able to incorporate these advances faster than other countries and make better use of the new technology (assisted, perhaps, by the industrial relations changes mentioned below).

The micro-chip hypothesis depends heavily on the assumption that adequate new investment embodying the latest technology has taken place since the recession of the early Thatcher years. But, as Nolan (1989) points out, this may not be the case. Manufacturing investment more or less collapsed during the first half of the 1980s, and although it recovered somewhat in the latter half of the 1980s, it only returned briefly to the levels attained in 1979 before falling again as the 1990–2

117

Table 6.8 International comparison of productivity for the business sector (average annual % changes)

	1960–73	1973–9	1979–88
Labour Productivity[1]			
UK	3.5	1.5	2.6
US	2.2	0.0	0.9
Japan	9.4	3.2	3.1
Germany	4.6	3.4	1.9
France	5.4	3.0	2.4
Italy	6.3	3.0	1.6
Canada	2.8	1.5	1.5
OECD Europe	5.0	2.7	2.1
OECD	4.3	1.4	1.7
Capital Productivity			
UK	−0.7	−1.6	0.2
US	0.2	−1.1	−0.7
Japan	−2.0	−2.8	−2.4
Germany	−1.3	−1.1	−1.4
France	0.5	−1.2	−0.7
Italy	0.2	0.2	−0.6
Canada	0.4	−0.7	−2.0
OECD Europe	−0.5	−1.5	−0.9
OECD	−0.3	−1.5	−1.0
Total Factor Productivity[2]			
UK	2.2	0.5	1.9
US	1.6	−0.4	0.4
Japan	6.4	1.8	1.8
Germany	2.7	2.0	0.7
France	3.9	1.7	1.5
Italy	4.6	2.2	1.0
Canada	2.0	0.7	0.3
OECD Europe	3.3	1.5	1.2
OECD	2.9	0.6	0.9

Source: OECD Economic Outlook, December 1989
Notes: [1] Labour Productivity is output per person employed.
[2] Total Factor Productivity growth is equal to a weighted average of the growth in labour and capital productivity. The sample period averages for capital and labour shares are used as weights.

recession began to bite. This interpretation is further reinforced by the historically high levels of capital utilisation recorded in the 1980s.

The 'capital scrapping and utilisation' hypothesis rests on:

1 the above-average capital scrapping and below-average capital utilisation which occurred over the 1973–80 period (following the large rise in energy prices);

2 the fall in capital scrapping and improved utilisation that occurred after 1981, thus assisting labour productivity growth to return to something like its pre-1973 rate.

The shedding of the below-average (or, as it is commonly called, the 'batting-average') hypothesis suggests that the improvement in the average quality of workers, management and plant results from the shedding of less productive resources – or, as Matthews (1988) puts it, 'the elimination of tail-enders' – and is responsible for a once-and-for-all improvement in productivity growth. However, some doubt has been expressed as to whether this has been of any practical importance. Oulton (1987) noted that it was the largest plants which were closed in the 1980–1 recession, with employment shifting away from the size of plant which had enjoyed the highest level of productivity in 1979 and the highest growth in subsequent years. Blackaby and Hunt (1989) find that the increase in total manufacturing labour productivity growth in the 1980s is attributable to the labour productivity growth of the individual sub-sectors of manufacturing and not to a re-allocation of resources from low-productivity to high-productivity sectors.

The 'labour utilisation' hypothesis rests on the idea that employers 'hoard' labour as output changes in order to cut hiring and firing costs. In other words, labour is treated as a quasi-fixed factor of production, so that firms facing large changes in output would incur large adjustment costs if they responded by hiring or firing workers. Instead, firms have responded by changing the rate at which the employed workers are utilised as demand for the product changes. Thus, if output falls, labour utilisation – but not the size of the workforce – falls, resulting in a fall in measured output per person employed. This, according to Muellbauer, is what happened in the early 1980s. Output collapsed during the 1979–80 period. The shedding of labour lagged behind, but eventually caught up as output stabilised at a lower level. Thus, after the initial fall in measured manufacturing productivity, adjustment did take place with rapidly declining employment and reasonably stable output, resulting in a short-term increase in manufacturing labour productivity.

Nolan (1989) casts some doubt on this hypothesis. Between 1986 and 1990, manufacturing output grew very fast. The 'labour utilisation' hypothesis would predict, therefore, that after the adjustment period had passed, there would have been a corresponding rise in employment over the second half of the 1980s. But this did not happen: although the decline in manufacturing employment temporarily slowed (even reversing slightly in 1988), the downward trend continued, with utilisation rates increasing as firms attempted to increase output without additional hiring and firing costs. This could, however, reflect a change in the attitude and expectations of managers about the Conservative government's ability or will to avoid future recession following the events of the late 1970s and early 1980s.

The hypothesis that has attracted the most attention has been the 'industrial relations' hypothesis (see also Chapter 10). This refers to the reduced strength of trade unions caused by the rise in unemployment and by the Conservative government's legislation: a development which enabled 'managers to manage' and to introduce new technology and flexible working practices. This, Muellbauer claims, would be consistent with a permanently higher rate of productivity growth. This view is supported by Boakes (1988), who claims that the most striking labour market development in the 1980s was the change in balance of power in industrial relations. Managers won back considerable control and successfully introduced widespread changes in work practices, leading to the general adoption of a more flexible working pattern in a large number of British companies. All of this combined to increase productivity growth.

Freeman and Medoff (1984) accept that the restrictive practices of unions could lead to lower productivity, but argue that two other channels exist whereby they could actually do the opposite. First, firms could respond to strong unions that push up the cost of labour by substituting capital and/or better quality workers for the existing labour. If the amount of capital per worker increases, labour productivity will increase. Second, by reducing turnover, the unions might raise productivity by lowering training and recruitment costs. In addition, the managers' response to unions may take the form of more rational personnel policies and more careful monitoring of work. All of this could help raise productivity by reducing organisational slack. Empirical evidence for Britain is mixed. Metcalf (1988) has suggested that unions tend to be associated with low productivity in the British economy; thus the diminishing influence of the unions in the 1980s has contributed to the improvements in productivity growth rates, particularly in manufacturing. This result is disputed by Wadhwani (1989) who finds that unionised firms actually experienced faster productivity growth than non-unionised firms over the period 1980–4, whilst there was no difference in productivity between the two sectors during 1975–9 and 1985–6.

AN ASSESSMENT AND A LOOK TO THE FUTURE

In returning to the first of the two questions posed at the end of the introduction, it is clear from the previous section that there is no unequivocal answer. Total manufacturing output only briefly returned to its 1979 level at the end of the 1980s, following the recession of 1979–80, before once again falling as recession began to bite. Although the increase in output that took place during the 1980s led to an increase in measured manufacturing labour productivity, it is not obvious that this constitutes a 'miracle'. This is also true of the sub-sectors of manufacturing, as highlighted in Table 6.9. Seven sectors during the period 1979–88 experienced positive average annual output growth, which is only a slight improvement over the earlier period. The figures for employment are more dramatic, with 'Chemicals and Man-Made Fibres' the only sector experiencing employment growth in the first period. No sectors at all experienced this in the latter.

Most sub-sectors experienced a bigger decline in employment over the period 1979–88 compared with 1973–9 (the 'All Other Manufacturing' sector being the exception). As a result, the low labour productivity growth in the first period was associated with a small decline in output and a slightly larger decline in employment, while in the latter period the so-called productivity 'miracle' is associated with negligible growth in output and rapidly declining employment. Thus, while the growth in total manufacturing productivity in the 1980s was a distinct improvement on the 1970s, this productivity 'miracle' was not evenly distributed across manufacturing and does not seem to have been accompanied by a supply-side output 'miracle'.

As for non-manufacturing, the picture is slightly different, as shown in Table 6.10. Most sectors experienced faster growth in output in the period 1979–88 compared with the period 1973–9 (the exceptions being 'Energy and Water Supply' and 'Education and Health Services'). The employment situation was slightly mixed. Most of the service sectors experienced positive growth in employment over the two periods ('Transport and Communication' and 'Public Administration and Defence' being the exceptions). The remaining sectors, 'Agriculture, Forestry and Fishing', 'Energy and

Table 6.9 UK manufacturing output and employment (average annual % changes)

1980 SIC	Sector name	Output 1973-9	1979-88	Employees in employment 1973-9	1979-88
21-4	Metals, Other Minerals and Mineral Products	-2.3	0.3	-2.1	-7.0
25-6	Chemicals and Man-Made Fibres	1.8	2.1	0.2	-3.5
31	Metals Goods n.e.s.	-2.5	-1.0	-1.6	-4.5
32	Mechanical Engineering	-1.0	-1.1	-0.3	-3.4
33-4, 37	Office Machinery, Electrical Engineering and Instruments	1.0	4.6	-1.0	-2.8
35	Motor Vehicles and Parts	-2.9	-1.1	-1.6	-5.9
36	Other Transport Equipment	-1.5	0.6	-1.0	-5.1
41-2	Food, Drink and Tobacco	0.8	0.6	-1.0	-2.8
43	Textiles	-3.4	-2.1	-4.1	-5.2
44-5	Clothing, Footwear and Leather	0.6	-0.7	-2.5	-3.2
47	Paper, Printing and Publishing	-0.3	1.5	-0.4	-1.4
46, 48-9	All Other Manufacturing (including Timber, Furniture, Rubber and Plastics)	-0.6	1.3	-1.5	-1.3
2-4	TOTAL MANUFACTURING	-0.7	0.8	-1.3	-3.6

Source: CSO data bank at the University of Bath and the Department of Employment
Note: See notes to Table 6.2

Water Supply' and 'Construction' all experienced negative growth over both periods, with the latter two sectors experiencing an even greater decline during the 1980s, similar to manufacturing. Thus, the improvement in the growth of productivity in services and non-manufacturing as a whole is attributable to slightly faster growth in output, coupled with positive but slower growth in employment.

Consequently, it would seem difficult to describe the recent British productivity performance as a 'miracle'. At best it appears that some structural changes took place in the deep recession of 1979-81 and led to increased productivity growth over the remainder of the 1980s. The real test of the 'miracle' hypothesis, therefore, lies in the second of the questions posed at the end of the introduction. This relates to whether or not the recent gains are sustainable across the whole of manufacturing (with productivity continuing to rise faster than its

Table 6.10 UK non-manufacturing output and employment (average annual % changes)

1980 SIC	Sector name	Output 1973-9	Output 1979-88	Employees in employment 1973-9	Employees in employment 1979-88
0	Agriculture, Forestry and Fishing	0.4	3.0	-2.7	-2.1
1	Energy and Water Supply	10.2	2.1	-0.2	-4.3
5	Construction	-1.8	2.6	-0.9	-1.9
6	Distribution, Hotels and Catering, and Repairs	0.2	2.7	1.2	0.4
7	Transport and Communication	1.5	3.0	-0.4	-1.2
8	Banking, Finance, Insurance and Business Services	3.7	5.7	2.2	4.6
91	Public Administration and Defence	0.0	0.2	0.6	-0.7
93, 95	Education and Health Services	3.4	1.4	2.6	1.1
92, 94, 96-9	Other Services	3.1	3.9	3.5	3.4
6-9	TOTAL SERVICES	1.8	2.8	1.6	1.2
0-1, 5-9	TOTAL NON-MANUFACTURING	2.1	2.9	1.2	0.7

Source: CSO data bank at the University of Bath and the Department of Employment
Note: See notes to Table 6.3

international competitors, accompanied by a continued growth in output and, possibly, stabilised employment) and even greater improvements in non-manufacturing productivity (with sustained improvements in both output and employment growth). The likelihood of this happening, however, depends upon a number of factors.

It is possible that the factors mentioned by Muellbauer may continue to help improve productivity in the years to come. In particular, the momentum of change (in terms of 'flexible working practices' and the managers' 'right to manage') that developed during the 1980s, is unlikely to diminish immediately. But this, in isolation, is unlikely to be enough for sustainable productivity improvements. Investment in new plant and equipment is essential for underpinning continuing productivity increases and it is clear that this investment was not taking place even in the 1980s; with the economy hit by the recession of 1990-2, levels of investment have fallen further still.

Manufacturing industry was particularly hard hit by the government's use of high interest rates to 'squeeze out' the upsurge of inflation between 1988 and 1990. High interest rates both directly and indirectly (via their effect on the exchange rate) damage manufacturing and so lead to adverse effects on investment as managers delay new investment or possibly cancel it altogether.

The shortfall in investment was highlighted by the strong growth of demand in the late 1980s, which was translated not just into rising domestic production, but also into rising prices and a widening trade deficit as the economy overheated. The inability of British manufacturing to respond to the increase in demand reflects the relatively low levels of investment undertaken by firms in the 1980s, which left British manufacturing short of capacity: real manufacturing investment in 1987 was, for example, approximately one-tenth lower than in 1979 (Glyn, 1989). Although investment per head was higher, due to the substantial falls in manufacturing employment, investment per head in British industry is still substantially below that found in important trading partners.

The CBI (1990) drew attention to this problem, showing Britain at the base of an investment league table in 1988 (and this was a very buoyant year for investment relative to the rest of the decade). The CBI estimates that annual fixed investment per person employed was £3,699 in Japan, £3,234 in the United States, £3,190 in France, £2,946 in Germany and only £2,318 in Britain (all at 1985 prices). The evidence generally suggests, however, that the link between higher investment and higher growth is rather uncertain and variable. Low levels of investment, particularly in manufacturing, resulted in a slowing down in the annual rate of growth of manufacturing capital stock to 0.7 per cent over the period 1979–88 (compared to 2.5 per cent in the period 1973–9), which has important implications for trading performances.

Furthermore, Britain is not only poor in terms of physical investment, but also in terms of investment in training and in research and development (R&D). The January 1989 CBI survey reported that 25 per cent of respondents felt that a shortage of skilled labour would be an important factor limiting future output, a similar percentage to 1978. This skills problem is further highlighted by the work of Davies and Caves (1987). They suggest that an important factor limiting growth of the British economy (and leading to a reduction in the quality of output compared to its competitors), is underinvestment in human capital, in everything from simple technical skills to business administration.

A continuing research project on international comparisons of workforce skills by the National Institute of Economic and Social Research (NIESR) has shown that there is a large gap in productivity between British plants and similar European plants[3]. The studies note that, generally, in European plants (in both the manufacturing and service sectors) the workforce is better trained and has greater skills, all of which is going to make it more difficult to close the productivity gap in the future. Ashton et al. (1989) also note the deficiencies in the general education system, Britain having one of the lowest participation rates in full-time education of those aged between 16 and 18 years of any country in Western Europe. Britain is well below Canada, France, Germany, Italy, Japan and the United States in the proportion of 17-year-olds receiving formal education. In addition, Prais and Wagner (1988) draw attention to the lower levels of mathematical attainment of those 15- to 16-year-olds in schools, particularly the less able academically. Only well-trained operatives, technicians and craftsmen and women can get the best out of technically intricate machinery. A technically advanced economy needs a well-trained and well-educated workforce across all occupational grades if the strong productivity growth is to persist in the future. The economy is only as healthy as the pyramid of skill on which it is based (Eatwell, 1982).

This, in conjunction with Britain's deteriorating position in the field of R&D, will possibly constrain future productivity growth. R&D employment fell by 5 per cent between 1981 and 1983 and by 16 per cent between 1983 and 1985, although the decline in supporting staff was greater than for scientists and engineers (*British Business*, 1987). In 1967 Britain was second in terms of the proportion of gross domestic product (GDP) spent on R&D, but by 1983 it was only sixth, with the lowest rate of the ten major OECD countries between 1967 and 1983 (Patel and Pavitt, 1987).

The amount of expenditure spent on R&D as a proportion of GDP relative to other European Community and OECD countries fell in the 1980s and this is especially true of non-defence R&D (Layard and Nickell, 1989). The appropriateness of the direction of R&D expenditure in Britain has also been questioned on two fronts. First, a large proportion of R&D expenditure has been on military projects, which by their very nature have only small spillover effects for the economy generally, while at the same time attracting a large number of the best engineers and scientists. Second, R&D expenditure has been heavily concentrated in just a few industries and in a similar pattern to that found in the United States. Given that the United States enjoys far greater resources, it was unlikely that Britain could have established technological leadership in these industries. In contrast, the countries with the fastest productivity growth have spread resources more evenly across the electrical and electronic industries.

CONCLUSIONS

It would appear that Britain's productivity growth in the 1980s represented an advance on the previous decade, with notable improvements *vis-à-vis* other countries. Whether this constitutes a 'miracle' or not is less clear. For anything like a 'miracle' to emerge, these improvements must endure for some time to come. Even after allowing for the fact that productivity growth will be temporarily held back by the effects of the 1990–2 recession, it seems possible that the growth rates enjoyed during the 1980s will not be resumed in the mid-1990s. With skills shortages apparent even at high levels of unemployment, and a slump in investment coming after a decade of relatively low capital spending, the prospects for continued productivity growth are not great.

NOTES

1 Budget speech, March 1988.
2 HM Treasury, Autumn statement, November 1988.
3 See, for example, Daly, Hitchens and Wagner (1985), Prais and Steedman (1986), Prais (1987), Steedman and Wagner (1987), Prais and Wagner (1988), Steedman (1988), Jarvis and Prais (1989) and Steedman and Wagner (1989).

7

THE CONSERVATIVE GOVERNMENT'S 'FIGHT AGAINST INFLATION'

Ten years without cheers

Nigel M. Healey

INTRODUCTION

The Conservative Party launched its 1979 election campaign with a firm pledge to conquer inflation, placing the need to restore 'sound money' above all other political objectives in its manifesto document:

> Sound money [. . . is] essential to economic recovery . . . Inflation . . . has come near to destroying our political and social stability. To master inflation, proper monetary discipline is essential, with publicly stated targets for the rate of growth of the money supply.[1]

Since that time, the government claims to have waged a ceaseless battle against inflation, reaffirming, for example, in the 1989 budget its conviction that 'inflation is a disease of money; and monetary policy is the cure'.[2] Long-standing, alternative weapons of anti-inflation policy like prices and incomes controls were eschewed on the grounds that they are ineffective at best and counterproductive at worst. The once-traditional, postwar commitment to maintain 'full employment' through active demand management has been sacrificed at the altar of price stability: 'fighting inflation' has meant not only accepting the highest real interest rates since records began, but also tolerating the deepest recession since the 1930s.

Yet, by the end of the decade, inflation was almost exactly at the levels inherited by the Conservative government, while over the intervening years the purchasing power of the pound had shrunk to less than 44p in 1979 terms. Britain's demonstrable failure to bring inflation under control, moreover, contrasted sharply with the success of our major trading partners during the 1980s. British inflation rates remained persistently above the OECD average by a margin which, in proportionate terms, grew rather than shrank. And by the time

Table 7.1 Inflation in Britain (annual average %)

	Retail prices	*Earnings*
1978	8.2	13.0
1979	13.3	15.5
1980	18.0	20.7
1981	11.9	12.8
1982	8.8	9.4
1983	4.6	8.4
1984	5.0	6.0
1985	6.1	8.5
1986	3.4	7.9
1987	4.2	7.8
1988	4.9	8.7
1989	7.8	9.1
1990	9.5	9.7

Source: CSO *Economic Trends*

Britain joined the European Monetary System (EMS) in 1990, thereby effectively transferring responsibility for anti-inflation policy to the German Bundesbank (see also Chapter 1), inflation was approximately twice the average of the industrialised world as a whole (see Table 7.2).

What went wrong? The government's anti-inflation policy was not 'blown off course' by the sort of external, oil price shocks which so rocked the economy in the 1970s. Nor was its strategy undermined by trade union 'militancy', since unlike past policies predicated on wage restraint, prices and incomes controls were written out of the script from the start. Could it be, then, that the strategy itself was inherently flawed in some way? Or was it that the government mishandled its execution? This chapter attempts to provide answers to these, and related, questions. It opens by documenting the government's inflation record since 1979, going on to outline the theoretical basis of its anti-inflation programme. It then examines the way in which policy has actually been conducted, arguing that the experience of the last decade suggests weaknesses in policy design and, perhaps more seriously, mismanagement in policy conduct.

TEN YEARS OF 'FIGHTING INFLATION'

The new Conservative government which took power in May 1979 inherited an inflation rate of 10.3 per cent, slightly up from the 8.2

Table 7.2 Consumer price inflation around the world (annual average %)

	1982–6 average	1987	1988	1989	1990
United States	3.8	3.7	4.1	5.0	5.4
Japan	1.9	0.1	0.7	2.6	3.1
Germany	2.6	0.3	1.2	3.0	2.7
European Community	5.0	3.1	3.3	4.9	5.1
OECD	5.0	3.2	4.0	5.2	5.3
Britain	5.5	4.1	4.9	7.7	9.3

Source: Barclays Review

per cent recorded in the preceding Labour government's last full year of office in 1978. Table 7.1 sets out inflation's roller-coaster ride during the 1980s. Two features are particularly notable, namely the surge in inflation during the new government's early years and the downward 'stickiness' of earnings growth which, even in the relatively low-inflation mid-1980s with unemployment at record levels, appeared to lodge at around 8 per cent.

Table 7.2 illustrates how starkly Britain's anti-inflation record contrasts with that of our major trading partners. Ten years after the government embarked on its crusade to restore price stability, inflation in Britain remained at almost twice the average of the main industrial nations, with the gap opening rather than closing as the decade ended. In 1990, the British inflation rate was nearly twice the OECD and European Community averages and more than three times the rate in Britain's most important trading partner, Germany.

THE THEORETICAL BASIS OF THE GOVERNMENT'S ANTI-INFLATION POLICY

In his 1984 Mais Lecture, the former Chancellor of the Exchequer, Mr Nigel Lawson, cleverly summarised the break with the past that his government's anti-inflation policy represented. He suggested that until 1979, governments had used 'microeconomic' policies (by which he meant prices and incomes controls) to contain inflation, while reserving 'macroeconomic' (i.e. demand-management) policies to promote full employment. In contrast, he claimed, his Conservative government had redirected 'macroeconomic' policy towards the control of inflation and used 'microeconomic' policy (now redefined to

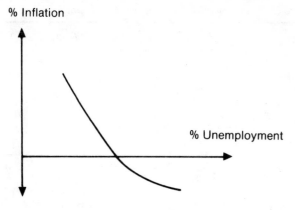

Figure 7.1a The Phillips Curve

mean 'supply-side' reform) to tackle unemployment, a radical reassignment of instruments to targets born of the conviction that:

> the proper role of each [policy] is precisely the opposite of that assigned by the conventional post-war wisdom.[3]

The essence of Mr Lawson's argument can be illustrated by considering the Phillips Curve diagrams in Figures 7.1a and 7.1b. Figure 7.1a shows the stable, negatively sloped relationship between inflation and unemployment which underpinned 'Keynesian' macroeconomic theory in the 1960s. According to Mr Lawson, chancellors of yore used demand-management policy to slide the economy up and down the Phillips Curve and thereby achieve objectives for unemployment. As their efforts were gradually undermined by the breakdown of this relationship in the 1970s, the rightward drift of the Phillips Curve was, in Mr Lawson's view, wrongly interpreted by his predecessors as the product of 'cost-push' inflationary forces. Prices and incomes policies were thus imposed in a (futile) attempt to push the Phillips Curve back to the left and prevent fiscal/monetary stimuli to aggregate demand being dissipated in rising prices.

Mr Lawson's perception of economic reality is shown in Figure 7.1b, which sets out the now more fashionable, 'expectations-augmented' version of the Phillips Curve model, which was first postulated by Friedman (1968). The trade-off between inflation and unemployment is recast as a purely temporary phenomenon, which persists only for the time it takes expectations to 'adapt' to changes in the actual rate of inflation. When expectations are fully adjusted (i.e.

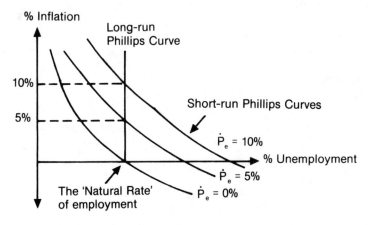

Key: $\dot{P}_e$ = expected rate of inflation

Figure 7.1b The expectations-augmented Phillips Curve in the short and long run

when the actual inflation rate is fully anticipated), the economy returns to its 'natural rate of unemployment'.

According to Mr Lawson's view of the world, demand management can only achieve transitory reductions in the rate of unemployment, at the cost of ever-accelerating inflation. By the same token, contractionary demand-management policy can be used to eliminate inflation and achieve price stability at the cost of purely temporary increases in unemployment above the natural rate. In the long run, unemployment (which will always converge on the natural rate) can only be reduced by using supply-side policy to 'set the market free'. To quote the former Chancellor:

> Right from the outset we have had . . . a macroeconomic and a microeconomic policy objective. The macroeconomic policy objective is the conquest of inflation, to be achieved by the monetary and fiscal stance . . . . The microeconomic policy objective is the improvement of the performance of the supply-side of the economy [thereby reducing the natural rate of unemployment] by the removal of unnecessary market distortions . . . and the enhancement of incentives.[4]

The theoretical basis of the Conservative government's approach to 'macroeconomic policy' and the role played by 'the monetary and fiscal stance' can best be considered by thinking of its anti-inflation strategy as a series of links in a long chain:

1 excessive public spending leads to budget deficits;
2 budget deficits add to the overall demand for credit in the economy, either contributing to monetary growth (see Gilbody, 1985) or forcing the government to raise interest rates in order to curb private sector borrowing by an offsetting amount (note that in the latter case, the rise in interest rates leaves the level of aggregate demand unchanged, but distorts its composition in favour of the public sector);
3 'the growth of the money supply . . . [is] the prime determinant of the overall level of [aggregate] demand';[5]
4 since real output (Y) is determined in the medium to long term by the same supply-side factors that determine the natural rate of unemployment, growth of aggregate demand (PY) in excess of the underlying growth of real output leads to inflation (i.e. an increase in the price level, P).

The prescriptions for monetary and fiscal policy which follow from this diagnosis of the inflation problem are clear. Monetary growth must be cut to the rate that permits aggregate demand to grow no faster than the underlying rate of real output growth, thereby guaranteeing price stability in the medium to long term (see Chapter 1). The budget deficit must be reduced, not because it has any direct effect on the level of aggregate demand *per se*, but because it can only be made consistent with the target rate of monetary growth by crowding out the private sector via higher interest rates (Robins, 1984). Finally, given the government's supply-side objective of reducing the tax burden, there must be deep cuts in public expenditure to allow both the budget deficit and taxes to be simultaneously reduced.

In operational terms, the appropriate, long-run monetary target (or 'rule') can be derived from the quantity theory equation of exchange (MV = PY). Aggregate demand (PY) is identically equal to the stock of 'money' (M) multiplied by its velocity of circulation (V). On the assumption that 'over the medium term the velocity of circulation is relatively stable and predictable',[6] the architects of the government's new anti-inflation policy were able to calculate the rate of monetary growth that appeared to be consistent with price stability, given their econometric estimates of the trend rate of change of velocity and the underlying (supply-side driven) rate of growth of real output.

The rule for fiscal policy is more straightforward, since a 'balanced budget' is the only way of ensuring the public sector neither fuels monetary growth nor crowds out the private sector in the long run; in the former Chancellor's words, 'a balanced budget is . . . a clear and simple rule, with a good historical pedigree'.[7]

Inflationary expectations clearly play an important role in the overall strategy, since the length of time they take to adjust to a fall in inflation determines the real, 'short-run' costs of fighting inflation. (In terms of Figure 7.1b above, a reduction in the growth of aggregate demand pushes the economy down its short-run Phillips Curve, so that unemployment rises above the natural rate; this situation persists until expectations 'catch up' with the change in actual inflation, shifting the short-run Phillips Curve vertically downwards and allowing unemployment to recover.) The rationale for publishing monetary targets is that, by preannouncing a change of policy regime, adjustment may be accelerated, so reducing the period spent in 'disequilibrium':

> monetary targets, openly proclaimed and explained, can have a crucial effect in reducing inflationary expectations.[8]

The statistical identification of the 'money' stock is central to the process of actually implementing such an anti-inflation policy. As already noted, the theoretical proposition underpinning the government's anti-inflation policy is that increases in the stock of 'money' cause increases in spending and, ultimately, inflation. Translating this abstract idea into operational reality means statistically measuring the stock of financial assets regarded by its holders as 'money' – that is, perceived as being readily 'spendable' or 'liquid'. Only if the authorities can statistically measure the stock of 'money' can they adjust the instruments of monetary policy to keep its growth on some target path. (Note that the financial system creates new 'money' by extending credit. By using fiscal policy to determine the government's own demand for credit and interest rates to affect the private sector's demand for credit, the growth of 'money' can be controlled.)

But whether an asset is regarded as 'money' depends on its particular characteristics, which are constantly changing in a dynamic financial system, and on the subjective perceptions of its holders, which may also change over time. In a statistical sense, therefore, there is no clear-cut dividing line between 'monetary' and 'non-monetary' assets. Regardless of the strength of the link between 'money' and spending – itself a source of continuing controversy between monetarists and Keynesians – monetary policy is only a useful tool for managing aggregate demand if the collection of liquid assets labelled as 'money' for policy purposes bears a stable relationship to the underlying 'money' stock. This may be the case in a world of monetary tranquillity, where the structure of financial portfolios is stable. However, if financial innovation is unpredictable, changing the nature of assets over time, then monetary targetry begins to break down (Laidler, 1987).

In an open economy, the alternative to relying on the growth of some statistical measure of 'money' to guide policy is to focus instead on its international price, the exchange rate. If the 'money' stock is growing rapidly relative to the demand for 'money', its holders increase their spending 'across the board', buying not just more domestic goods, but more foreign goods and assets as well. *Ceteris paribus*, the exchange rate comes under downward pressure and the domestic price of imports rises, reinforcing the inflationary impact of the higher spending on domestic goods. In an open economy, the exchange rate is thus an integral part of the transmission mechanism, providing a useful, additional guide to the stance of monetary policy.

The obvious difficulty with going beyond this and enlisting the exchange rate as an intermediate target of monetary policy is that it can also be affected by, *inter alia*, changes in the monetary stance of the country against whose currency its value is being targeted. For example, pegging the exchange rate may mean having to relax monetary policy to counter a rise in the exchange rate caused by monetary expansion abroad. Only if the 'partner' country has precisely the same objectives for monetary policy would an exchange rate target be rational. And at the beginning of the last decade, the new Conservative government was quite clear that no other nation shared its anti-inflationary zeal, so that the exchange rate was to be allowed to float cleanly, leaving the authorities free to pursue their monetary targets without external distractions.

Against this technical background, the following sections now examine the way in which the government set about implementing this anti-inflation strategy, focusing both on the robustness of its theoretical underpinnings and the authorities' performance in executing the programme as planned.

ANTI-INFLATION POLICY IN PRACTICE

The government's anti-inflation policy is enshrined in the so-called 'Medium-Term Financial Strategy' (MTFS), an annual policy document which, since its inception in March 1980, has been published each year at the time of the budget (see Table 7.3). The MTFS sets out targets for monetary growth (the precise definition of 'money' changing from time to time) and the budget balance – a deficit being termed the 'public sector borrowing requirement' (PSBR) and a surplus, the 'public sector debt repayment' (PSDR) – over a medium-term planning horizon varying between three and five years.

The target monetary aggregate chosen by the government to launch its fight against inflation was M3 (then called £M3), which basically comprised currency and sterling bank deposits (both current and deposit accounts). It was theoretically appealing, embracing most assets which were, at the time, regarded as readily 'spendable'. Statistical work undertaken in the 1970s also appeared to confirm that its relationship with spending, as measured by its velocity of circulation, was reasonably stable and predictable, suggesting that it was an acceptable proxy for 'money'. Over the last decade, however, the government has also used M1 (currency plus current bank accounts), M5 (then called PSL2, a very 'broad' measure of 'money' which incorporates a variety of liquid assets, including building society deposits) and M0 (the narrowest definition of 'money', which is basically currency alone). Table 7.3 sets out the targets and outturns for the different target aggregates employed, as well as the government's objectives and outturns for the PSBR (the PSDR appears as a negative sign on the PSBR figure).

The conduct of anti-inflation policy falls into five broad phases: 1979–82 (the 'monetarist experiment'); 1982–5 (the 'retreat from naïve monetarism'); 1985–8 ('targeting the exchange rate'); 1988–90 (the 'fight against inflation renewed'); and 1990–date (the 'Euro-solution'). The next five sections consider each of these periods in turn.

1979–82: The 'monetarist experiment'

This early period of policy is thoroughly documented elsewhere (e.g. Healey, 1987c) and so is only briefly reviewed here. The name derives from the single-minded fashion in which the government sought to control monetary growth (M3), arguing that there was 'no question of departing from the money supply policy',[9] regardless of the short-run costs. Interest rates were raised to record levels and automatic fiscal stabilisers were overridden in an attempt to bring M3 under control, despite the deep recession assailing the real economy. Unemployment doubled to over 3 million in the first eighteen months of the new government and real output fell sharply; one-fifth of British manufacturing 'went to the wall'.

As the recession deepened and M3 continued to overshoot its target band, it became increasingly apparent that, far from losing control of monetary growth as the M3 statistics suggested, the government had been misled into unwittingly engineering a catastrophic 'credit crunch'. Other indicators of the monetary stance provided evidence of the scale of the monetary squeeze: the 'narrow' measure of money, M0, grew by only 2.6 per cent in 1981, while the exchange rate soared from \$2.07 in May 1979 to peak at \$2.45 in October 1981 (Niehans, 1981). The problem, it gradually transpired, was that M3 had become subject to special distortions which had destroyed the previous relationship between its growth and that of 'liquidity' generally. Specifically, the removal of legislative restrictions in 1980–1 and the acceleration in the pace of financial innovation had allowed the banks to take business away from other institutions, increasing the ratio of bank deposits to total liquid assets (Podolski, 1987).

Faced with mounting evidence of its monetary 'overkill', the government overhauled the MTFS in 1982 (see Table 7.3). The M3 targets were all raised in an effort to allow for the continuing structural change in the financial markets, while M1 and M5 were drafted as additional target aggregates; moreover, thenceforth 'interpretation of monetary conditions . . . [was] to take account of all available information, including the behaviour of the exchange rate'.[10] Virtually at the outset, the government's anti-inflation policy had been undermined by the collapse of the central relationship upon which it depended, namely the link between its target for monetary growth and spending (Healey, 1987a).

1982–5: The 'retreat from naïve monetarism'

In the years immediately following the ill-fated 'monetarist experiment', the government's anti-inflation policy drifted largely rudderless. Disillusioned by the M3 débâcle, the government experimented half-heartedly with targets for M1 and M5, and later M0, but its faith in monetary targets had been badly dented (Goodhart, 1989). The exchange rate began to play an increasingly important role, but at this stage the government's declared approach was to react (by tightening or loosening the monetary stance) to exchange rate fluctuations caused by internal monetary imbalances only (i.e. to exchange market developments that were accompanied by confirmatory movements in the domestic monetary aggregates), ignoring external shocks so that its anti-inflation policy could not be 'blown off course' by, say, a monetary expansion overseas. In practice, identifying the immanent causes of exchange rate fluctuations proved impossible, given the invariably contradictory signals sent out by the government's three (later two) monetary aggregates. The modified 'MTFS Mark II' was thus little more than a confused ragbag of monetary and exchange rate targets, devoid of any clear-cut rationale.

Not only was its anti-inflation policy in considerable disarray by 1982, but the government's anti-inflation resolve was also seriously weakened by the dramatic – and largely unanticipated – doubling of unemployment between 1979 and 1982. As the rate of inflation tumbled in the wake of the recession, monetary and fiscal policy were gradually relaxed. Despite its declared intention of achieving price stability, no further attempt was made to reduce inflation below the levels at which it stabilised after 1982. In 1982 and 1983, for example, budget 'giveaways' (i.e. deliberate cuts in net tax revenues) of approximately £2bn in each year were engineered by revising upwards the earlier MTFS targets for the PSBR (see Table 7.3), while interest rates were gently eased down from the peak reached in October 1981 (when base rates were 16 per cent) to reach 8.75 per cent by March 1984.

The government's change of heart was highlighted by a particularly illuminating exchange during the Chancellor's traditional cross-examination by the Treasury and Civil Service Select Committee after the 1984 budget:

Committee member: We are putting it to you that you have no serious intention of getting down to zero inflation at all and that you are in fact willing to grin and bear 3, 4 or 5 per cent inflation.

Mr Lawson: Our objective is to get stable prices within the Green Paper period [ten years] . . . [but] it is a matter of what is realistic. . . . There is no point in kidding yourself, there is no point in self-delusion.[11]

The Governor of the Bank of England subsequently explained the

Table 7.3 The MTFS 1980–9, targets and outturns

MTFS targets	1980	1981	1982	1983	1984	1985	1986	1987	1988	1989	Outturns
M3 (% p.a.)											
1980/81	7–11										20.0
1981/82	6–10	6–10									14.5
1982/83	5–9	5–9	8–12								10.0
1983/84	4–8	4–8	7–11	7–11							9.8
1984/85			6–10	6–10	6–10						9.5
1985/86			5–9	5–9	5–9	5–9					14.8
1986/87					4–8	4–8	11–15				18.0
1987/88					3–7	3–7		***			22.1
1988/89					2–6	2–6					22.4
M1 (% p.a.)											
1982/83			8–12								11.0
1983/84			7–11	7–11							11.0
1984/85			6–10	6–10	***						
1985/86				5–9							
M5 (% p.a.)											
1982/83			8–12								9.0
1983/84			7–11	7–11							12.3
1984/85			6–10	6–10	***						
1985/86				5–9							

M0 (% p.a.)

1984/85	4–8					5.5
1985/86	3–7	3–7				3.5
1986/87	2–6	2–6	2–6			4.0
1987/88	1–5	1–5	2–6	2–6		5.0
1988/89	0–4	0–4	1–5	1–5	1–5	7.5
1989/90			1–5	1–5		6.0
1990/91			0–4	0–4		2.7
1991/92				0–4		
1992/93					0–4	

PSBR (% of GDP)

1980/81	3.75										6.00
1981/82	3.00	4.25									4.50
1982/83	2.25	3.25	3.50								2.75
1983/84	1.50	2.00	2.75	2.75							3.25
1984/85			2.00	2.00	2.25						3.25
1985/86				2.00	2.00	2.00					2.00
1986/87					1.75	1.75	1.75				1.00
1987/88					1.75	1.75	1.50	1.00			−0.75
1988/89						1.75	1.50	1.00	−0.75		−3.00
1989/90							1.50	1.00	0.00	−2.75	−0.25
1990/91								1.00	0.00	−1.75	1.00
1991/92									0.00	−1.00	
1992/93										−0.50	

Source: Medium-Term Financial Strategy, published in HM Treasury, *Financial Statement and Budget Report* each March; CSO Financial Statistics (various)

Key: *** = Target Range abandoned

government's loss of appetite for price stability in the following terms:

> I think there is a sound barrier [for inflation] at around 5 per cent where a lot of people think it is not too bad . . . . [It] is going to be very difficult to get down to the general expectation of 2 or 3 per cent which is acceptable in Germany and Japan.[12]

The effect of the disastrous 'monetarist experiment', therefore, was not simply to throw the government's anti-inflation strategy into confusion, but to break its will to drive inflation completely out of the system. In the years that followed, 5 per cent effectively became the 'target' inflation rate, with the government only tightening policy when inflation looked set to breach this ceiling; the goal of price stability, like full employment before it, became a vague, political aspiration, rather than a concrete policy objective.

1985–8: 'Targeting the exchange rate'

1985 marked the start of the third phase of anti-inflation policy. In January of that year, a speculative run on sterling – triggered, it appeared, by nothing more than a misinterpreted Lobby briefing on exchange rate policy (e.g. *The Sunday Times*, 6 January 1985) – pushed its value to a record low of $1.04. This event, which caused Britain to 'import' a sharp, albeit short-lived, inflationary shock, taken together with the 'quite inappropriate'[13] behaviour of the US dollar between 1982 and 1985, appears to have severely undermined the government's previous faith in the ability of the foreign exchange markets to maintain 'fundamental equilibrium'.[14]

As already noted, the logic of the government's anti-inflation strategy makes the (nominal) exchange rate a viable substitute for a monetary target only if the 'partner' country – or group of countries in the case of a composite exchange rate measure like the European Currency Unit (ECU) – is pursuing 'suitable stable policies' (Walters, 1986). But by the mid-1980s, the anti-inflation success of Britain's major trading partner, Germany, was becoming widely appreciated in official circles, convincing many that a deutschmark target might provide an acceptable, alternative basis for policy. The success of other, formerly high-inflation European countries like France and Italy, which had tied their monetary policies to Germany's through their membership of the EMS, strengthened the position of those pressing for an exchange rate target. Moreover, as a bonus, more active exchange rate management would, it was argued, also help to avoid the sort of short-run dislocation suffered in early 1985, by reassuring the financial markets about the future course of the currency.

The government's drift towards a formal (although undisclosed) exchange rate target was hastened by contemporaneous negotiations amongst the 'G3' countries (the 'Group of Three' major trading nations: the United States, Japan and Germany). The 'Plaza Accord' in October 1985 marked a period of closer international policy co-ordination, which reached its high point with the 'Louvre Accord' in February 1987, when the G3 Finance Ministers agreed to peg their currencies within secret 'target zones' of approximately ±5 per cent. Following the latter agreement, the government embarked on a period of 'shadowing the EMS', operating a deutschmark peg between March 1987 and March 1988 (Goodhart, 1989).

Unlike the then Chancellor, Nigel Lawson, Mrs Thatcher was, however, unconvinced of the need for a formal (as opposed to an undisclosed and hence movable) exchange rate target, and the EMS 'experiment' was plagued by a series of often-public disagreements between the two on this question. It is now clear with hindsight that Mr Lawson favoured completing the transition from monetary to exchange rate targets by locking sterling into the Exchange Rate Mechanism of the EMS, while the former Prime Minister remained strongly sceptical, retaining much of her original faith in domestic monetary targets (Keegan, 1989). Mrs Thatcher's hand was strengthened by the surge in broad monetary growth, which had begun in 1985 but continued to gather pace throughout 1987. So long as Mr Lawson was committed to using interest rates to keep the pound stable against the deutschmark, the government could not unilaterally raise British interest rates to head off what the Prime Minister's advisers regarded as a major, impending inflationary threat. When M0 finally broke through its target ceiling in early 1988, convincing Mrs Thatcher that the earlier surge in broad money growth had finally started to spill over into higher spending, she overruled her Chancellor and ordered that sterling be 'decapped' in order to re-establish control over domestic credit (Riddell, 1989).

1988–90: The 'fight against inflation renewed'

As inflation accelerated through the 5 per cent barrier, interest rates were pushed back to the levels last witnessed during the 'monetarist experiment'. The difference was that, internally divided over the relative merits of monetary and exchange rate targets, the government no longer appeared to have any clear guideline for policy. Indeed, it sometimes seemed that the government had dispensed with intermediate targets altogether, distrusting both monetary aggregates and the exchange rate and preferring to keep monetary policy tight until inflation itself finally began to fall. On a number of occasions, the previous Chancellor, Nigel Lawson, said:

> interest rates will stay as high as is needed, for as long as is needed. For there will be no letting up in our determination to get on top of inflation.[15]

The worrying suggestion was that not until inflation is 'under control' would monetary policy be relaxed (Healey, 1989). Given the 'long and variable' time lags between changes in the monetary stance and inflation – estimated to be in the region of three years by Friedman (1980) – such an approach risked repeating the monetary 'overkill' of 1979–82. Shades of this earlier experience were also apparent on the fiscal front. Despite its continued public commitment to a balanced budget, fiscal policy was also tightened, with the government radically rewriting its MTFS targets for the PSBR (which in 1988 had been set at zero for 1989–90 onwards) in March 1989, a change which was explained by the Chancellor in the following terms:

> given the particular uncertainties there are at the present time, I believe it would be right to budget for 1989–90 for a surplus . . . of some £14bn.[16]

Britain entered the 1990s with inflation rising towards 10 per cent, higher unemployment and a less favourable external outlook, with world commodity prices – the collapse of which helped bring down inflation in the mid-1980s – trending upwards. With North Sea oil revenues dwindling, the trade deficit (which exceeded £20bn in 1989) contrasted sharply with the huge surpluses enjoyed in the early 1980s, limiting the government's scope for again using an exchange rate appreciation to put downward pressure on domestic prices. Having let inflation wriggle out of its control between 1985 and 1988, the Conservative government was faced with a difficult and politically damaging run-up to the next election which was due in 1992.

1990–date: 'The Euro-solution'

The confusion that characterised the government's anti-inflationary policy in the period 1988–90 masked an intensifying struggle between the former Prime Minister – who remained committed to the basic principles of monetary targetry, despite the absence of a reliable monetary aggregate – and her Chancellor, Nigel Lawson, who was convinced that an exchange target against the deutschmark was the only long-term solution. Overshadowing this essentially technical conflict was Mrs Thatcher's deep antipathy to the idea of giving up political sovereignty to outsiders. Since an exchange rate target against the mighty deutschmark effectively entailed handing over monetary policy to the German Bundesbank, the former Prime Minister set her face firmly against this option.

As the decade ended and the pace of European economic integration accelerated (spurred on by the European Community's '1992' programme to 'complete the internal market'), the 'monetary versus exchange rate targets' debate became entangled in the broader political discussion about Britain's links with the Community. During an extraordinary twelve months, the Chancellor, Nigel Lawson, and the Foreign Secretary, Sir Geoffrey Howe (himself a former Chancellor), both left the Cabinet in protest at Mrs Thatcher's intransigence. The new Chancellor, John Major, managed to persuade the Prime Minister that not only was full membership of the EMS ultimately unavoidable, but that early entry would provide the Conservative Party with its best chance of re-election in 1992.

Eventually, in October 1990, Mrs Thatcher finally agreed and Britain joined the EMS as a full member, albeit with a wider target band (±6 per cent) than the standard ±2.25 per cent respected by other EMS members. The Prime Minister had, however, been so politically damaged by the divisions that her hostility to membership had opened up within her party that she was forced to resign as leader the following month. As in the early 1980s, subsequent events proved that during the frenzied renewal of the 'fight against inflation', monetary conditions had been excessively tight. Once a target rate of DM2.95 (only marginally below the target adopted by Nigel Lawson between 1987–8) had been established within the framework of the EMS, the government was able to cut interest rates so that they quickly came into line with those in Germany (see p. 141). However, in contrast to the earlier episode when interest rate cuts had triggered a credit explosion, the preceding monetary squeeze of 1988–90 had pushed the economy into such a deep recession that the interest rates cuts which followed in 1990–2 served only to moderate its decline, rather than pump up inflation. As inflation fell steadily throughout 1991, the irony was that not until the government had completely and irrevocably given up any attempt to operate its own anti-inflation policy did the inflation rate fall in a sustainable fashion.

CONCLUSIONS

In 1979, the Conservative government embarked on a radical econ-omic strategy, designed to exorcise inflation and thereby provide a stable financial environment in which a revitalised market economy could flourish. Yet, despite explicitly abandoning 'full employment' as a policy goal, so allowing demand-management policy to be used exclusively to achieve the objective of price stability, inflation cont-inued to remain endemic in the British economy throughout the 1980s. So what went wrong? Was the government's anti-inflation programme theoretically flawed or was it simply bungled at the operational level, whether for technical or political reasons? In fact, the review of the 1980s set out above suggests that both the design and the execution of policy were deficient.

The most striking weakness in the strategy's design was that it was constructed around the key theoretical propositions that there exists a 'natural rate of unemployment' which depends only on supply-side factors (see Figure 7.1b) and that, once inflationary expectations have fully adjusted, factor and product markets clear. In such a world, were it to exist, reducing the rate of growth of aggregate demand (PY) would indeed have allowed inflation to be 'squeezed out of the system' with only transitory, real side-effects (i.e. in terms of higher unem-ployment and lower output). In the real world, however, life is more complicated. The natural rate of unemployment can be altered in an enduring way by changes in aggregate demand – in technical terms, unemployment is subject to strong 'hysteresis' effects (see Wilkinson, 1988; Healey and Parker, 1990), so that periods of high unemploy-ment can significantly raise the underlying rate of unemployment consistent with stable inflation. Real markets are not perfect and prices are not flexible. In the labour market, for example, trade unions represent only the interests of their current members and so quite rationally continue to bid for large wage rises when unemployment is high – wage inflation never fell below 6 per cent per annum in the

1980s, despite record unemployment – thereby denying potential jobs to those in the jobless queues.

During the early years of the new anti-inflation policy, there was no shortage of economists warning the government that, for these sorts of reasons, it faced a negative trade-off between unemployment and inflation which was more unfavourable and would persist for far longer than ministers appeared to believe. And in the event, it is hard to deny that these doubters were proved correct. By engineering a severe recession between 1979 and 1982, albeit one deeper than planned (see also Chapter 4), the government did temporarily reduce inflation, but at the cost of unemployment levels unprecedented in the postwar era. More significantly, as inflation (and inflationary expectations) stabilised in the mid-1980s (at around 5 per cent), unemployment lodged for an extended period at 3 million rather than automatically recovering in the way that the government had envisaged. In other words, the trade-off between inflation and unemployment persisted for long after inflationary expectations had fully adjusted to the slowdown in the rate of growth of aggregate demand. Only after the government let the growth of demand accelerate out of control between 1986 and 1988 did unemployment begin to fall and by then, of course, the inflationary threat was once more looming.

A second notable weakness of the strategy, this time at the operational level, was the means by which aggregate demand was controlled during the 1980s (i.e. the chosen instruments of policy). The government's heavy reliance on monetary policy, as opposed to fiscal policy, was extremely unfortunate. Having almost completely deregulated the financial system over the last decade, the government unwittingly created the conditions for the explosion in credit which drove the consumer boom of the late 1980s. By refusing to use fiscal policy – for example, by raising income tax rates to curb consumption – the government found itself forced to try and limit the growth of spending by levering up interest rates to punitive levels. High interest rates are a notoriously blunt tool at the best of times and their effects have fallen disproportionately hard on those sectors of the economy – notably, manufacturing and construction which rely on borrowed funds to finance their investment – whose vitality is so crucial to Britain's long-term, supply-side performance.

Third, and still concerning the issue of the way in which the strategy was executed, the government's choice of intermediate targets in the 1980s must be questioned. To the government's credit, it abandoned broad monetary targets as soon as M3's unreliability became clear. And to the extent that the behaviour of M0 – 99 per cent of which comprises the notes and coin that the Bank of England automatically supplies as the public's need for currency grows in line with its spending – is nothing more than a reflection of changes in aggregate demand, it played a useful role in informing policy stance. But by clinging to the rhetoric of monetary control for so long, the government gave undue weight to monetary variables rather than alternative leading indicators like corporate stockbuilding or housing starts' which may have been telling a different and more realistic story (as in the period 1985–9); moreover, by not dumping the baggage of monetarism early on, the authorities were forced on occasion to make otherwise unnecessary policy changes because their lip service to monetary targets fostered the expectation of policy action in the financial markets (e.g. the view that interest rates would rise whenever M0 was over target) which they were obliged to fulfil.

The government must also be taken to task for its confused attitude towards the exchange rate, which became the main intermediate target of policy after 1982. By delaying the decision to take the logical next step and place sterling in the Exchange Rate Mechanism of the EMS for so long, the government paid all the costs (e.g. greater interest rate volatility) of pegging the exchange rate for few of the benefits (e.g. greater long-term stability). Even more damning, by the time the government finally accepted the futility of continued resistance to EMS membership and joined in October 1990, its earlier confused monetary policy had allowed inflation to accelerate to over three times the German rate, thereby making the unemployment costs of living with the DM2.95 target higher than they needed to have been.

Several lessons emerge from Britain's unhappy experience with anti-inflation policy during the 1980s. First, inflation is not an evil which can be permanently driven out of the economy by a once-and-for-all deflation; nor is 'inflation psychology' something which can be decisively smashed by a 'short, sharp shock'. The real costs of fighting inflation are significant and enduring and the path of real variables like unemployment and output should not be ignored in deciding the thrust of anti-inflation policy. While the government did ease policy after 1982, when it became clear that forcing inflation below 5 per cent would involve causing even higher unemployment, its early determination to avoid a 'U-turn' undoubtedly resulted in years of unnecessary hardship for hundreds of thousands of jobless people.

Second, the government should use all the weapons at its disposal when it comes to controlling demand and not keep one hand tied behind its back. Mr Lawson's successors (John Major and Norman Lamont) have both used fiscal policy in a more activist fashion – for example, allowing the PSBR to grow due to the operation of automatic stabilisers during the 1990-2 recession. This change of heart is to be applauded, but various forms of direct financial controls (especially in the consumer credit and mortgage markets) do not deserve the sneering condescension of Treasury ministers and could play a useful supporting role in future boom periods. Indeed, with EMS membership obliging the Chancellor to set interest rates at whatever level the exchange rate demands, the need for an extra instrument of policy to make occasional adjustments to the growth of aggregate demand is now greater than it was in the 1980s.

Finally, the government should realise that its long-overdue entry to the EMS – which completed its protracted transition from monetary to exchange rate targets – is not an easy option. Given Germany's enviable record of fighting inflation, Britain can look forward to an era of much greater price stability in the 1990s. But EMS membership will achieve nothing that the successful implementation of the MTFS could not have achieved, had the original strategy been seen through to the bitter end. For all the technical difficulties of targeting the money supply, the fundamental reason why the government relaxed the discipline imposed by the MTFS in the early 1980s was that it judged the unemployment costs of price stability to be too high in political terms. It remains to be seen whether a future British government will be prepared to suffer years of 3 million-plus unemployment to keep inflation at German levels in the 1990s.

NOTES

1 *The Conservative Manifesto*, Conservative Central Office, 1979.
2 Budget speech, 14 March 1989, reprinted in the *Financial Times*, 15 March 1989.
3 'The British experiment', the Mais Lecture by Nigel Lawson, City University Business School, 1983.
4 'The Budget strategy', speech by Nigel Lawson to the Institute of Fiscal Studies, March 1981.
5 ibid.
6 'The fight against inflation', the Mais Lecture by Sir Geoffrey Howe, City University Business School, 1983.
7 See note 2.
8 *The Right Approach to the Economy*, Conservative Central Office, 1977.

9   *Financial Statement and Budget Report*, HMSO, 1980.
10 *Financial Statement and Budget Report*, HMSO, 1982.
11 Treasury and Civil Service Committee, *Fourth Report on the 1984 Budget*, Cmnd 341, HMSO, 1984.
12 Treasury and Civil Service Committee, *Fourth Report on the 1986 Budget*, Cmnd 313, HMSO, 1986.
13 McMahon, K., evidence to Treasury and Civil Service Committee, *Third Report on International Monetary Co-ordination*, Cmnd 384, HMSO, 1989.
14 'The state of the market', speech by Nigel Lawson to the Institute of Economic Affairs, 21 July , 1988.
15 See note 2.
16 See note 2.

Part II

CONTEMPORARY MICROECONOMIC ISSUES

8

GOVERNMENT POLICY, TAXATION AND SUPPLY-SIDE ECONOMICS

Phil Robins

INTRODUCTION

For more than a decade, the centrepiece of the Conservative government's macroeconomic policy has been the Medium-Term Financial Strategy with its formal monetary growth targets (see Chapter 7). The prime aim of these targets was the reduction of the rate of inflation in order to establish a favourable environment for sustainable non-inflationary growth in the economy. This strategy for growth did not rely solely on a spontaneous recovery of the economy as inflation fell. The government had, in addition, a parallel strategy to encourage growth by means of a radical reform of the microeconomic structure or 'supply-side' of the economy. An integral part of this 'supply-side' reform programme was the desire to restructure the tax system, especially direct taxes, to encourage enterprise, effort and innovation.

In the 1979 budget, the government took the first steps by reducing the basic rate of income tax from 33 per cent to 30 per cent and the top rate from 83 per cent to 60 per cent. At the time the Chancellor of the Exchequer, Sir Geoffrey Howe, made his intentions clear:

> We need to strengthen incentives, by allowing people to keep more of what they earn, so that hard work, talent and ability are properly rewarded.[1]

Over the following years the government's views did not change, but financial and economic circumstances prevented further progress until 1986. Sir Geoffrey Howe's successor, Nigel Lawson, then felt able to reduce the basic rate of income tax to 29 per cent with the clear intention still being to stimulate a 'supply-side' revolution:

> Reductions in taxation motivate new business and improve

incentives to work. They are the principal engine of the enterprise culture, on which our future prosperity and employment opportunities depend.[2]

The ultimate aim of Sir Geoffrey Howe was a basic rate of income tax of 25 per cent and Nigel Lawson confirmed that this continued to be the government's long-term objective. After 1986, progress became more rapid with a reduction in the basic rate of income tax from 29 per cent to 27 per cent in 1987. In 1988 the original long-term objective was achieved with the basic rate reduced to 25 per cent and, in addition, all higher rates above 40 per cent abolished. Thus, in the space of nine years, basic rate taxpayers saw their nominal rate of income tax fall from 33 per cent to 25 per cent and, more dramatically still, higher rate taxpayers saw their top level income tax rate fall from 83 per cent to 40 per cent, and for investment income the rate fell from 98 per cent to 40 per cent.

At the time the Chancellor was in no doubt as to the benefits that such reductions would bring to the economy:

> Excessive rates of income tax destroy enterprise, encourage avoidance, and drive talent to more hospitable shores overseas. As a result, so far from raising additional revenue, over time they actually raise less.[3]

The notion that tax cuts can be used to stimulate economic recovery is hardly novel. A conventional Keynesian analysis would argue that tax cuts increase private sector disposable income, which in turn leads to a rise in aggregate demand and thereby to higher output and employment. The present government's support for tax cuts is, however, based upon an entirely different view of the economic system. The role of tax changes is not to increase aggregate demand but to improve the workings of the 'supply-side' of the economy by altering the structure of relative prices and thereby incentives to workers, savers and entrepreneurs.

THE SUPPLY-SIDE ANALYSIS OF TAX CUTS

In the Keynesian view, the supply capacity of the economy is assumed to be determined by long-run exogenous forces such as demographic and technology changes and natural resource discoveries. The task of economic management is seen as that of ensuring adequate aggregate demand exists to utilise fully available capacity and thus prevent large-scale unemployment of economic resources, especially labour.

In contrast, supply-side policy concentrates on the impact of tax changes on relative prices and therefore on individual behaviour. The two sets of relative prices that are often the focus of supply-side policy are:

1 the relative cost of work as against leisure, affected by changes in income tax, which influence individuals' decisions as to how many hours of labour to offer at the margin. As well as the quantitative effect there may also be a qualitative effect, influencing the effort, innovation and efficiency with which individuals are prepared to apply their labour;

2 the relative cost of saving and investment as against consumption, affected by changes in income and company taxation and the direct/indirect tax mix. After-tax rates of return on savings and investment will influence the type and the pace of capital accumulation and thus the level and rate of growth of efficiency and innovation in the economy.

The implication for tax policy is that it is changes in the average rate of taxation, affecting the level of disposable income, that are significant for Keynesian demand-side policy, whereas it is changes in the marginal rate of taxation, affecting relative prices and thus individual choice decisions, that is significant for supply-side policy. One consequence of this supply-side analysis is that a budget-deficit (i.e. aggregate demand) neutral set of tax changes can be either expansionary or contractionary, depending upon the impact on relative prices (Ture, 1983).

The difference in emphasis on the role of taxation between the demand-side and the supply-side views can be illustrated with a simple diagrammatic example. In Figure 8.1, we have an economy where the production possibility frontier (PPF) with full utilisation of existing labour and capital resources and the use of the best technology is A_0B_0. The particular combination of public and private sector goods and services that is chosen to be produced is indicated at point X – A_x private sector output and B_x public sector output. To shift the PPF outwards requires either an increase in the supply of labour and/or capital or an improvement in technology, to improve the productivity of the existing supply of factor inputs. The PPF will contract inwards if either labour and/or capital supplies fall or if the efficiency with which they are utilised is reduced.

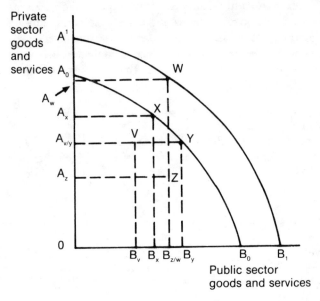

Figure 8.1 Production possibility frontier of a two-sector economy

The contention of 'supply-side' theory is that conventional (i.e. Keynesian) macroeconomic policies designed to generate an expansion of the economy can significantly reduce the productive potential of the economy. The tax and expenditure changes entailed in conventional 'demand-side' policies will, it is argued, generate individual choices and behaviour patterns which will reduce the current and future availability of resources and the efficiency of their employment. For example, if over time the productive potential of the economy has shifted out to A_1B_1, then a conventional fiscal policy response might be to cut taxes and increase public expenditure to ensure adequate demand so that unemployment does not rise. If such a policy is successful, then the output of the economy will rise to point W with A_w private sector and $B_{z/w}$ public sector output. The supply-side contention is that such a policy will generate serious consumption and investment choice distortions, whose effect will be to reduce both the quantity of resources supplied and the efficiency with which they are employed. The net effect would be to reduce aggregate supply and lead to a contraction of economic activity so that the level of output and employment would fall to something like point V where private sector output is to $A_{v/y}$ and public sector output is B_v.

154

Where the object of policy is to re-allocate resource use in the economy, for example, to provide more public sector goods and services, the government may use tax and public spending policies to shift the output mix from point X to point Y. Again, such fiscal policy changes will generate distortions in the economy so that productive potential is reduced. The net result may well be a relative shift of resources to the public sector but the supply-side effects will lead to a contraction of economic activity so that the output mix of the economy moves not from point X to point Y but from point X to point Z. Public sector output rises only marginally from B_x to $B_{z/w}$ and does not reach the expected level of B_y. On the other hand, the cost in terms of lost private sector output is far greater than anticipated, falling from A_x to A_z rather than just to $A_{v/y}$.

The supply-side solution would be to recommend that the government cut marginal tax rates to utilise the incentive effects that they are supposed to generate. Such a policy will encourage greater supplies of labour and capital resources to be provided and used more efficiently. The PPF will expand to A_1B_1 and total output in the economy will rise from point X to point W. Private sector output increases from A_x to A_w and public sector output rises from B_x to $B_{z/w}$. It is notable that this 'private enterprise' orientated policy in fact generates far more public sector output than the failed 'Keynesian' expansionary policy ($B_{z/w}$ instead of B_v), and just as much public sector output as the redistributive policy, but with much higher private sector output than in either case (A_w as opposed to $A_{v/y}$ or A_z).

THE IMPLICATIONS FOR FISCAL POLICY

Crucial to the above analysis is the belief that there are serious negative supply-side effects created by conventional economic policies. For example, a 'balanced budget' fiscal expansion aims to increase demand, but the associated tax increases will, in the supply-side view, lead to a contraction of economic activity. First, owners of labour resources faced with a rise in taxes may decide to offer less labour for sale and to use the time released at home or for leisure. Second, owners of capital resources may react to increased taxes by reducing the use of existing plant, lengthening the useful life of assets, and spending the proceeds of current capital resources on consumption as investment is now less attractive. And third, owners of all types of resources may continue to supply them to the marketplace, but try increasingly to divert them to lower or non-taxed uses. Such a reaction will increase inefficiency since resource use is subject to artificial distortion and is therefore sub-optimal, and valuable time and effort will be diverted from productive uses to tax avoidance or evasion activities.

If a fiscal expansion is carried out by generating a budget deficit (i.e. government expenditure increases are not fully offset by tax increases or tax cuts are not fully offset by expenditure cuts), then bond sales will tend to 'crowd-out' private sector investment (see Robins, 1985; Healey and Parker, 1990) and thus neutralise the expansionary effect as well as distorting the optimum allocation of resources. If the deficit is financed by monetary expansion, then this too can have negative supply-side effects. Monetary expansion will generate inflation, since real output has not increased but the money supply has. In such circumstances, inflation reduces economic efficiency by creating uncertainties about how to interpret price changes and distorts resource allocation as scarce resources are used to economise on the higher cost of holding money.

In contrast, a supply-side policy of tax cuts allied with reductions in government expenditure should lead to an expansion of economic activity via the incentive effects of the tax cuts and the shift of resources to the 'productive' and more efficient private sector. Such a policy, however, may not be revenue-neutral if it proves, in practice, impossible to cut expenditure as much as taxes. As a consequence, a budget deficit can be generated by a 'one-sided' supply-side policy. Such deficits represent a problem to the non-Keynesian economist, since attempts to finance them can cancel out the expansionary effect of the supply-side tax cuts, as outlined above. On the other hand, limited tax cuts which can be financed by expenditure reductions may be insufficient to generate maximum economic growth. The essence of this choice between maximum revenue (at higher tax rates) and maximum economic growth (at lower tax rates) is illustrated by the 'Laffer Curve' concept.

In the mid-1970s, Professor Arthur Laffer resurrected a well-established concept that there is a logical linkage between the rate of taxation and the amount of revenue raised. At a tax rate of 0 per cent, revenue will clearly be zero. At a tax rate of 100 per cent, revenue will also be zero since there is no financial incentive to work in a taxable activity. Between these two extremes, therefore, there will be a function relating the amount of tax revenue to the tax rate which will be positive and obviously at some point reach a maximum, producing the distinctive 'humped' shape of the 'Laffer Curve'. Such a curve is

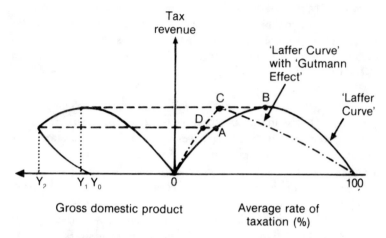

Figure 8.2 The 'Laffer Curve' and the 'Gutmann Effect'

Notes: 1 'Laffer Curve'
— Tax rates O to A: income effect is greater than the substitution effect, giving a net incentive effect.
— Tax rates A to B: income effect is less than the substitution effect, giving a less than proportionate disincentive effect.
— Tax rates greater than B: income effect is much less than the substitution effect, giving a more than proportionate disincentive effect.

2 'Gutmann Effect'
— As above but with tax rates O to D, D to C, and greater than C respectively.

shown in the right-hand sector of Figure 8.2, in which the level of tax revenue raised at any given level of taxation is plotted.[4]

The 'Laffer Curve' can be divided into separate sectors that correspond with both the revenue raised and the associated levels of economic activity as measured by gross domestic product (GDP), as shown in the left-hand sector of Figure 8.2. At a 0 per cent tax rate, no revenue is raised and the associated level of GDP is Y_0, equivalent to a market economy operating without any form of public sector intervention or regulation. As the tax rate rises above 0 per cent, so economic activity is affected: firstly, and positively, by the income effect whereby taxpayers have to work harder to maintain their post-tax income; secondly, and negatively, by the substitution effect whereby taxpayers find leisure and consumption progressively more

157

attractive, compared to work and saving, as the post-tax reward declines. Between 0 per cent tax rate and point A, the positive income effect outweighs the negative substitution effect and, as a consequence, GDP rises from Y_0 towards its maximum of Y_2. At tax rates beyond point A, the substitution effect outweighs the income effect and GDP falls.

Note, however, that tax revenue will continue to rise so long as the proportionate rise in the tax rate exceeds the proportionate rise in the net disincentive effect on taxpayers – and hence the tax base. Eventually, when the tax rate reaches point B, the rise in the proportionate net disincentive effect will equal the proportionate rise in the tax rate and tax revenue peaks. However, the erosion of the tax base means that GDP has now fallen to Y_1. At tax rates beyond point B, the net disincentive effect is so strong that it erodes the tax base faster than the tax rate can rise, and total tax revenue starts to fall. As the tax rate approaches 100 per cent, the net disincentive effect completely destroys the tax base and revenue falls to zero, as does recorded GDP.

If the government is faced with an economy where existing tax rates are higher than point B, then no policy problem exists since a cut in tax rates will not only stimulate GDP growth but also increase revenue. If tax rates are below point A, then again GDP and tax revenue will move in the same direction. A rise in taxes will lead to growth in GDP and tax revenue. A policy problem does arise if the existing tax rates lie between points A and B, as GDP and tax revenue will move in opposite directions. For example, if the tax rate is at point B and therefore GDP is equal to Y_1, then a cut in tax rates could stimulate a growth in economic activity towards Y_2 but at the cost of a decline in tax revenue. In the absence of balancing expenditure cuts, the result will be a rise in the budget deficit leading to the financing problems already discussed. Some empirical evidence for Britain (e.g. Beenstock, 1979) indicates that governments are likely to find themselves facing such a policy dilemma with current tax rates fairly centrally placed between points A and B.

However, Gutmann (1983) argues that high tax rates have driven a substantial amount of economic activity underground or into the so called 'black economy'. Thus the recorded, and therefore taxable, level of economic activity understates the real level with this discrepancy becoming greater the higher the tax rate. As a consequence a cut in tax rates has a twofold effect on the tax base. The 'Laffer Curve' as shown here only captures revenue changes due to changes in the legitimate level of economic activity, but once allowance is made for the 'Gutmann Effect', then revenue turns out to be substantially higher than expected at lower tax rates. This is because at lower levels of taxation not only is there real growth in the economy due to the incentive effect, but there is growth in the recorded tax base in addition to this, as more and more underground activity comes back into the legitimate economy. If the 'Gutmann Effect' is combined with the 'Laffer Curve' it may be that revenue-neutral or even revenue-positive tax cuts would be possible at much lower tax rates than previously thought. Thus in Figure 8.2, the revenue-maximising level of taxes is shifted from point B to point C and the GDP-maximising tax rate is shifted from point A to point D.

The actual magnitude of importance of the black economy is open to serious question. In the United States, Gutmann (1983) estimated it to be as much as 10 per cent of GNP. In Britain, Sir William Pile has suggested that the black economy could amount to 7.5 per cent of GDP. However, the Central Statistical Office (CSO), using an income and expenditure analysis of National Accounts data, has suggested a level of 4 per cent of GDP. Dilnot and Morris (1981) produced an even lower estimate of between 2 and 3 per cent of GNP, with about one in ten households actually participating in the black economy.

At the lower end of the range of estimates, it is clearly open to question as to how beneficial a 'purge' of the black economy would be. Indeed, it might be argued that accepting the existence of a limited amount of economic activity with a nominal marginal tax rate of 0 per cent might actually be beneficial. Attempts to tax such activity may merely result in more determined attempts at evasion or the abandonment of the activity altogether and thus a real decline in total output.

A further problem that faces supply-side, tax-cutting programmes is identified by Elwell (1983), who argues that whilst such policies might, over time, generate appropriate supply-side responses, the reaction may be slow and long-term in nature. The problem is that such changes have revenue consequences which affect the government's budget deficit and private sector disposable income fairly quickly. Thus, a short-term demand-side response can be expected from such policies. The result could be that in the short term the rise in aggregate demand outstrips the rise in aggregate supply, leading to inflationary pressure and rising interest rates. These effects, when

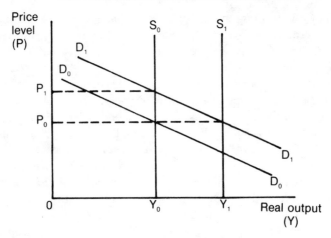

Figure 8.3 Supply-side policy and the price level

combined with fear amongst firms as to the government's policy responses to restrain inflation, could damage prospects for a supply-side recovery.

On these grounds, a successful supply-side policy may need to be co-ordinated with a policy of demand restraint – including reduced government expenditure, reduced growth of the money supply and lower tax cuts than average for the less supply-side-responsive sectors of the economy. In addition, lower government expenditure would alleviate the budget deficit problem and reduce the risk that the financing of the deficit would undermine growth prospects via such mechanisms as crowding-out.

Elwell's point is illustrated in Figure 8.3, in which supply-side tax cuts aim to shift the long-run equilibrium level of aggregate supply from S_0 to S_1 and raise national income from Y_0 to Y_1. In the short run, the demand response to the tax cuts will shift aggregate demand from D_0 to D_1, leading to a rise in the general price level from P_0 to P_1 and a rise in the rate of interest. Both of these effects will tend to undermine the growth stimulus provided by the supply-side policy. An appropriate strategy might therefore be to restrain the growth of aggregate demand so that it only increases in line with the gradual adjustment of aggregate supply. The result of such a policy would be to co-ordinate the rightward shift of both aggregate demand and aggregate supply in Figure 8.3, thus preventing a rise in the general price level.

160

THE CONSERVATIVE GOVERNMENT'S RECORD: TAXING HOUSEHOLDS

Notwithstanding the weakness of empirical evidence supporting the existence of significant positive supply-side benefits arising from tax cuts (e.g. Sandford, 1978; Thompson, 1986; Brown, 1988; Dilnot and Kell, 1988), the government has been committed to just such policies since coming to office in 1979. To assess the extent to which they have succeeded, we can consider the impact of tax changes on households, and thus the supply of labour, and on firms, and thus the utilisation of labour and the supply and utilisation of capital.

The supply-side effects of tax changes on households depend upon the effect they have on incentives. Whether tax changes generate incentive effects or not will depend not only on characteristics of individual taxes that are introduced or withdrawn but also on the combined effect of all tax changes and how they interact with each other. (See Table 8.1 for a summary of the main tax changes affecting households since 1979.)

The net incentive effect of tax changes on households will depend upon: the magnitude of the income effect, where increased taxation encourages more work effort, which will depend upon the average rate of taxation; the magnitude of the substitution effect, where increased taxation reduces work effort, which will depend upon the marginal rate of taxation; and the progressivity of the tax system, which depends upon the mix of tax allowances and tax rates. A more progressive tax system will have larger allowances and higher marginal tax rates: such a structure may tend to reduce incentives. A less progressive tax system will have smaller allowances and lower marginal tax rates and may tend to increase incentives.

Since indirect taxes are generally less progressive than direct taxes, a switch from direct to indirect taxation, as happened in the 1979 and 1991 budgets, could have a substantial effect on incentives, depending upon the extent to which the progressivity of the tax system is changed as a result. However, the precise effect may be quite complex. For example, VAT is nominally a proportional tax, but since it only applies to households' net (i.e. after direct tax) income, then in a regime of progressive direct taxation, a lower proportion of higher-income households' income will be exposed to VAT, compared to lower-income households. In principle therefore, an increase in VAT is regressive.

This effect is, however, offset by the effective incidence to pay VAT

Table 8.1 Main tax changes affecting households since 1979

1979 budget
- substantial reductions in higher rates of income tax including lowering top rate for earned income from 83 per cent to 60 per cent (affects 3 per cent of tax units);
- major shift from direct to indirect taxation involving increase in VAT standard rate from 8 per cent to 15 per cent;
- reduction in the basic rate of income tax from 33 per cent to 30 per cent;
- income tax allowances increased by 8 per cent more than inflation;
- extension of the basic rate income tax band.

1980 budget
- income tax allowances increased in line with inflation;
- specific duties increased in line with inflation;
- reduced rate (25 per cent) band of income tax abolished;
- National Insurance contributions rate increased by 0.25 per cent.

1981 budget
- no increase in income tax allowances to take account of inflation;
- specific duties increased by more than inflation;
- National Insurance contributions rate increased by 1 per cent.

1982 budget
- income tax allowances increased by slightly more than inflation;
- National Insurance contributions rate increased by 1 per cent;
- National Insurance surcharge reduced by 1 per cent.

1983 budget
- income tax allowances increased by 8 per cent more than inflation;
- National Insurance contributions rate increased by 0.25 to 0.6 per cent;
- specific duties increased in line with inflation;
- National Insurance surcharge reduced by 0.5 per cent.

1984 budget
- income tax allowances increased by 7 per cent more than inflation;
- higher-rate tax thresholds increased in line with inflation;
- coverage of VAT widened to include building alterations and take-away food;
- specific duties restructured but the total increase in line with inflation;
- National Insurance surcharge abolished.

1985 budget
- income tax allowances increased by twice the rate of inflation;
- higher rate tax thresholds increased in line with inflation;
- National Insurance contributions rate reduced for low-paid workers and upper limit to employers' contributions for higher-paid workers abolished;
- coverage of VAT widened to include advertising and credit card companies;
- specific duties increased by more than the rate of inflation.

1986 budget
- basic rate of income tax reduced from 30 per cent to 29 per cent;
- income tax allowances increased in line with inflation;

- higher rate tax thresholds increased by less than the rate of inflation;
- specific duties increased overall in line with inflation but mainly weighted on petrol and tobacco;
- Capital Transfer Tax abolished and replaced by Inheritance Tax.

1987 budget
- basic rate of income tax reduced from 28 per cent to 27 per cent;
- income tax allowances increased in line with inflation;
- no increase in specific duties;
- first higher-rate tax threshold increased in line with inflation; the second threshold by £200 and the remainder left unchanged;
- tax relief for profit-related pay schemes

1988 budget
- basic rate of income tax reduced from 27 per cent to 25 per cent;
- all higher rates of income tax over 40 per cent (i.e. 45, 50, 55 and 60 per cent) abolished;
- income tax allowances and the remaining higher-rate threshold increased by twice the amount of inflation;
- specific duties raised differentially, spirits and vehicle excise duty not raised at all but petrol duty raised by more than rate of inflation;
- Capital Gains Tax to be charged at income tax rates and no charge on pre-1982 gains.

1989 budget
- reform of National Insurance contributions for employees with 2 per cent rate on earnings below lower earnings limit;
- income tax allowances and thresholds increased in line with inflation;
- no increase in specific duties on alcohol, tobacco and leaded petrol. Duty on unleaded petrol cut.

1990 budget
- independent taxation of husband and wife;
- income tax allowances raised in line with inflation;
- basic rate tax band unchanged;
- specific duties generally increased in line with inflation but higher increases for petrol, tobacco and spirits. No increase in vehicle excise duty;
- Tax Exempt Special Savings Accounts (TESSA) to allow saving free of all tax to be introduced in January 1991.

1991 budget
- abolition of mortgage interest tax relief at higher rate;
- higher rate tax threshold increased by £1,000 more than rate of inflation;
- income tax allowances raised in line with inflation but no increase in the married couple's allowance;
- employers' National Insurance contributions extended to company cars;
- increase in the rate of VAT from 15 per cent to 17.5 per cent;
- specific duties on fuel and tobacco raised by more than rate of inflation, on alcohol by rate of inflation, and vehicle excise duty unchanged;
- doubling of tax relief available to employees in profit-related pay schemes.

which varies between income groups because of their different patterns of expenditure and thus their consumption of VAT and non-VAT liable goods and services. As a consequence, higher-income households are likely to spend a larger proportion of their net income on VAT-liable goods and services, so that in practice VAT does turn out to be a roughly proportional tax. In the case of excise duties, however, and especially with regard to tobacco, the spending pattern effect tends to reinforce the regressive nature of any increase in such taxes. Finally, it should be remembered that even if VAT is a proportional tax, the shift from progressive taxes to proportional taxes is a regressive change in itself.

Bearing these factors in mind, we can now assess the supply-side contribution of government tax changes as they have affected households. Turning first to the income effect, this will tend to reduce incentives if the net result of tax (and benefit) changes is to increase household income, and would tend to increase incentives if household income were reduced. In Table 8.2, the changes in net income for the working population caused by government policy between 1979 and 1986 compared with what would have been the case if the previous Labour government's policies had simply been indexed in line with inflation is shown. During that period, 67 per cent of households were poorer by more than 1 per cent (see also Chapter 12).

The principal factors that made the system less generous were the increase in National Insurance contributions, the substantial rise in VAT, increases in the real levels of other indirect taxes and the abolition of the reduced rate band of income tax. Increases in the real value of tax allowances (after 1982) and the reductions in the basic rate of tax in the 1979 and 1986 budgets were not sufficient to offset these losses. As well as one-parent families, the other main section of the working population to gain were higher-rate taxpayers, representing at that time just 3 per cent of tax units, who were the major beneficiaries of the large reductions in higher-rate tax bands made in 1979.

Thus up to 1986, so far as the income effect is concerned, the government's policy had, for the majority of working households, probably had some incentive effect. The irony is that the mechanism by which this was achieved was a reduction in net income, thus forcing households to work harder just to maintain existing living standards. This is almost certainly not the result the government would have wanted (or, at least, for which it would want to claim the credit). In addition, the effect on high-income households, which

Table 8.2 Percentage changes in net income for working population: 1979 indexed compared with post-1986 budget

	−5 or more	−3 to −5	−1 to −3	−1 to +1	+1 to +3	+3 to +5	+5 or more	1979–86 change
Single	25	22	30	14	4	2	3	−2.2
Couple (0)	14	21	34	21	6	2	2	−1.8
Couple (2)	14	23	39	13	5	1	4	−1.9
OPF	4	3	10	11	4	3	67	+5.5
TOTAL	16	20	31	17	6	2	8	−1.4

Source: Fiscal Studies
Notes: Couple (0) = married couple with no children
     Couple (2) = married couple with two children
     OPF = one-parent family

presumably provide key managerial and technical staff and the entrepreneurial drive to commerce and industry, was perverse from the incentive point of view. They experienced a sharp rise in after-tax income and, via the income effect, experienced a reduction in incentives.

Clearly the analysis in Table 8.2 does not include the major tax changes of the 1987 and 1988 budgets. When these are included the picture does change, but not necessarily in a way that improves incentives. Looking at the cumulative effects over ten years from 1978/9 to 1988/9, the proportion of gross income paid in income tax, National Insurance, VAT, other indirect taxes and rates of a married couple with two children on male average earnings, rose from 38.5 per cent to 40.5 per cent. Rises in rates, National Insurance and VAT more than offset income tax reductions and falls in the real value of specific duties. For poor households, on three-quarters average earnings, the rise is even larger; whilst for better-off households, the rise is less.

Concentrating on the impact of income tax and National Insurance only for similar households, the burden is marginally higher for those on three-quarters average earnings, very slightly down for those on average earnings, about 4 per cent lower for households on one-and-a-half average earnings, and for those on five times average earnings over 14 per cent lower. This compares with a 4 per cent increase for households on half average earnings. Such comparisons suggest that the incentive to work harder, via the income effect, has been considerably eased by the 1987 and 1988 tax changes for all but the

Table 8.3 Single-earner couple: effective marginal tax rate (%)

	78–9	79–80	80–1	81–2	82–3	83–4	84–5
Inc. Tax	29.1	26.1	25.7	25.7	26.1	26.2	26.5
Nat. Ins.	15.6	16.5	17.8	18.9	18.7	18.3	17.6
VAT	4.4	8.0	7.9	7.8	7.7	7.8	7.8
Other indirect	10.5	10.2	10.2	10.6	10.4	10.6	10.2
TOTAL	59.6	60.8	61.6	63.0	62.9	62.9	62.1

Source: Fiscal Studies

very low paid. Indeed, for the well paid the income effect continued to act as a disincentive to harder work (Johnson and Stark, 1989).

Turning to the impact of the substitution effect on households, the key indicator to consider is the effective marginal tax rate. The substitution effect will reduce incentives if the marginal tax rate rises and increase incentives if it falls. In Table 8.3, we can see the impact on a specific household type between 1978–9 and 1984–5. The significant reduction in the marginal rate of income tax in 1979 was more than offset by increases in National Insurance and VAT marginal rates up to 1982, and the overall effective marginal rate actually rose by over 3 per cent. From 1982 to 1985, there was some easing of the overall marginal rate – due almost exclusively to reductions in National Insurance. By 1984/5, the overall marginal rate was still 2.5 per cent above that inherited from the last Labour government.

Even after the tax cuts of 1987 and 1988, the overall marginal rate including income tax, National Insurance and VAT was still above the 1979 level. The impact of increases in allowances is also interesting, especially as this is an aspect of policy that has had increasing emphasis laid upon it by the Conservative government. The argument put forward for increases in the real value of allowances is that they improve incentives by taking a lot of low-income households out of tax altogether so that their nominal marginal tax rate falls by the full amount of the basic tax rate and the disincentive effects of the 'poverty trap' are significantly eased. In fact, the actual impact on incentives of such a policy is very limited, because unless there is a huge increase in allowances, the effect is only felt by those at the bottom end of the poverty trap. However, there are far more families with earnings near the top end of the poverty trap and they remain unaffected by the increase in allowances (Dilnot and Stark, 1986).

In addition, many of those taken out of tax by increased allowances are either not economically active or are secondary income earners on whom the incentive effect may be limited. Dilnot and Stark (1986) calculate that, at 1985–6 tax rates, over three-quarters of those taken out of tax by a 30 per cent increase in tax allowances would be married women, pensioners or single parents. Furthermore, although in some budgets, especially towards the end of the 1980s, tax allowances were raised by more than inflation, they did not, over the decade, do more than keep pace with earnings. Thus in 1988/9, the married person's tax allowance was virtually the same proportion of average earnings as it had been in 1978/9.

Turning finally to the progressivity of the tax system, it is very difficult to assess this precisely, since it depends upon the particular circumstances of different households. Looking again at the household type studied above, we can get some idea of what has happened. A less progressive tax system, which should increase incentives, will be characterised by low tax allowances and low marginal tax rates. Between 1978–9 and 1984–5, the real value of tax allowances fell by nearly 9 per cent while the effective marginal tax rate rose by over 2.5 per cent. Thus, in the first half of the 1980s the combination of conflicting movements in allowances and tax rates made it unclear as to whether the tax system had become more or less progressive for the basic-rate taxpayer.

In the second half of the 1980s, the trend to over-index tax allowances in successive budgets led to an increase in real terms of nearly 27 per cent compared with 1979 levels. The second half of the 1980s also saw the threshold pattern of the income tax and National Insurance rate structure radically altered. In Figure 8.4, the rate structure prior to the 1988 budget can be compared with that after. The regressive feature of a drop in the marginal rate faced by those with incomes above the National Insurance upper earnings limit and the first higher-rate threshold remains, but the five-step rise in tax rates above the basic rate to a maximum of 60 per cent has been reduced to one step, to a maximum of 40 per cent.

Combining this change with the fact that there was no significant increase in the real value of allowances as a proportion of earnings tends to indicate an overall reduction in progressivity by the end of the 1980s. In supply-side terms, this should have a clear incentive effect for those able to go well into the 40 per cent band, but for those hovering just below it in the National Insurance 'trough', the sudden imposition of a 15 per cent increase in marginal rates on additional

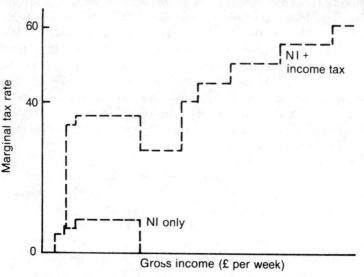

(a) Direct tax marginal rate structure before the 1988 budget

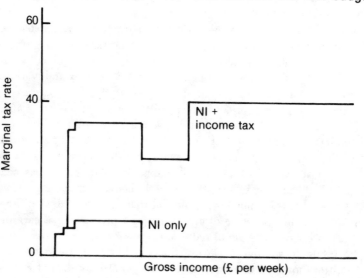

(b) Direct tax marginal rate structure after the 1988 budget

Figure 8.4 Tax structures before/after 1988 Budget

earnings may be regarded as a significant disincentive. Clearly, the numbers affected by this constitute only a small proportion of the labour force, but they will be on income levels associated with 'middle' management, whose motivation may be seen as critically important to the efficiency of the economy.

The overall impression from the above assessment is that there is really no clear evidence of a substantial boost to incentives for households. Since the income and substitution effects may have different strengths of influence on households, it is not clear what the net result of a weak income incentive combined with a substantial substitution disincentive would be, but it is certainly not the stuff of which a dramatic supply-side revolution is likely to be made.

THE CONSERVATIVE GOVERNMENT'S RECORD: TAXING COMPANIES

The supply-side objective of the government for business taxation was also set out in the 1979 budget:

> to enable the economy to work better . . . to stimulate enterprise and set British business on the road to profitable expansion . . . that will help to bring new jobs.[5]

In the event, major changes to corporation tax were not announced until the 1984 budget, when the Chancellor made it clear that he wished not only to see

> very substantial reductions in the tax [that companies] pay [and a more neutral tax regime that] . . . would encourage the search for investment projects with a genuinely worthwhile return, and . . . discourage uneconomic investment.[6]

This latter objective aimed to remove the existing, historically evolved structures of discrimination in business taxation between different types of investment and between investment and other uses of funds by firms. Such an objective was not going to be an easy one to achieve as, in the pre-1984 tax system, the effective tax rate faced by a firm could be influenced by a range of factors such as the type of asset, type of industry, method of finance and the financier's tax status. For example, under the tax regime current in 1980, up to 81 effective tax rates could be faced by firms, ranging from plus 130 per cent to minus 312 per cent (Sargent and Scott, 1986). In addition, over time there had been a consistent tax bias in favour of plant and machinery

169

compared with other forms of business investment. Evidence submitted to the Treasury and Civil Service Committee indicated that the 1984 budget changes (see Table 8.4) would substantially reduce the discrimination between different forms of investment, but still leave a considerable problem (see also Devereaux, 1988).

In the event, the post-1984 system did not deal satisfactorily with the effects of inflation and might even exacerbate them as the new writing-down allowances were based on historical cost. Edwards (1984) argued that unless future inflation were zero, the new corporation tax regime would levy tax on fictional rather than real profits. The new corporation tax system was introduced over a transitional period from 1984 to 1986. During this period after-tax profits were distorted, as the tax rate was reduced from 52 per cent to 35 per cent on returns from investment which had already benefited from 100 per cent initial allowances. This represented a temporary windfall gain to existing shareholders rather than an incentive to new investment. The short-term effect therefore of the new tax regime was to generate a temporary increasing tax subsidy on low-yielding assets.

At the end of the transitional period in 1986, the effective rate of tax rose sharply to create on average a larger marginal tax 'wedge' under the post-1984 system than under the pre-1984 system. Thus, whilst the old system increased the cost of capital by about 0.8 per cent, the new system increased it by over 1.7 per cent (Devereaux, 1988). As well as reducing distortions, the Conservative government predicted that the 1984 reforms would reduce companies' tax bills. This was based on the belief that the benefit of lower tax rates would more than offset the reduction in allowances. In fact, corporation tax revenues rose rapidly in the mid-1980s. Part of this rise could be attributed to rising company profitability as the economy recovered from the 1979–81 recession, but part was also due to the effects of the 1984 reforms which widened the tax base and reduced the proportion of 'tax-exhausted' companies. As a result, mainstream corporation tax liabilities rose faster than the underlying increase in profits. In the longer term, the value of writing-down allowances will build up and may reduce the amount of corporation tax paid, but this depends critically on the rate of inflation. If inflation rates of 4 per cent are the norm, then they should reduce substantially the tax payable by firms, but if inflation rates exceed 8 per cent, then the tax burden would rise above that under the pre-1984 system (Devereaux, 1987).

Table 8.4 Main tax changes affecting companies since 1979

1980 budget
- Initial allowances of 50 per cent for industrial buildings increased to 100 per cent for small (i.e. workshop) industrial buildings.

1981 budget
- Initial allowances for industrial buildings increased from 50 per cent to 75 per cent;
- Capital allowances of 75 per cent introduced for the first year only for the construction of properties for letting (five-year experimental scheme).

1984 budget
- main rate of corporation tax to be reduced in stages from 52 per cent to 35 per cent by the end of 1986-7;
- phasing out of initial allowances of 100 per cent for plant and machinery and of 75 per cent for industrial buildings by 1986;
- introduction of 25 per cent reducing balance writing-down allowance for plant and machinery and 4 per cent straight line writing-down allowance for industrial buildings but no allowances for commercial buildings;
- abolition with immediate effect (i.e. from 13 March 1984) of stock relief.

1991 budget
- main rate of corporation tax on profits earned in 1990/1 reduced from 35 to 34 per cent;
- main rate of corporation tax to be further reduced to 33 per cent on profits earned in 1991/2.

The 1984 tax changes also represented an effective increase in the tax burden faced by unincorporated businesses, which lost the benefits of initial allowances and stock relief, but did not gain the compensation of reduced tax rates as incorporated firms did. The financing problems of small firms were accordingly made more difficult, a policy outcome that is very much at odds with the government's often expressed desire to encourage small firms. Another problem is that the 1984 changes ignore an alternative route of tax reform proposed by the Meade Committee in 1978, which argued for a so-called 'take-out' tax. Such a tax would be levied on the net cash flow to shareholders in the form of dividends plus net repayments of share capital less new share issues. The real rate of return on all marginal investments is the same both before and after tax, irrespective of the type of asset or method of finance considered. Such a tax would also be unaffected by any realistic rate of inflation. This tax regime would therefore neither discourage worthwhile investment nor encourage uneconomic investment. Sargent and Scott (1986) and Edwards (1984) argue that the pre-1984 corporation tax system, despite its failings, had in fact moved quite a distance towards a 'take-out' tax system, but that the post-1984 system really represented in some respects a step away, with no conclusive evidence that the changes had dramatically improved the supply-side impact of company taxation.

Finally, we might note that the government's concern with 'supply-side' corporate tax reform came quite late in the day. As Table 8.4 indicates, no major initiatives were attempted until 1984 and those changes that were made in 1980 and 1981 consisted of increases in initial allowances designed to assist selectively particular types of investment by specific types of businesses. Yet this was precisely the sort of policy that the 1984 changes were designed to sweep away.

CONCLUSIONS

The supply-side approach provides a novel and interesting analysis of how tax-cutting policies might stimulate economic recovery. Unfortunately, the empirical evidence to support it is relatively unspectacular. In addition, supply-side policies are not, by their very nature, geared to achieve short-run stabilisation. Thus, the results of such policies will, if they work at all, primarily benefit long-run growth prospects rather than improve short-term economic performance.

At a practical level, the government's tax policies have to cater for a whole range of concerns and pressures as well as supply-side interests. Not surprisingly, the evidence suggests that despite good intentions, little real progress has been made to stimulate either households' or firms' supply responses.

The conclusion must therefore be that supply-side effects might just be a possible additional benefit to be derived from a policy of tax cuts, in the long run, over and above the far more certain demand-side effects. In such circumstances, to abandon demand-side policy in order to rely exclusively on supply-side effects is more an act of faith than of sound and measured economic judgement.

NOTES

1 Sir Geoffrey Howe, budget speech, 12 June 1979.
2 Nigel Lawson, budget speech, 18 March 1986.

3 Nigel Lawson, budget speech, 15 March 1988.
4 Strictly speaking, of course, for supply-side analysis it is the marginal tax rate that matters, but so long as there is a reasonable coincidence in the movements of marginal and average tax rates, then the latter can act as a useful proxy for the former.
5 Sir Geoffrey Howe, budget speech, 12 June 1979.
6 Nigel Lawson, budget speech, 13 March 1984.

9

PRIVATISATION TEN YEARS ON

A critical analysis of its rationale and results

David Parker

INTRODUCTION

Just as the 1940s decade is remembered as the era of nationalisation, the 1980s will be remembered as the decade of privatisation. It therefore seems timely to review the achievements of the privatisation programme. The programme has had two main strands: (i) the sale of state assets (denationalisation); and (ii) the introduction of competition into areas previously monopolised by state-owned suppliers (liberalisation). It is, however, the former programme which has captured the most attention and which is the primary focus of this chapter.

Table 9.1 lists all of the major privatisations to date and Table 9.2 the amounts raised from each sale; in total the government has sold almost £40bn of state assets. In 1979 the state had a major stake in many of Britain's most important industries, namely steel, motor vehicles, aero engines, aerospace, coal, rail, road haulage, air travel, oil, telecommunications, electricity, gas and water. By 1991, however, only the coal industry and the railways remained in the state sector.

Three broad reasons have been put forward in support of privatisation:

1 it raises efficiency in 'sleepy' state monopolies;
2 it widens share ownership with important gains in terms of raising public sympathy for private enterprise and profit-making; and
3 it provides useful funds to augment the Exchequer's coffers at a time when macroeconomic policy dictates a reduction in the public sector borrowing requirement (PSBR).

In this chapter, each of the above rationales is critically assessed in the light of a decade's experience. An attempt is made to answer the question, to what extent has privatisation achieved its objectives?

However, since the first rationale, the efficiency argument, is the most contentious, the chapter concentrates upon the theoretical grounds for expecting privatisation to improve performance, examining the available data on actual performance changes.

THE EFFICIENCY ARGUMENT

The economic argument against state ownership in the 1970s came from the 'New Right' and drew on the public choice and property rights theories. Both theories are rooted in neoclassical economics and the concept of the rational utility maximiser and are worth reviewing in some detail.

According to public choice theory, boards of state industries, civil servants in sponsoring departments, and politicians in government and parliament are no different from other people. Whereas earlier in the century Weber had popularised the notion of disinterested state officials pursuing the 'public interest', public choice theory argued that government employees are strongly motivated by their own self-interest. According to one of its leading exponents, Niskanen (1971), this translates into the pursuit of 'salary, perquisites of the office, public regulation, power, patronage, output of the bureau, ease of making changes, and ease in managing the bureau'. For politicians, it means attempting to maximise the chances of remaining in office by shaping policies to gain votes justifying any kind of policy as being in the 'public interest', even one which results in considerable burdens on taxpayers.

In this atmosphere, public choice economists considered it inevitable that the management of state industries would become demoralised in the face of shifting and inconsistent objectives and that the industries would fall under the influence of pressure groups, notably rent-seeking trade unions. Consequently, the industries would suffer both overmanning and wasteful investment. This pessimistic view of public ownership seemed to be borne out in Britain. In the 1970s, productivity growth in the nationalised sector lagged well behind growth in the private sector and profits net of state subsidies were negative (Pryke, 1981).

Property rights theory complemented the public choice critique. This argued that the source of the differing levels of efficiency in the public and private sectors lay in the capital market. State industries raised external funding through government, by loans with state guarantees, or directly from taxpayers. The public, which, in princ-

Table 9.1 Major British privatisations

Sale of government holdings in:		Dates
British Petroleum	various dates	1979 to 1987
National Enterprise Board investments	various dates	1980 to 1986
British Aerospace		1981, 1984
Cable and Wireless		1981, 1983, 1985
Amersham International		1982
National Freight Corporation		1982
Britoil		1982, 1985
British Rail Hotels		1983
Associated British Ports		1983, 1984
British Leyland (Rover)	various dates	1984 to 1988
British Telecom (BT)		1984, 1991
Enterprise Oil		1984
Sealink		1984
British Shipbuilders and naval dockyards	from	1985
National Bus Company	from	1986
British Gas		1986
Rolls-Royce		1987
British Airports Authority	first issue	1987
British Airways		1987
Royal Ordnance Factories		1987
British Steel		1988, 1989
Water		1989, 1990
Electricity distribution		1990
Electricity generation		1991

Source: Cmnd 1021 (1990)

iple, 'owns' the state assets, has no formal property rights in the industries. They do not own tradable shares or have rights to attend annual general meetings (AGMs) of the firms to censure management. By contrast, in the private sector, AGMs are held and shares are traded. Owners of shares are free to buy and sell them – buying further shares in companies which are well run, hence raising the share price, and selling them in firms considered to be failing, thus deflating the share price and leaving the company exposed to a hostile takeover bid.

Ultimately, according to property rights theorists, it is the vulnerability of companies to takeover by new management which is the vital spur to managerial efficiency in private enterprises and this is missing in the public sector. Inefficient nationalised industries are

Table 9.2 Privatisation proceeds (£bn)

Year	Proceeds
1979/80	0.4
1980/1	0.2
1981/2	0.5
1982/3	0.5
1983/4	1.1
1984/5	2.1
1985/6	2.7
1986/7	4.5
1987/8	5.1
1988/9	7.1
1989/90	4.2
1990/1	5.3
1991/2	5.5

Sources: Cmnd 1021 (1990); HM Treasury, *Financial Statement and Budget Report*, 1991–2, March 1991, HMSO

immune to takeover. From a property rights perspective, the attenuation of property rights in the public sector inevitably leads to lower efficiency. No matter how good the intentions of civil servants and politicians, the agent-principal relationship in the public sector leads to a waste of resources.

In sum, the idea in the early 1980s that privatisation would improve operating efficiency was based on removing political control and making firms rely on the private capital market. This is illustrated in Figure 9.1 by a movement from west to east – that is, away from direct political control towards reliance on the private capital market.

The public choice and property rights literature was popularised in Britain by the Institute of Economic Affairs and the Adam Smith Institute. It undoubtedly had a major influence on thinking about the public and private sectors in the 1970s and early 1980s, notably in the Conservative Party. However, it is not free from problems. In particular, studies of the operation of private capital markets have not demonstrated conclusively that a more active market in shares with an openness to hostile takeover bids is economically beneficial. There is some suggestion that it might lead to an overemphasis on short-term profits over long-term investment, thus lowering economic well-being. The economies of Japan and Germany, with capital markets in which hostile bids are rare, have performed much better

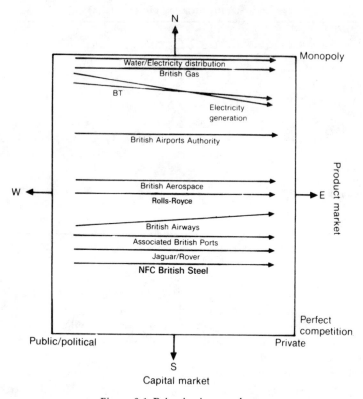

Figure 9.1 Privatisation: a schema

since the Second World War than Britain and the United States, where such bids are more commonplace. Of course, the capital market may not be a reason for this, but at least their experience demonstrates that an open capital market is not necessary for high efficiency.

It is also difficult to square the notion of the takeover threat as the key motivator for managerial efficiency, with the government's retention of a 'golden share' in a number of privatised firms. The golden share was introduced precisely to prevent unwelcome (especially foreign) takeovers of companies considered to be of strategic importance (e.g. British Aerospace and Rolls-Royce). The removal of the golden share which led to Ford's takeover of Jaguar may be seen as a belated recognition of the contradiction in government thinking about the desirability of takeovers.

Turning to motivation in the public sector, which lies at the heart of the public choice literature, detailed studies of the working of government suggest that the idea of self-interested individuals is a crude caricature. For example, the civil service went about cutting its own manning levels in the 1980s with an enthusiasm which is hard to square with the idea of 'looking after number one' (Dunsire and Hood, 1989).

The economic case for believing that privatisation will necessarily raise efficiency is therefore not clear-cut. Indeed, some economists have argued that increasing competition in the product market is a more reliable way of creating an environment in which management has the necessary incentives to operate enterprises efficiently (Millward and Parker, 1983; Kay and Thompson, 1986). The role of competition in allocative efficiency is, of course, central to the neoclassical models of perfect competition and monopoly. Also, Leibenstein (1966) has emphasised the link between product market competition and 'X-efficiency'.

The allocative and X-efficiency gains from increasing competition are illustrated in Figure 9.1 by a movement from north to south; that is, from monopoly towards more competitive markets. By combining the capital market and competition arguments, and accepting the notion that private capital markets are beneficial for economic performance, it appears that the largest efficiency gains can be expected where there is an ownership change which leads to both more competition and more reliance on private capital markets – a movement from north-west to south-east in Figure 9.1.

The actual movement of a number of privatised firms has been plotted in Figure 9.1. It can be seen that very few privatisations have been associated with a significant movement from north to south – in other words, with an increase in competition. Firms such as the National Freight Corporation (NFC), which while in the state sector always had less than 10 per cent of the British haulage market, have continued to compete as before. The same applies to Jaguar cars. State monopolies, in particular the water industry, are no more open to competition now than before privatisation. BT faces competition from Mercury Communications and in the future from cable and PCNs, but in 1991, seven years after privatisation, it still retains 95 per cent of the British telecommunications market. British Gas remains the monopoly supplier of domestic gas, though, following a Monopolies Commission report in 1988, it is being forced to permit increased competition in the industrial market. At the present time, even electricity generation offers only a promise of more competition. Also, there is a case where competition has actually declined (a south-to-north move). British Airways strengthened its market power, in an industry where competition is already highly regulated, when it was allowed to take over a major rival within Britain, namely British Caledonian.

Given the earlier reservation about the role of the capital market in ensuring efficiency, the fact that the opportunity was not taken to inject more competition into state firms at the time of privatisation must remain a source of regret. Also, it is worth recalling that privatisation was not a necessary step in increasing competition. The legislation which created Mercury as a rival to BT, which liberalised coach and later bus services, and which enabled any energy supplier to utilise the gas and electricity distribution systems, preceded privatisation of the relevant industries.

SHARE OWNERSHIP

Reversing the decline in individual share ownership has been a goal of the Conservative government. Since the end of the Second World War, the proportion of shares held by the large institutional investors has grown at the expense of individual share ownership. By giving priority to the small shareholder when selling state assets, the proportion of adults owning shares has trebled from around 7 per cent to 25 per cent since 1979. Small shareholders have been enticed through expensive advertising campaigns of the 'Tell Sid' variety, and by the offer of bonus shares or vouchers against their telephone and gas bills.

There are obvious political gains for the Conservatives in fostering a 'property-owning democracy', but ministers from time to time have also hinted at a possible economic dividend. It has been suggested that private shareholders will be more supportive of the goals of capitalism. Also, where employees of privatised firms hold shares – and employees have been given preference in share flotations – it has been argued that they now have a direct interest in the financial health of their companies. The implication is that they will work harder and strike less.

When governments attempt to pursue more than one economic objective using only one policy instrument, contradictions can arise. This has been true of privatisation. There appears to be a contradiction between creating large numbers of small shareholders and the argument that the capital market is important in producing more efficient industries following privatisation. The mechanism in the property rights literature by which the capital market promotes efficient operation is arguably more consistent with a capital market dominated by a few large shareholders rather than by many small investors. This follows because it is rational for a person who has only a small stake in an enterprise to invest little time and effort in monitoring its performance. The costs of continuous monitoring and consequent share dealing will far outweigh any benefits. Rather, detailed scrutiny of industries and managements is an economic proposition for the large institutional investors who have a lot more funds at stake in a firm. Similarly, because of transactions costs, notably brokers' charges, small shareholders are less likely to trade actively in the shares, thus it is the large investors who are the ones to be courted during a takeover bid.

It is also easy to exaggerate the impact of privatisation flotations on the composition of share ownership in Britain. The government likes to emphasise the rise in the proportion of adults holding shares since 1979, but 54 per cent of investors hold shares in only one company and only 17 per cent have shares in more than four enterprises (Treasury, 1991). Privatisation has widened share ownership but it has not deepened it, nor has it reversed the relentless growth in the financial power of the City institutions. During the 1980s, the institutional investors continued to raise their proportion of share-holdings at the expense of the private investor, whose share of the market fell from 30 per cent to 20 per cent. However, in so far as the capital market is an important constraint on management behaviour in the private sector, this may be a desirable development.

RAISING FUNDS

Just as there is an apparent conflict between the policy objective of promoting shareholding and that of promoting efficiency, there is also a conflict with the goal of raising funds for the Exchequer. If the priority had been to spread wealth through maximising the number of small shareholders, the shares could simply have been given away. Instead, the shares have been sold, though usually at far less than their opening market value on the first day of trading (see Figure 9.2). This has raised funds for the Exchequer but at the cost of reducing the potential spread of share ownership. It has also provided windfall capital gains to 'stags' at a cost to taxpayers in general (as Figure 9.2 illustrates, the government's ability to set a flotation price close to the

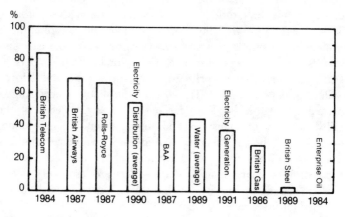

Figure 9.2 Privatisation new issues; premium after first day's trading

true market valuation does not appear to be improving with experience).

Figure 9.3 illustrates the effect of privatisation revenues on the PSBR since 1980. The revenues are treated as negative public spending under British public sector accounting convention and thus they reduce the size of the government's financial deficit. Although much play has been made of the way privatisation receipts have improved the look of the public finances, in fact only in one year, 1987–8, did they turn a positive PSBR into a debt repayment. At best, privatisation receipts have provided a useful but small supplement to taxation. Suggestion that the privatisation receipts have 'massaged' government finances in some dramatic way cannot be supported. In terms of the share of public spending in gross domestic product (GDP), they reduced the percentage by 1.5 points in 1988–9, but in other years by less.

We saw earlier that privatisation is most likely to raise the operating efficiency of the enterprises concerned when it is coupled with more competition in the product market. We now turn to consider the evidence to date on the impact of privatisation on efficiency. This is approached by looking at some of the available economic and financial data relating to privatised companies and by reviewing research recently undertaken at the University of York into the effects in terms of Figure 9.1 of west-to-east shifts in ownership. The discussion concludes by considering some of the issues for

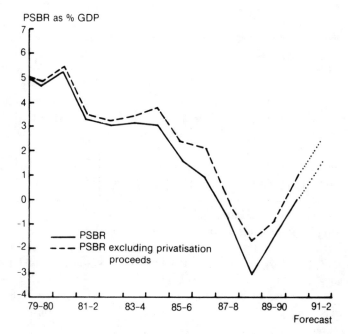

Figure 9.3 Privatisation: impact on the public sector borrowing requirement
Source: HM Treasury, 1991, *Financial Statement and Budget Report 1991-2*,
HMSO, London, p. 67

efficiency raised by the need for ongoing regulation of natural monopolies.

PRIVATISATION: THE RESULTS SO FAR

Since most privatisations occurred after 1983, it is still too early to make conclusive judgements on the impact of ownership change on many of the companies concerned. What we can say is that the experience of privatised firms to date is mixed. In 1990, Britain's most profitable companies in terms of profits per employee included four former nationalised industries in the top twenty. The star performers were the British Airports Authority in eighth position, followed by five water companies, British Steel and BT. However, profitability is generally considered on its own to be an inadequate indicator of gains in economic efficiency, and the level in one year tells us nothing about trends in the enterprise resulting from privatisation. Perhaps these enterprises would have been just as profitable had they remained in the state sector.

Table 9.3 gives a series of financial performance indicators for a selection of companies since their privatisation. It is apparent from the figures that, while top manager salaries have risen impressively, improved performance has not always resulted. The return on capital has improved marginally in the case of British Gas, BT and Rolls-Royce, but has declined badly at Associated British Ports, Enterprise Oil and Jaguar cars (the latter two firms were affected by adverse demand movements). Sales per employee (a crude productivity indicator) improved most at Associated British Ports but not dramatically in the other firms; and it actually declined at Rolls-Royce and Enterprise Oil.

The idea that privatisation leads to a shake-out of labour as wasteful working practices are terminated receives some support in the cases of British Gas and Associated British Ports, where employment declined, but elsewhere employment rose (though since 1989 BT has also begun a major programme of redundancies). Of course, many of the improvements in performance may have occurred before privatisation, but this raises the question: was privatisation really necessary? Interestingly, nationalised industries raised their profitability as a percentage of GDP and also increased their productivity faster than the private sector in the 1980s (Table 9.4). Bishop and Kay (1988) concluded that the growth in total factor productivity between 1979 and 1988 in the privatised firms they studied appeared 'wholly unrelated to privatization'. After also studying accounting data similar to that reproduced in Table 9.3, they observed:

> The overall picture to emerge . . . is one of substantial change. Output and profits have grown, margins have increased, employment has declined. But the relationship of these changes to the fact of privatization is not immediately apparent from the data. The privatized industries have tended to be faster growing and more profitable, but it seems that the causation runs from growth and profitability to privatization, rather than the other way round.

THE YORK RESEARCH PROJECT

The research undertaken at the University of York between 1986 and 1990, in which the author of this chapter was involved, consisted of a

Table 9.3 The record since privatisation: some performance indicators

	British Gas 31/3/87	British Gas 01/3/90	British Telecom 31/3/85	British Telecom 31/3/90	Rolls-Royce 31/12/87	Rolls-Royce 31/12/89	Assoc. British Ports 31/12/86	Assoc. British Ports 31/12/90	Jaguar 31/12/85	Jaguar 31/12/88	Enterprise Oil 31/12/85	Enterprise Oil 31/12/89
Return on capital employed (%)	22.7	23.4	18.3	21.3	15.2	16.3	14.9	8.8	47.7	13.2	27.8	10.7
Sales per employee (£000 real terms)	86.2	90.1	34.9	43.0	49.0	46.4	21.8	43.5	65.6	70.0	2,443	1,251
Total no. employees	88,469	80,481	238,000	248,000	42,000	55,475	6,401	3,633	9,662	12,835	109	374
Highest director's salary (£000 real terms)	109	183	172*	308	130	171	79	155	86	180	98	167

Source: Datastream
Key: * = 1986

Table 9.4 Performance of nationalised industries, 1979–87

Year	Gross trading surplus		Labour productivity (annual % change)		
	£bn	% GDP	Nationalised industries	Whole economy	Manufactur- ing
1979/80	1.1	0.5	0.1	0.7	0.9
1980/1	1.5	0.6	–0.5	–3.8	–5.3
1981/2	2.1	0.8	6.5	3.5	6.9
1982/3	2.7	1.0	2.4	4.0	6.4
1983/4	2.7	0.9	7.2	4.0	8.3
1984/5	3.1	0.9	6.0	2.9	4.8
1985/6	3.9	1.1	9.6	1.1	2.4
1986/7	4.5	1.2	6.2	3.6	4.8

Source: HM Treasury, *Economic Progress Report*, no. 193, December 1987, p. 5

study of the effects of ownership on economic and financial performance.[1] The organisations studied had either crossed the public–private boundary (privatisation or nationalisation) or had undergone major changes of status within the public sector. These changes of status involved the introduction of more commercial management and financial independence and a reduction in direct political involvement in day-to-day operations. The organisations studied and their changes in ownership status are summarised in Figure 9.4. Only two of the Conservative government's privatisations, British Aerospace and the National Freight Corporation, were included; but since all of the other cases test for the effects of a Figure 9.1 west-to-east movement, the results have general relevance to a discussion of privatisation.

Performance was measured three ways:

1 in terms of employment efficiency using an established employment function;
2 in terms of labour and total factor productivity;
3 through an analysis of a basket of standard accounting ratios.

The productivity results were compared with national trends to ensure that the changes observed were not simply the product of productivity trends in the wider economy.

Table 9.5 summarises the results of the study. The hypothesis that a movement away from political control improves performance was generally supported in six out of the ten organisations studied – the

Type of change	Organisation	Date of change
1 Movements within the public sector		
(a) Government department to trading fund	Royal Ordnance Factories	July 1974
	Royal Mint	April 1975
	HMSO	April 1980
(b) Government department to public corporation	Post Office (Postal)	April 1969
	Post Office (Telecommunications)	April 1969
(c) Public corporation accountable to local government	London Transport	Jan. 1970
(d) Local government accountability to normal public corporation status	London Transport	June 1984
2 Ownership change		
(a) Private to public	Rolls-Royce	Feb. 1971
	British Aerospace	April 1977
(b) Public to private (privatisation)	British Aerospace	Feb. 1981
	National Freight	Feb. 1982
(c) Anticipating privatisation	British Airways	1980–7

Figure 9.4 The organisations

Royal Mint, HMSO, London Transport (1984 change), National Freight, British Airways and the privatisation of British Aerospace. This includes both of the 'privatisation' cases. However, the results for Rolls-Royce consistently contradicted the hypothesis (performance improved following nationalisation) and performance failed to improve as expected in the cases of the postal and telecommunication services and the Royal Ordnance Factories.

What the results imply is that a Figure 9.1 west-to-east shift may improve performance, but that this improvement is not guaranteed. Performance improvement may depend upon factors other than ownership. Simple propositions about ownership and performance need to be qualified and treated with some caution. This implies that future research needs to focus on other sources of efficiency which may or may not be associated with changes in ownership – namely,

Table 9.5 Summary of the York research results: did performance improve as expected?

Organisation	Performance Measure			
	Employment function	Labour productivity	Total factor productivity	Financial ratios
Royal Mint	Confirmed	Confirmed	Confirmed	N/A
London Transport (1970 change)	Not confirmed	Not confirmed	Confirmed	Not confirmed
London Transport (1984 change)	Mainly confirmed	Confirmed	Confirmed	Confirmed
British Airways	Confirmed	Confirmed	Confirmed	Confirmed
British Aerospace (nationalisation)	Mainly confirmed	Confirmed	Unclear	Not confirmed
British Aerospace (privatisation)	Confirmed	Confirmed	Unclear	Confirmed
National Freight	Confirmed	Confirmed	Confirmed	Confirmed
Post Office Postal	Not confirmed	Confirmed	Unclear	Confirmed
Post Office Telecommunications	Mainly confirmed	Confirmed	Unclear	Unclear
HMSO	Confirmed	Unclear	Not confirmed	Confirmed
Royal Ordnance Factories	Not confirmed	Not confirmed	Unclear	Confirmed
Rolls-Royce	Not confirmed	Not confirmed	Not confirmed	Not confirmed

Notes: N/A = not available
For financial ratios, 'confirmed' applies to those cases where 40 per cent or more of the results supported the central hypothesis.

greater competition in the product market, improvements in management, and changes in employment contracts which encourage improved performance.

THE PROBLEM OF REGULATION

The conclusion that economic performance depends upon many factors, of which ownership status may only be one, is supported by international studies of the relative efficiency of public and private enterprises. Studies of publicly and privately owned firms operating in the same or similar markets have not demonstrated that private firms are always more efficient, especially in terms of costs of production and productivity, though they usually record higher profits (for reviews of the evidence see, for example, Borcherding *et al.*, 1982; Millward and Parker, 1983). What these studies do suggest is that competition in the product market is often a key variable, with the efficiency of both publicly owned and privately owned firms enhanced by rivalry – a conclusion which accords with our earlier discussion of the relevant economic theory. Where competition is precluded by natural monopoly factors, most especially in the electricity, gas and water industries, there are reported cases of lower cost production in the public sector.

A likely explanation of this result lies in the need to regulate private suppliers. In other words, the choice is not between dynamic, competitive private firms and sleepy state monopolies, but between private monopoly and state monopoly. In both cases, to protect consumers from monopoly exploitation, some form of government regulation must exist. Under public ownership, this is hidden within the bureaucratic mechanism and is likely to be flexible and reactive to political as well as economic pressures. Privatisation pushes regulation into the open and makes it more visible and structured.

In Britain, the privatised monopolies are now regulated by terms laid down in their privatisation legislation and their operating licences. For example, BT, which was the first public utility to be privatised, has an operating licence which runs for twenty-five years in the first instance, and which sets out the terms under which the utility must operate, including the supply of rural services, call boxes and 999 emergency calls. Prices are largely regulated by formula and the regulatory system is policed by the Office of Telecommunications (OFTEL). This structure has been copied for gas, water and electricity.

The impact of a regulatory system depends upon its influence on managerial behaviour. In the United States, where private monopoly suppliers of electricity, gas and water have existed for many years, the regulatory system has led to confusion, litigation and commercial disaster. The regulations control, *inter alia*, the level of service, environmental considerations, and pricing, much as in Britain.

Three broad problems have been experienced in the United States. First, the quasi-judicial system has given too many opportunities to lobbyists and lawyers. Consequently, resources are used up in lengthy 'rent-seeking' operations. Second, the regulatory agencies in the United States have been criticised for siding with the supplier against the consumer. Although to date the British regulatory bodies have shown commendable independence, the American experience suggests that 'regulatory capture' is an ever-present threat where private regulated monopolies exist (Peltzman, 1976; Stigler, 1971). Third, prices have generally been regulated with a view to achieving or preserving a 'satisfactory' rate of return on capital. But where a ceiling on the rate of return on capital exists, the incentive for management to control costs is reduced, and an incentive exists to extend the capital base through more investment – the so-called Averch–Johnson effect (Averch and Johnson, 1962).

The method of price control introduced in Britain when BT was privatised, and subsequently extended to the other privatised monopolies, is summarised in Figure 9.5. It was designed to overcome the distortionary effects of US-style regulation. The 'RPI minus X' formula was intended to control prices while permitting increased profits resulting from lower costs. However, despite its advantages over direct rate of return control, it does contain a major flaw which can lead to precisely the same inefficiencies as US-style regulation.

The flaw lies in the 'X' factor. For example, initially BT could raise its tariffs by the RPI less 3 per cent; therefore when inflation was 7 per cent, the charges covered by the formula could rise by up to 4 per cent. This was designed to leave an incentive for management to reduce costs by more than 3 per cent, thereby boosting profits to shareholders. However, this will only work if cost savings are not clawed back when the pricing formula is reviewed. In other words, if OFTEL decides that profits are 'too high' following a BT efficiency drive, and the 'X' factor is therefore increased, consumers benefit but shareholders lose out. Thus shareholders can gain only from the time of the efficiency improvement to the time when the price formula is renewed – at most, five years.

In practice, it appears that the 'X' factor is indeed being set at renewal with a view to what the regulatory body considers to be a 'satisfactory' rate of profit. In the face of increasing profits, BT's 'X' was raised to 4.5 per cent in 1989 and to 6.25 per cent in 1991. James McKinnon, Director General of OFGAS (Office of Gas Supply), has made it known that he considers that gas prices should be set to earn a rate of return of around 5 to 7 per cent on regulated gas supplies. In May 1991 the Office of Water Supplies (OFWAT) expressed concern

Organisation	Main feature of price regulation	Comment
British Telecom (BT)	RPI–3% 1984–9 RPI–4.5% 1989–91 RPI–6.25% 1991–	Initially applied to around one-half of turnover. Now extended to 80% of turnover.
British Gas	RPI–2% 1986–92 RPI–5% 1992–	Excludes input costs from North Sea which can be passed through to the consumer; applies to domestic market only.
British Airports Authority (BAA)	Maximum annual revenue per passenger	Duty-free shops franchised.
Water	RPI + k	'k' varies for each company and reflects agreed future capital investment programmes, e.g. to improve water quality. Allowed to pass through costs of complying with new statutory obligations.
Electricity Distribution	RPI–X + y	Allowed to pass through certain generation costs (the 'y' factor). The initial value of X has been set at zero for all the regional electricity companies.
Scottish Electricity Companies	RPI–X	Generation, transmission and distribution have separate 'X' factors.

Figure 9.5 UK privatised monopolies: price regulation

about the growth of profits in the water industry, which is ahead of estimates made at the time of privatisation.

Profits gained through monopoly exploitation are unacceptable. But threatening noises made about the growth of profits by the regulator, especially when accompanied by an upgrading of the 'X' factor, destroy managerial incentives to reduce costs and become more efficient. Also, in so far as investors take account of the risk of a change in the 'X' factor, this raises the firm's cost of capital. Moreover, the regulatory bodies have to prevent the monopolies increasing profits by raising prices unduly in services not covered by the pricing formula or by lowering the quality of the service. Recently, OFGAS informed British Gas that if it discovered that the quality of service was being sacrificed, the 'X' factor might be raised as a penalty. The use of the 'X' factor in this way, however, risks a further blurring of its purpose.

Therefore, the 'RPI minus X' formula has not overcome the distortionary effects on resource allocation associated with American-style regulation. Also, there is no sign of new competition in the foreseeable future removing the need for pricing and service regulation. Indeed, quite the reverse. Since privatisation, OFTEL has been drawn into regulating international calls and interconnection charges, and OFGAS into monitoring industrial gas pricing, precisely to facilitate new entry.

CONCLUSIONS

Britain in the 1980s was subjected to a privatisation experiment, now much copied around the world (Hemming and Mansoor, 1988). But like nationalisation, privatisation has been surrounded by more rhetoric than objective research. Only now are economists able to begin to analyse its theoretical rationale alongside its actual effects. Two possible conclusions suggest themselves:

1 Privatisation is sound in principle but the policy could have been better executed – the attempt to pursue three broad goals: increasing efficiency, widening share ownership, and reducing the PSBR led to inevitable conflicts in policy.
2 Privatisation is defective in principle, there are no sound theoretical or empirical underpinnings for a policy of transferring large chunks of the public sector to private enterprise.

At present it is not possible to be sure which of these conclusions is correct. The theoretical case for privatisation relies upon a particularly pessimistic view of motivation in the public sector, alongside what some would consider an overly optimistic view of the disciplining effect on management of exposure to the private capital market. At the same time, the available empirical evidence on the effects of privatisation on operating efficiency is ambiguous. Some organisations have registered improved performance after privatisation, while others seem to have recorded large efficiency gains while in the public sector.

Economic theory and the international evidence suggest that

competition is a key factor in ensuring high operating efficiency, and this is also borne out by Britain's experience of competitive tendering for government services during the 1980s, where cost savings of around 20 per cent or more were recorded (Parker, 1990). Belatedly, the government has recognised this. During the privatisation of the electricity industry, some competition was injected into electricity generation and, since 1989, 10 per cent of gas from new North Sea fields has been sold through suppliers other than British Gas. Also, in March 1991 the government announced an end to the duopoly in telecommunications, permitting new applications to run trunk networks.

In at least the immediate future, however, the privatised public utilities will remain dominant in their industries. After seven years of competition from Mercury Communications, BT still controls 95 per cent of the British telecommunications market; while the private sector's share of gas and electricity supplies is limited to a small amount of the industrial market. In much of the water industry it is difficult to see how competition can develop.

The existence of privatised monopolies has necessitated the creation of a regulatory structure for each industry. Hence, privatisation has altered the form of regulation – from political direction to arm's-length control by the means of legislation, operating licences and regulatory bodies. Given the pivotal role of the telecommunications, gas, electricity and water industries in the economy, it is difficult to see how any government could have abdicated responsibility for their behaviour. But while privatisation has removed the inefficiencies resulting from direct political intervention, it has introduced distortions, notably in terms of price control. Moreover, based on the American example, there remains an ever-present threat of regulatory capture and regulatory muddle (the regulatory structure of the water industry appears to have been designed to maximise the chances of confusion – the industry is now subject to the scrutiny not only of OFWAT, but also HM Inspectorate of Pollution, the Department of the Environment, the Ministry of Agriculture, the Monopolies and Mergers Commission, the European Commission and the National Rivers Authority!).

Consequently, the 1990s is likely to see heated debate about the form and extent of regulation and its impact on the way that firms behave. Britain has created the regulatory structure without much thought as to whether it is to be temporary or permanent or as to its economic effects. This is particularly surprising given the evidence on regulatory failure in the United States – evidence available to the government at the time of privatisation. If regulators get involved in questions of costs, prices, rates of return, and service quality, they are almost managing the industries. With what consequences?

NOTE

1 The research was funded by the Economic and Social Research Council as part of its Management in Government Initiative (Project no. E0925006). Other members of the research team included Professors Keith Hartley and Andrew Dunsire.

10

THE ECONOMICS OF TRADE UNION POWER

Ian Paterson and Leslie Simpson

INTRODUCTION

Labour market reform was at the forefront of the Conservative government's supply-side strategy during the 1980s. Ministers variously accused trade unions of:

1 inhibiting economic progress and blunting Britain's overseas competitiveness by the use of restrictive work practices and overmanning; and

2 preventing the flexible operation of the labour market, by holding wages above their market-clearing levels and thereby causing higher unemployment.

This chapter examines the operation of the labour market and considers the role of trade unions in altering the equilibrium outcomes for wages and employment. It then reviews the changes in trade union legislation that have taken place over recent years, before surveying the empirical evidence on the effects of trade unions.

LABOUR MARKET THEORY AND THE ROLE OF TRADE UNIONS

The labour market is concerned with the supply and demand for labour and the consequent wage and employment level. As in the market for goods and services, the forces of a competitive market give rise to an equilibrium situation where supply and demand for labour are equated. In Figure 10.1, SL is the labour market supply curve. It shows that the higher the wage rate, the higher will be the supply of labour. The market demand curve for labour, DL, is the summation of the labour demand curves of individual firms. Where employers are profit-maximisers, more labour will be demanded up to the point

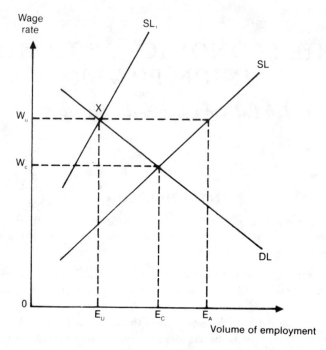

Figure 10.1 Labour market equilibrium

where the marginal cost of labour, the wage rate,[1] equals the marginal revenue product of labour. Given diminishing marginal returns in the short run, this means that the lower the wage rate, the higher the quantity of labour that individual firms can profitably employ and, therefore, the higher will be market demand. In this competitive model, the labour market is in equilibrium when wages are equal to W_C and the level of employment is E_C.

Where employees are represented by a trade union, the consequences for wages and the level of employment may be different from that indicated by the competitive model. For example, a powerful trade union may be able to force wages above the competitive level, but in so doing reduces the level of employment. Figure 10.1 shows two ways in which this result may be achieved. The first method is to negotiate a wage rate that moves firms up their demand curves for labour. A move to point X would give an increase in the wage rate to W_U. If the trade union is able to persuade the employer to pay a wage rate of W_U, the volume of employment will fall from E_C to E_U and an

196

excess supply of labour will exist (E_A-E_U). However, the union may be strong enough to insist that the firm maintain the level of employment at E_C. Clearly, such action will result in overmanning and reduce profitability, with the consequence that some firms may be forced to close down.

In the second case, wages are forced up by restricting the supply of labour. This might be achieved by controlling employee training or selection arrangements, or by restricting access to jobs by making union membership a condition of employment; that is, imposing a 'closed shop'[2] Such tactics will make it more expensive or otherwise more difficult for people to enter that employment and so, at any given wage rate, the quantity of labour supplied will be reduced. In other words, the market supply curve will move to the left. This is shown in the diagram with a move to SL1. The result is an increase in the wage rate to W_U and a reduction in employment to E_U.

In the absence of trade unions, individual employees would be obliged to negotiate their own wage contracts with employers. Far from presenting an ideal situation for wage bargaining, this scenario would put too much power in the hands of the employer. The theoretical analysis of trade union behaviour discussed above implicitly assumes that the trade unions are well organised and able to use union power, whilst employers are operating in a competitive environment and are completely disorganised. In reality, employers are in a significantly more powerful bargaining position than individual employees. This is particularly so where employers are themselves organised and where unemployment is high. In these circumstances, the wage rate and the level of employment will be lower than that in a competitive market.

This is demonstrated in Figure 10.2, with the extreme case of the monopsonist, where the firm's marginal revenue product of labour schedule is the market demand curve DL. The supply of labour schedule, SL, shows the volume of labour that is available for employment at each wage rate. However, the marginal cost of employing an additional unit of labour will be above the wage rate.[3] A profit-maximising monopsonist will employ additional units of labour as long as the marginal cost of labour is below its marginal revenue product. In Figure 10.2, the monopsonist employs E_M units of labour at wage rate W_M. This contrasts with the competitive market equilibrium of E_C and W_C. Trade union activity that succeeds in raising the wage rate from W_M to W_U will also result in an increase in employment from E_M to E_U.[4] Only when the wage rate rises above W_C

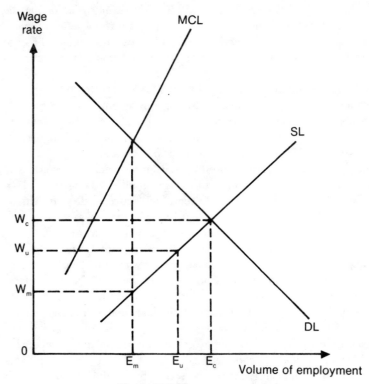

Figure 10.2 The monopsonist

will the volume of employment start to fall. In this example, there is scope for bargaining between the employer and the trade union.

TRADE UNION POWER

What is required is a balance of power between employees and employers. Trade unions can provide that balance through collective bargaining. The collective bargaining power of trade unions varies considerably from industry to industry and is not concerned solely with wages. Whilst it may appear that trade unions spend their time negotiating for higher wages, their overall objective is the improvement of working conditions, which could take many forms. If agreement is not reached, then collective industrial action may be taken in order to enforce trade union demands.

Union power manifests itself in a number of ways, the most

Table 10.1 Stoppages of work due to industrial disputes in the UK, 1960–89

Year	Average no. of stoppages per year	Average no. of working days lost per year (000s)
1960–4	2,512	3,180
1965–9	2,380	3,929
1970–4	2,885	14,077
1974–9	2,310	11,663
1980–4	1,351	10,486
1984–9	881	3,940

Source: Calculated from various issues of *Employment Gazette*

obvious of which is the ability of unions to persuade workers to take strike action. As in other countries, the level of strike activity in Britain has varied considerably over time. This is demonstrated in Table 10.1, which shows the annual average figures for the number of strikes and the number of working days lost during six five-year periods. Strike activity built up during the 1960s and peaked during the first half of the 1970s, since when it has greatly declined. It should be pointed out that considerable fluctuations in strike activity may occur from one year to the next, especially working days lost, which in 1972, 1979 and 1984 exceeded 20 million.

Strikes are very costly, not only in terms of lost output and good-will for a firm, but also to the union and its members. A protracted strike, even if eventually successful, is likely to lead to a loss of income. Consequently, a strike is more likely to be a last resort rather than the first sanction adopted. Trade unions often prefer to use other means of putting pressure on employers – for example, an overtime ban, work to rule, go-slow, or some other form of industrial action. The study undertaken by Millward and Stevens (1986) indicated that firms facing industrial action by manual workers were equally likely to experience non-strike and strike action.

THE BACKGROUND TO THE REFORMS OF THE 1980s

During the 1960s, politicians and others became increasingly critical of trade unions and the British industrial relations system in general. It was argued by many observers that some trade union activities were having a negative macroeconomic impact by slowing down the rate of economic growth and increasing the rate of inflation. At the microeconomic level, the existence of work rules and other formal and informal restrictions on the use of labour were seen as a serious problem which reduced productivity and caused overmanning (see Chapter 6). Concern was also expressed over the tactics used in the pursuit of pay claims with the frequency of strike action, especially unofficial strikes, being a particular cause of anxiety. The closed shop was another much-debated matter, because of the control it gave to a union over its members' livelihoods as well as the restriction on individual liberty which it imposed.

A Royal Commission on Trade Unions and Employers' Associations, chaired by Lord Donovan, was set up in 1965 to consider these problems. Its report, published in 1968, was mainly concerned with remedying the causes of shortcomings in the industrial relations system – such as informal and fragmented bargaining at workplace level in manufacturing industry – rather than the symptoms produced by them, like the high level of unofficial strikes. The report recommended a greater degree of formality in industrial relations, particularly at company and plant level. Although it proposed substantial institutional and legal changes, it took a pessimistic view of the effectiveness of legal sanctions.

In 1969, the Labour government unveiled its proposals for reforming industrial relations. Some of the legislative changes outlined went beyond the recommendations of the Donovan Commission by including legal sanctions for controlling industrial disputes. Strong opposition from trade unions and its own backbenchers, however, forced the government to drop these controversial measures. Two years later a Conservative government did legislate substantial reform. The Industrial Relations Act of 1971 introduced a new and comprehensive legal framework, including a National Industrial Relations Court. A number of forms of behaviour were classified as 'unfair industrial practices', with legal remedies for those found to have been unfairly treated. A new system of registration for trade unions was also introduced, with the rules of registered unions subject to stringent requirements. Union hostility and management indifference severely limited the effectiveness of the Act, however, and it was repealed in 1974 by the next Labour government.

By the late 1970s, there was a growing public conviction that the trade unions had become too powerful. This conviction was reinforced during the so-called 'Winter of Discontent' of 1978–9, when there were major disputes in the health service and the road haulage industry as unions challenged the government's pay guidelines.

Unions continued to be criticised for their refusal to abandon restrictive practices which hindered technological change and discouraged high levels of labour productivity. Overmanning was also seen as a major problem, caused by demarcation rules and a general lack of flexibility among employees.

A number of reasons have been put forward to explain the strengthening position of trade unions in the 1970s. First, legislation introduced by the Labour government between 1974 and 1979 added to the powers of trade unions at the expense of public and private sector employers. The major statute during this period was the Employment Protection Act of 1975, which was one of the results of the agreement between the Labour government and the Trade Union Congress (TUC) known as the 'Social Contract'. The Act was designed to strengthen and extend collective bargaining. As well as putting the Advisory, Conciliation and Arbitration Service (ACAS) on a statutory footing, it introduced a number of positive legal rights for trade unions and individual employees.

There were three main rights given to independent unions by the Employment Protection Act:

1 the right to be consulted in advance by employers about proposed redundancies;
2 the right to receive information from employers to enable them to bargain effectively;
3 the right to seek statutory support for claims for recognition by particular employers.[5]

The individual employee rights bestowed by the 1975 Act, such as the right to attend union meetings during working hours, were designed to protect and support union membership and activity at the workplace, and thus complement the rights given to unions as organisations.

Second, trade union membership grew rapidly during the period 1968–79, both in absolute and relative terms. As Table 10.2 shows, the membership of trade unions rose by more than 3 million (an increase of 30 per cent) in only eleven years, and the density of membership, or degree of unionisation, went up from 44 per cent to 54 per cent. The bulk of this growth occurred among men in non-manual occupations and among women in both manual and non-manual work. The ability of unions to succeed in attracting previously unorganised groups between 1968 and 1979 has been largely attributed by Price and Bain (1983) to price and wage inflation.

Table 10.2 Trade union membership and density in the UK: selected years 1960–88

Year	Union membership (000s)	Potential union membership (000s)	Union density %
1960	9,835	22,229	44.2
1964	10,218	23,166	44.1
1968	10,200	23,203	44.0
1970	11,187	23,050	48.5
1974	11,764	23,317	50.5
1977	12,846	23,987	53.6
1979	13,289	24,393	54.5
1980	12,947	24,485	52.9
1982	11,593	24,170	48.0
1984	10,994	24,193	45.4
1986	10,539	24,807	42.5
1988	10,238	24,612	41.6

Sources: Price and Bain (1983); various issues of the *Employment Gazette*; *Employment Gazette Historical Supplement*, April 1985

However, a change in outlook among employers in favour of the extension of collective bargaining as a result of the recommendations of the Donovan Commission was also seen as significant. Union membership began to decline after 1979, as Table 10.2 illustrates.

A third point to be noted is that trade unions acquired an increasing political and economic influence. Throughout the 1970s, trade unions were exercising power on three levels. One was at the workplace level in manufacturing industry where, with a considerable rise in the number and influence of shop stewards, shop-floor bargaining became wider in scope and greater in significance. Another was at the industrial level in the public sector, in which there were several major strikes over pay that arose from attempts by the government to control inflation by incomes policies and other means. The third was at the level of the TUC and its relations with the government of the day – the Employment Protection Act, for example, was largely drafted by the TUC.

The fourth factor explaining the position of trade unions concerned the closed shop. Between the late 1960s and the late 1970s there was a growth of formal closed-shop arrangements, interrupted only whilst the Industrial Relations Act of 1971 made enforcement of closed shops an unfair practice. As Dunn and Gennard (1984) showed, by 1978 closed-shop arrangements affected at least 5.2 million employees (23 per cent of the labour force) compared with 3.75 million employees (16 per cent of the labour force) in 1962. This growth of the closed shop, which was particularly noticeable in the public sector and in large companies, was attributed in part to changing management attitudes. The appreciation of a need to reform industrial relations brought a recognition of the fact that the closed shop could be of mutual benefit to management and unions in their search for stability and order. The law on the closed shop was amended in 1976 to permit employers to dismiss anyone for non-membership of a union where a closed-shop agreement was in force, unless an employee had a genuine religious objection to union membership.

TRADE UNION LEGISLATION SINCE 1979

In 1979 the Conservative Party won the general election and Mrs Thatcher became Prime Minister. The new government's economic strategy had two main objectives. The first was to defeat inflation. The second was to improve the supply-side of the economy by removing impediments which prevented firms responding quickly to changing economic circumstances worldwide. This emphasis on supply-side economics meant, among other things, limiting the power of trade unions in order to make labour markets more responsive to changing economic conditions. As noted in the introduction, the government blamed the unions for a number of economic problems, including high wage settlements, low productivity, and unemployment.

Since 1979, a series of statutes has placed restrictions on trade union activity, particularly in relation to industrial action and the closed shop.[6] As far as strikes and other forms of industrial action are concerned, the legislation has limited the extent of the immunities which are involved in such action. The Employment Act of 1980 restricted picketing to an individual's place of employment, thereby making secondary picketing unlawful. Consequently, persons picketing at locations other than their own workplace became liable to civil action for interfering with employment or commercial contracts. The 1980 Act also restricted the legality of other forms of secondary industrial action, such as the 'blacking' of goods. The action had to be confined to a direct customer or supplier of the employer with whom the union was in dispute.

The Employment Act of 1982 narrowed the definition of a trade dispute and its accompanying immunity from civil damages. It specified that a trade dispute must be between workers and their employer; disputes between workers and workers lost their immunity. Furthermore, it required that a trade dispute must 'wholly or mainly' relate to employment matters – an attempt to prevent political strikes. The 1982 Act also enabled unions to be sued in their own names. It laid down that a union would be liable for unlawful industrial action authorised or endorsed by a responsible person from the union concerned, although limits were placed on the damages that courts could award. Previously, only union officials were liable for organising unlawful industrial action on behalf of the union – the union's funds were protected.

The Trade Union Act of 1984 restricted a union's immunity to those cases in which industrial action has been formally approved in advance by the union members concerned. It provided that a union would lose its immunity in cases where it did not obtain majority support in a secret ballot before authorising, or endorsing, any form of industrial action which interfered with or broke employment contracts. This was followed by the Employment Act of 1988, which gave union members the right to apply for a court order restraining their union from organising industrial action in the absence of a ballot approving such action. The 1988 Act also gave union members the right not to be disciplined by their union for failing to take part in industrial action.

A second dimension to legislation relating to trade unions concerned statutory support for the closed shop, which was gradually removed during the 1980s. The Employment Act of 1980 extended the grounds on which employees could object to union membership and tried to protect existing employees when a closed shop was introduced. It became unfair for an employer to dismiss anyone for non-membership of a union who had conscientious or deeply held personal reasons for not wishing to join, or who had been engaged before a closed-shop agreement was concluded. The 1980 Act also attempted to ensure that future closed shops would only come into existence with the overwhelming support of the employees affected. It stipulated that if any new closed-shop agreement was not approved by at least 80 per cent of those to be covered by it, it would be unfair for the employer concerned to dismiss anyone for not being a union member.

The Employment Act of 1982 sought to encourage periodic reviews of existing closed shops. It made it unfair for an employer to dismiss anyone for non-membership of a union unless a closed-shop agreement had been the subject of a ballot within the previous five years and in which 80 per cent of those employees covered by it (or 85 per cent of those actually voting) supported it. The 1982 Act also substantially increased the level of compensation payable to those unfairly dismissed in a closed-shop situation.

The Employment Act of 1988 gave increased protection to employers and employees against the operation of closed shops. It repealed the earlier provisions that had permitted dismissal for non-membership of a union where an 'approved' closed shop was in operation, thereby making dismissal for non-membership of a union automatically unfair. It also removed all legal immunity for industrial action taken by a union to force an employer to create or maintain any sort of closed-shop practice.

Further legislation concerning both industrial action and the closed shop came into force at the end of the decade. The Employment Act of 1990 made it unlawful to deny people a job because they are not union members.[7] The Act also outlawed all secondary industrial action by making a union legally liable when it takes action against any customer or supplier of the employer with whom it is in dispute. In addition, the Act made unions legally responsible for unofficial strikes called by shop stewards or any lay officer – when industrial action is organised by any union official (full-time or part-time), the action will have to be either put to the test of a secret ballot or repudiated in writing by the union concerned. Finally, the Act enabled employers selectively to dismiss workers taking unofficial industrial action.

THE EFFECT OF TRADE UNIONS ON WAGES

Empirical studies which have investigated the effect of trade unions on wages have shown that the impact is positive and can be large (see also Chapter 4). Freeman (1989) claims that in the United States during the postwar period the wages of union members have been on average 15 to 22 per cent higher than those of the equivalent non-union employees. The effect of this 'union mark-up' is not uniform across workers, nor is it constant over time. In Britain, the union mark-up is lower on average than in the United States. A survey undertaken by Blanchflower and Oswald (1988) cautiously concludes that the average wage premium for union members over non-union members is 10 per cent or just under. Most of this premium is associated with closed shops, with pre-entry closed shops having the greatest impact on wages.

This argument is supported by Stewart (1987), who found that for semi-skilled manual workers, the union mark-up was on average 7.8 per cent, but increased to about 9 per cent where a post-entry closed shop existed and to 15 per cent in the case of a pre-entry closed shop. For skilled workers, the average differential associated with union membership, *ceteris paribus*, was found to be insignificant, but rose to 7.5 per cent where a pre-entry closed shop existed. In a minority of pre-entry closed shops, Stewart calculated that the union wage premium exceeded 25 per cent. Layard and Nickell (1987) show that until 1982 the trend in the mark-up of union over non-union wages was upward. Since 1982 the decline in union membership and the impact of trade union legislation has caused the gap to close.

THE EFFECT OF TRADE UNIONS ON EMPLOYMENT

The theoretical argument, discussed in the introduction to this chapter, indicates that trade unions that manage to push wages for their members above the competitive level will do so at the cost of lower employment. There is very little microeconomic evidence to support or reject the argument empirically because of a lack of reliable data. However, Layard and Nickell (1985), in examining the causes of unemployment in Britain, estimated that the direct impact of unions on aggregate employment in the postwar period was of the order of two percentage points. One study which throws some light on the issue was undertaken by Blanchflower and Millward (1988), using data from the Workplace Industrial Relations Surveys of 1980 and 1984. Their study classified workplaces into three categories:

1 non-union, where trade unions are not recognised for collective bargaining;
2 weak union(s), where recognition exists but there is no closed shop agreement;
3 strong union(s), where a closed-shop agreement exists, at least for some workers.

A simple examination of the relationship between these categories and employment growth does suggest that an inverse relationship exists, especially in the private sector for the period 1980–4, as Table 10.3 shows.

Table 10.3 Employment changes 1980–4*

	Decrease of 20% or more	Decrease of 5–20%	Stable	Increase of 5–20%	Increase of 20% or more
			Percentage		
Private sector	22	23	15	16	25
Non-union	15	19	16	17	33
Weak-union(s)	27	25	14	17	18
Strong-union(s)	37	30	13	12	9

Source: Blanchflower and Millward (1988)
Note: * Percentage of surveyed firms reporting employment changes of different magnitudes

It would appear from Table 10.3 that for establishments in the non-union category, 33 per cent achieved over 20 per cent employment growth, whilst 15 per cent experienced a decrease in employment of over 20 per cent. This compares with establishments in the strong union(s) category where only 9 per cent of establishments achieved over 20 per cent employment growth, whilst 37 per cent experienced over 20 per cent employment contraction. However, this data must be treated with caution. Using multiple regression analysis, Blanchflower and Millward discovered that establishment size is the dominant factor explaining this relationship, with larger organisations being associated with low employment growth. Thus, new small establishments, which tend to be non-union, account for the greater proportion of employment expansion, whilst large traditional establishments, which tend to be highly unionised, are in many cases in decline. Subject to further research they conclude that, contrary to expectations, there is no strong statistical evidence of a relationship between employment change and trade union presence once other significant influences are accounted for.

THE EFFECT OF TRADE UNIONS ON PRODUCTIVITY

The overall effect of trade unions on productivity may be seen as the net effect of forces pulling in opposite directions (see also Chapter 6).

Thus the existence of trade unions may increase labour productivity where good industrial relations and co-operation between employees and employers is encouraged. Unions may be persuaded to support management in their attempts to reduce inefficiency, and output and productivity may increase as a result. If, on the other hand, industrial relations are poor with employers and employees often in conflict, labour productivity is likely to be lower. Similarly, higher productivity may be expected when union activity keeps managers aware of, and alive to, what is happening around them.

However, if restrictive practices are permitted, productivity tends to be adversely affected. Such practices may be the result of agreement between management and workers' representatives over wages and effort. Work rules and agreement on manning levels can reduce effort and efficiency and result in labour being underemployed. Bargaining over work arrangements has been common in British industry, particularly manufacturing industry, and even though a decline in such joint regulation occurred in the early 1980s, Millward and Stevens (1986) show that in 1984 bargaining over manning levels for manual workers was still taking place in 40 per cent of manufacturing establishments in which trade unions were recognised.

Empirical studies designed to test the impact of trade unions on labour productivity do not provide clear evidence to support the view that the presence of unions is generally associated with lower productivity. There appears to be no straightforward association between trade union activity and productivity. Machin (1987) investigated the impact of unionisation on productivity in the engineering industry and concluded that unions had no damaging effect on productivity except in large firms with more than 1,000 employees – in small firms the effect was neutral. Another study by Wilson (1987), which used the same data set, found that in firms where the level of unionisation was below 50 per cent or over 80 per cent, unions had a negative effect on productivity, but where the level of unionisation was between 50 per cent and 80 per cent, the effect was positive.

Edwards (1987) examined the situation in manufacturing plants with more than 250 employees and concluded that unionisation had little or no effect on productivity. Research reported by Freeman and Medoff (1984) indicates that in the United States, productivity is in general higher in unionised firms than in otherwise comparable companies that are non-union, although there are notable exceptions. Freeman and his associates at Harvard University have argued that unions can contribute to increasing productivity by giving employees a 'collective voice' in the firm, thereby reducing labour turnover by improving communications and reducing waste, and by adopting more productive techniques by 'shocking' management into tightening production standards.

Trade unions are not homogeneous organisations and are likely to have different impacts on productivity over time and space. Different union structure and organisation, different attitudes to flexibility and technological change, will have different effects on productivity even if levels of unionisation are similar. Management behaviour and other company characteristics are also important factors to consider.

CONCLUSIONS

It is difficult at this stage to draw any firm conclusions regarding the impact of trade union legislation since 1979 on wages, employment and productivity. What is clear, however, is that over the course of the 1980s the number of strikes and days lost through strikes declined, and the level and density of union membership fell considerably. Although unemployment was a major factor in dampening strike activity and in reducing support for trade unions, legislative changes also appeared to have had an effect.

As far as union membership and density are concerned, the restrictions on union activity and the withdrawal (as early as 1980) of the right of unions to be recognised by employers, encouraged some companies to limit or push back such recognition, and this had an adverse effect on union membership. This may well be significant in explaining why union membership and density continued to fall after 1986 when unemployment was also falling. There was an upsurge during 1987 and 1988 in the number of employers withdrawing recognition from trade unions for certain grades of staff, and sometimes this was accompanied by pressure from the employer for staff to withdraw from union membership.

As for strike activity, the restrictions on picketing, secondary industrial action and on what constitutes a trade dispute all had some impact, but the most important change in the law was undoubtedly the strike ballot requirement introduced in 1984. Since then, ballots have become an increasingly common feature of the negotiating process, with union members in general now regarding them as a prerequisite for industrial action. Indeed, ballots have sometimes been used to put pressure on an employer to make a better offer, which is then accepted. So the increasing use of ballots has helped to reduce the number of strikes, not only by making it less likely that a stoppage will take place without the support of the majority of employees affected, but also because employers often respond to a ballot result that is clearly in favour of industrial action by making a further offer that leads to a settlement without a strike taking place.

NOTES

1 In a perfectly competitive market, the supply of labour for individual firms will be perfectly wage-elastic, since no one firm is able to influence wages by its own actions. Consequently, the marginal cost of labour is equal to the wage rate.
2 There are two types of closed shop. A post-entry closed shop exists when employees must join a trade union within a short time of being engaged. A pre-entry closed shop exists when there is insistence on union membership before engagement and is always associated with the aim of controlling, or restricting in some way, entry to employment.
3 If a monopsonist employing 100 workers at a wage rate of £200 a week increases the wage rate to £201 in order to attract an additional employee, the marginal cost of labour will be £201 + (100 x £1) = £301.
4 This is because the marginal cost of employing additional units of labour up to E_u, which is constant and equal to the union negotiated wage rate W_u, will be less than the marginal revenue product of labour.
5 This provision was repealed by the Employment Act of 1980.
6 The legislation has also tried to make trade unions more democratic by requiring that the members of a union's executive committee be elected by a secret ballot of all the union's members at least once every five years.
7 A National Opinion Poll survey in 1989 suggested that there were 1.3 million workers in jobs where they either had to be union members before being considered for employment or had to join a union before starting work.

11

NEW FIRMS
The key to employment creation?
Peter Johnson

INTRODUCTION

The role of new firms in the British economy has attracted much attention from both policymakers and researchers in recent years. Since 1979, the Conservative government has consistently argued that business formation plays a key part in the creation of new jobs. Such formation is also seen as a means of increasing and maintaining competitiveness, and of introducing innovations in products and processes. New and small business activity is regarded as an essential element in the development of the 'enterprise culture'. This policy interest has been translated into a range of measures, some of which are considered below in the section discussing policy initiatives. On the academic front, research into new and small firms has expanded dramatically. No self-respecting business school is now without its small business unit. Interestingly, economists have contributed relatively little to this work, although they have stimulated a revival in interest in the analysis of entrepreneurship (e.g. Casson, 1982).

In this chapter, the nature, extent and employment effects of formation activity are explored. The first section asks: what is a new firm? The second section presents some measures of the scale of formation activity, while the third section reviews the evidence on the impact of new firms. The fourth section briefly outlines some of the policy initiatives that have been introduced and looks at issues associated with the evaluation of policy in this field. The final section provides a summary of the chapter.

WHAT IS A NEW FIRM?

At first sight it might seem that the definition of the new firm is straightforward and that it should include any recently formed proprietorship, partnership or company. However, such a definition would include not only the entirely new 'start-up' established by someone going into business for the first time, but also organisations which have been 'spawned' by existing firms. Such extensions of existing interests may occur in a wide variety of ways. For example, a new subsidiary company may be set up by a parent company which has been trading for many years. More indirectly, the director of a company may – with the profits obtained from that company – set up a sole proprietorship or enter into a partnership. Or a major shareholder in one company may decide to launch another and become its major shareholder. In this case, the new company may not, in legal terms, be a subsidiary of the first, but clearly it is closely linked to it. Some investigators have also argued that changes in ownership should constitute formation. It should be noted that 'new' is not synonymous with 'small'. The former describes a firm which has been formed in some specified recent time period; the latter describes the size of a firm – whether new or well established – at some point in time.

The different types of 'newness' referred to in the previous paragraph are associated with different economic phenomena. It would therefore be a mistake to attempt to analyse the formation of a subsidiary in the same way as an entirely new start-up. The focus of discussion in this chapter is with the latter, although, as we shall see, the available data often use more wide-ranging definitions.

THE SCALE OF FORMATION ACTIVITY

Of published data, Value-Added Tax (VAT) registrations probably provide the best guide to formation activity in this country. Every firm with an annual turnover greater than the registration threshold (£22,100) is required to register unless they are in one of the (few) exempt trades, such as undertaking. Firms which sell zero-rated products, such as most foodstuffs, may apply for exemption from registration. Some firms whose turnover is below the registration limit may still apply to be registered voluntarily. The main advantage of VAT data for our purposes is that registration is a legal requirement for most new firms. The principal disadvantages are that, as indicated above, some new firms may not be covered by the statistics and that some registrations may result from business reorganisations, rather than from the formation of entirely new businesses. Despite these drawbacks, it is likely that the trends in VAT registrations between 1975 and 1987 shown in Figure 11.1 broadly reflect changes in formation activity.

Between 1975 and 1981, there were two periods (1976–8 and 1979–81) in which registrations declined. However, between 1981 and 1988, the trend was strongly upward, although there was something of a plateau in 1983–5. In each year between 1983 and 1988, the number of registrations was higher than that achieved in the peak years of the 1970s. Significantly, however, Figure 11.1 shows that deregistrations – or business 'deaths' – also rose substantially over the 1980s. Although births have exceeded deaths since the late 1970s – thus ensuring that the stock of VAT-registered businesses has continued to grow – the rise in both births and deaths has meant an increase in 'industrial turbulence': the 1980s saw much more movement into and out of business. While this rise in turbulence may do much to sharpen the competitiveness of industry, it may also bring substantial costs. The processes of birth and death both generate costs for those involved.

Another indication of formation activity is data on self-employment – any person working on an 'own account' basis. Unfortunately, we do not have statistics on flows into and out of self-employment. However, data are available on trends in the 'stock' of self-employment (Figure 11.2). These show a very substantial increase in self-employment activity over the 1980s. The self-employment figures must be treated very cautiously for a number of reasons. First, we do not know how far the recent expansion in self-employment numbers reflects movement from the 'black' to the 'white' economy. As tax rates in the latter have fallen, so the relative disadvantages of trading 'officially' have been reduced. To the extent that the increase in self-employment relates to such transfers, it does not reflect any 'real' rise in the numbers of people working for themselves.

Second, we know nothing about the hours worked by the self-employed. It may be that recent years have seen an increase in part-time self-employment by older people, who are working simply to supplement their incomes following redundancy or premature retirement. This may be one explanation for the decline in average real income among the self-employed (see below). Third, the figures do not capture all those who set up companies of which they then become employees. Such founders are probably more likely to be those who develop rapidly growing businesses. Finally, it must be remembered that the surge in self-employment may yet generate, after a lag, a substantial corresponding increase in 'deaths' as the new

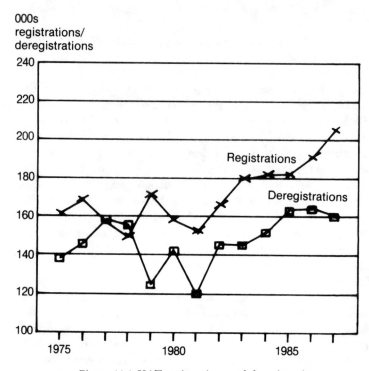

Figure 11.1 VAT registrations and deregistrations

business founders find that they are not really viable in the longer term.

Before we examine some of the reasons behind this increase, it is worth noting what has been happening to real self-employment income also shown (again in index form) in Figure 11.2. In the second half of the 1970s, income showed a slightly overall upward trend, while numbers fell. Thus average self-employment income rose. In the 1980s, both income and numbers have grown, but the former did so at a slower rate than the latter, thus causing average self-employment income to fall.

The reasons behind the increase in formation activity in the 1980s are complex. However, at least three key influences have been at work. First, the stimulation of an enterprise 'culture' has made own-account activity much more socially acceptable. The small businessman now has a status which is probably higher than it has been at any time in the postwar period. Government pronouncements have

214

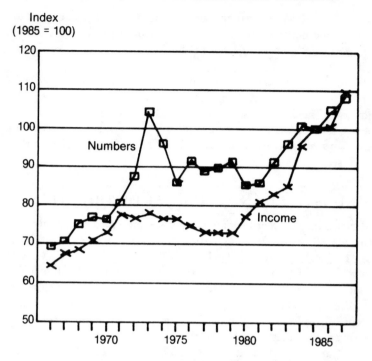

Index
(1985 = 100)

Figure 11.2 Self-employment: numbers and income, 1966–87
Sources: DE *Gazette*, UK *National Accounts*, various years

encouraged the perception that such businesses are the key element in economic revival.

Second, the high levels of unemployment in the 1980s (unemployment only briefly fell below 2 million at the very end of the decade) made setting up in business relatively more attractive. The potential founder may be viewed as comparing – usually implicitly – the expected returns from paid employment (obtained by working as an employee) with those from self-employment. Economic recession and unemployment reduces the former, and thus makes self-employment seem a relatively better prospect.

Of course, recession may also lead potential founders to revise downwards their expected returns from self-employment; however, this is less likely as such founders are not usually so aware of the link between economic recession and self-employment prospects as they are of that between the former and paid employment opportunities. A number of studies have shown that actual or potential unemployment acts as a stimulus to formation (see P. S. Johnson, 1986). It remains to be seen whether the temporary reductions in unemployment at the end of the 1980s lead to a lagged reduction in the level of formation activity.

Finally, the Conservative government's policies have almost certainly had a positive impact on formation activity. Such policies have provided general encouragement for business start-ups, as well as specific forms of assistance which, in various ways, have reduced the new firm's costs. These policies are given some consideration in the fourth section.

INDUSTRIAL AND REGIONAL DISTRIBUTION

Industries vary in their formation rates – as measured by the number of new VAT registrations expressed as a percentage of the stock of VAT businesses – as the first column in Table 11.1 shows. The 'Other' category – which includes a wide range of personal and commercial services – shows the highest 'fertility', followed some way below by 'Finance' and 'Wholesaling'. It is perhaps striking that in all industries except 'Agriculture', the formation rate is higher than 85 per cent. However, the table also shows that all sectors, apart again from 'Agriculture', also had a death rate (column 2) which exceeded 80 per cent, illustrating the high level of turbulence that has existed in industry in the 1980s. The net effect in column 3 shows that 'Finance' and 'Other' had the biggest proportionate increases (although 'Wholesaling' and 'Finance' had roughly similar birth rates, the former had a much higher death rate).

Across regions formation rates (VAT registrations as a percentage of the stock in 1979) also vary considerably (see also Chapter 13). Not surprisingly, the South-East has the highest rate, at 113 per cent. Northern Ireland has the lowest figure at 58 per cent. When the percentage net change – which in all regions is less than 20 per cent – is considered, the less prosperous regions tend to have lower rates. For example, Yorkshire and Humberside, the North West, the North and Wales all have rates under 10 per cent, whereas the South East, East Anglia and the East Midlands have rates of 19, 15 and 14 per cent respectively (the figure for Britain as a whole is 14 per cent). The main exception to this pattern is Northern Ireland, which has a relatively high net change (16 per cent) despite its relatively low birth rate.

The difference in the percentage net change across regions is in

Table 11.1 VAT registrations and deregistrations

	Registrations 1980-6 as % of stock at end of 1979	*Deregistrations 1980-6 as % of stock at end of 1979*	*% net change in stock 1980-6*
Agriculture	25.6	24.1	1.5
Production	101.3	83.6	17.8
Construction	99.1	80.5	18.5
Transport	95.3	86.0	9.3
Wholesaling	112.7	92.0	20.7
Retailing	87.5	90.1	-3.4
Finance, etc.	111.5	70.5	41.0
Catering	103.6	98.6	5.0
Motor trades	93.6	85.5	8.2
Other	154.7	105.4	49.3
TOTAL	93.9	80.0	13.9

Source: Derived from *British Business*, 12 August 1988

part explained by variations in industrial structure: some regions are better endowed with industries that have relatively higher proportionate net changes. Adjustment for differences in industrial structure alters the ranking of regions. For example, an 'adjusted' South-East has a net change which is the same as Britain (14 per cent), while Northern Ireland and Wales exceed the national average (19 and 15 per cent respectively). Clearly, the figures must be interpreted cautiously.

THE EMPLOYMENT IMPACT OF NEW FIRMS

Most research and policy interest in the assessment of the economic effects of new firms has focused on the capacity of such firms to generate jobs, and it is therefore on this issue that this section concentrates. It is perhaps worth stressing at the beginning of this section that many new firms have short lives and that of those that survive for any length of time, only a few reach a significant size. VAT data suggest that well over 50 per cent of all registrations have deregistered within six years (Johnson, 1986). We also know that over 60 per cent of companies were born less than nine years ago.

On the growth of surviving new firms, Storey (1982), using data for Cleveland and the East and West Midlands, has shown that in manufacturing, the probability of any new firm growing to 100 employees within a decade of its birth is less than three-quarters of 1 per cent. (It is likely that those that do not reach 100 employees within a decade will never do so.) The experience of new firms in other regions may be different, but it is unlikely to be dramatically so. We have little data on employment profiles for new firms in non-manufacturing, but it is almost certainly the case that the probability of achieving high employment levels is lower in this sector.

The substantial death rate in the early years of life and the very modest growth in those new firms that do survive means that many formations are unlikely to have any significant employment impact. However, the constant turnover of firms may nevertheless help to maintain the competitiveness of industry generally. It may also be the case that while a new firm may not itself survive for more than a short period, its economic impact may nevertheless be significant and long lasting. For example, an innovative firm may be taken over – and thus 'die' as far as the statistics are concerned – by a larger organisation, which then develops the innovation. It must also be remembered that although few new firms will grow to any size, those that do may become of major importance in the longer term. All of today's giants were new at some point!

One way in which the contribution of new firms to employment may be assessed is through the construction of job accounts. These accounts give, for the period and region in question, figures for gross job gains and gross job losses. Gross job gains may be categorised as follows:

1 births (creation of new firms as defined above), measured by the employment at the end of the period of firms formed during the period and surviving to its end. Such births are the primary concern of this chapter;
2 expansion of existing firms, measured by employment at the end of the period less employment at the beginning of the period, of firms which were in existence throughout the period and which expanded (such expansion may or may not involve the opening of plants).

Gross job losses may be similarly defined as:

1 deaths (cessation of independent existence of a firm), measured by the employment at the beginning of the period of firms dying during the period;
2 contraction of existing firms, measured by employment at the

beginning of the period less employment at the end of the period of firms which were in existence throughout the period and which contracted (such contraction may or may not involve the shutting of plants).

Gross job gains represent the flow into employment in the economy; gross job losses are the flow out. Net job change is gross job gains minus gross job losses. Where these gains and losses cancel each other out, net job change will of course be zero. Column 3 in Table 11.2 gives some research findings on the share of gross job gains coming from births for different parts of Britain. The studies for manufacturing are not wholly comparable as far as data sources are concerned and hence precise comparisons should not be made. Furthermore, for obvious reasons, the results are affected by the length of the time period under consideration. However, it is probably fair to say that over a ten-year period, between 5 and 20 per cent of gross job gains come from new firms, with perhaps a rather lower percentage for depressed regions.

In a major study, Gallagher and Stewart (1986) found figures for all British industry which are very substantially higher. Even allowing for the possibility that a number of gross job gains that in the other studies would have been classed as 'expansion' may be labelled as 'births' in the Gallagher and Stewart analysis, it is likely that the contribution of births to gross job gains is still substantially higher when 'all industry' rather than manufacturing alone is considered, because of the much higher turnover in service activities.

Job accounts also permit comparisons to be made between the extent of gross job losses (from contractions and deaths) and the jobs provided by new firms. These comparisons have been used to estimate how important new firms are as a mechanism for replacing lost jobs. It is clear from the fourth column in Table 11.2 that the scale of gross job loss in recent years has been much larger than the new employment arising from formations. In manufacturing, over a ten-year period, employment from births is unlikely to exceed 20 per cent of gross job losses. Even Gallagher and Stewart (1986) found that births accounted for substantially less than a half of all gross job losses between 1971 and 1981.

The broad conclusions of the job accounting studies are that:

1 In manufacturing, over a ten-year period, new firms account for less than 20 per cent of both the 'inflow' of new jobs and the 'outflow' of lost jobs.

Table 11.2 The relative contribution of new firms to employment

Region	Period	% of gross job gains accounted for by births	Jobs in new firms as a % of gross job losses	Source
Manufacturing				
E. Midlands	1948–67	28	N/A	Gudgin (1978) p. 62
	1968–75	15	14	Fothergill and Gudgin (1979)
North	1965–78	12	8	Storey (1985) pp. 16, 24
	1958–68	7	6	Firn and Swales (1978)
Scotland	1968–77	10	6	Cross (1981) pp. 50, 58
All industry				
UK	1971–81	59	43	Gallagher and Stewart (1986)
	1982–84	34	29	*British Business* 17 October 1986

2 In industry as a whole, the figures are considerably higher: over 50 per cent of the 'inflow' and over 40 per cent of the 'outflow'.

It is clear from these figures that employment in new firms should be seen as one mechanism only for job generation; other sources of job creation are required. Data on output from new firms are not available, although broadly similar results are likely to apply.

Unfortunately, we are unable to provide pre- and post-1979 comparisons on job creation in new firms. Such comparisons would be valuable in assessing the Conservative government's policy emphasis on new firms. The Gallagher and Stewart figures in Table 11.2 do, however, imply an increase in the relative importance of new firms in job generation, although much of this increase may be due to increases in the turnover of firms.

Since the job accounting approach is now firmly entrenched as a research technique for analysing the employment contribution of new firms, it is appropriate to be aware of the issues that it does not address. First, and most important, it gives no indication of the interrelationships that exist between the different categories of job change. For example, some births may – through competitive forces – cause other firms to contract or die. Thus it may sometimes be valid to argue that births generate job losses. Births may also generate further births or expansions. For example, a new innovatory firm may stimulate others to imitate its products. On the other hand, deaths and/or contractions may provide market 'space' which, in turn, stimulates births. In this way, it might be argued that deaths generate jobs! Again, expansion by others may provide opportunities for new firms to operate as satellites.

The interrelationships between employment generation in new firms and that in other firms may itself be the result of more fundamental forces in the economy. Recession and/or greater competitive pressures, for example, may cause larger firms to shed some of their peripheral activities. Such contraction may provide the opportunity for the formation of a new firm. Indeed, formations and 'buy-outs' may be encouraged by the larger firm in order to minimise the problems caused by large-scale redundancies. Such a shift of employment shows up in the job accounts as an employment gain from a birth, but as an employment loss from a contraction. In this case, net job change may be very small or even zero.

Such rearrangement of jobs is primarily a reflection of the underlying state of the economy, however. It is also likely to be the case – as we have seen earlier – that recession itself makes self-employment a relatively more attractive option. Thus births may be a direct consequence of a reduction in the prospects for paid employment. It may also be the only way in which an individual can offer himself for lower than the going wage rate in paid employment: while workers may be unable, because of institutional rigidities, to negotiate their own lower rate with an employer in order to secure or maintain a job, they do not face the same constraints when they offer labour services directly to the market.

Changes in consumer demand, brought about by long-term secular developments in tastes, may lead to a greater emphasis on those industries in which the new small firm has – for various reasons – a relative advantage. A full understanding of job creation and destruction processes would require a knowledge of precisely what these interrelationships are. To say that it is 'newness' or 'smallness' *per se* that is generating jobs is to ignore the complex nature of dynamic change in an industrial economy.

Second, job accounts do not typically distinguish between different types of job: the nature of the data sources used usually restricts the analysis to a head count. But one very highly paid job may have a bigger impact on overall employment than a few poorly paid, part-time jobs. Again, some new firm jobs may be more important in terms of the generation of further jobs than others, because of their more strategic nature. For example, a formation based on an inno-vation may generate substantial employment 'knock-on' effects. These issues are important in any assessment of the employment impact of new firms, especially given the fact that small firms tend to pay less well than large firms and that the vast majority of new firms are not technologically innovative (Gudgin, 1978).

Finally, the job accounting approach does not indicate why, in some industries, job gains from formations are relatively more important than in others. Thus, while this approach may be strong on descrip-tion, it offers little in terms of explanation. Despite these difficulties, however, it constitutes a useful first step in the analysis of job change.

GOVERNMENT POLICY TOWARDS NEW FIRMS

Over the past fifteen years, but particularly since 1979, a number of policy measures designed, *inter alia*, to assist new firms have been introduced (some of these measures are relevant to small firms generally and not simply to those that are newly formed). These initiatives have not generally sought to increase employment in new firms by direct means, for example, through employment subsidy, but indirectly by encouraging formation activity and by enhancing survivability and growth potential.

It is not possible to review here all the measures that have been introduced. However, some of the more important areas in which initiatives have been taken, together with relevant examples, are given below.

1 Advisory and information services
The government's Small Firms Service has a network of centres which provides information and advice to established small firms and would-be founders. As part of this activity, a low-cost counselling service is also provided. In 1987/8, 265,000 enquiries were received by the service and 28,200 clients were counselled. Seventy-two per cent of these clients were potential founders. The total cost of the service was £5m.

2 Tax advantages
A key initiative here is the Business Expansion Scheme (BES), under

which long-term investors in 'eligible' small companies obtain tax relief on their investments. In 1987–8, it is estimated that the relief given was £80m. In 1986–7, about 600 start-up companies (£151m of investment) received funds under the scheme.

3 *Financial assistance*

The most well-known form of assistance is the Small Business Loan Guarantee Scheme (SBLGS). The scheme is operated through the commercial banks, who are offered a 70 per cent guarantee on loans which they would not otherwise make on normal commercial terms. To finance this guarantee, the government levies a premium – based on the guaranteed amount – on the borrower. In 1987–8 there were 1,234 new loans involving £46m under the scheme.

Another form of financial assistance is given by the Enterprise Allowance Scheme (EAS), under which unemployed individuals who set up in business are paid £40 per week for up to a year, thereby overcoming the financial disincentive which would otherwise arise from the loss of entitlement to unemployment benefit. In 1987–8, 106,000 individuals joined the scheme. Gross expenditure was £196m.

4 *Training*

A range of publicly financed schemes designed to encourage and equip various groups to go into business are available. In 1987/8, some 52,000 individuals went through some form of publicly financed, start-up training. The gross cost of this training was £8.2m.

Evaluating the employment effects of particular policies directed towards new firms is fraught with difficulties. Two problems in particular may be mentioned. The first concerns how to estimate the difference a policy makes to employment in the 'direct beneficiary' firms (the 'direct effect'). To identify this difference, it is necessary to assess what the employment position would have been in the absence of the policy – an assessment that raises important methodological issues. Yet some attempt must be made: what evidence there is suggests that 'deadweight' – that is, the extent to which a policy benefits people and/or firms who adopt a course of action which is supposed to be induced by the policy, but which they would have taken anyway – is often substantial. For example, one study of the Enterprise Allowance Scheme (see *Employment Gazette*, August 1984) suggested that about 50 per cent of the firms formed under the scheme would have been set up anyway. There is also evidence that deadweight has been substantial under the SBLGS and BES (respectively, Department of Trade and Industry, 1984; Knowlman *et al.*, 1985).

The second problem relates to the measurement of a policy's indirect employment effects. These indirect effects may be positive or negative. Positive effects will occur where, for example, a new firm which has been founded as a result of a policy stimulated demand for inputs from other firms (and hence their employment) or produces an innovation that enables other firms to expand. Indeed, a new firm may contract out production and distribution as a deliberate policy, so that its management is not overstretched. Thus, any employment resulting from the formation occurs primarily in other firms. On the negative side, existing firms may be displaced by competition from the new firm or through the newcomer making their products obsolescent.

Estimates of these indirect effects are likely to be crucial for evaluating the effects of policies aimed at encouraging new firms, since they may sometimes negate much of the direct effect. For example, a policy designed to encourage people to set up in business as hairdressers may be highly successful in achieving its aim; that is, the direct effect may be high. But this market is already highly competitive and total demand is likely to be fairly static. Consequently, established hairdressers may find themselves forced out by the newcomers.

Such displacement may or may not be desirable; in any event it must be taken into account in policy evaluation. Unfortunately, despite its importance, relatively little is known about the displacement effect. Negative indirect effects are likely to be lower the more the new firm is orientated towards export markets. The evidence, however, suggests that for most new firms, local markets are their main target (e.g. Lloyd and Dicken, 1981). The presence of indirect effects means that employment within the boundaries of a firm that receives benefit from a policy measure may not be a very good guide to the overall job-creating effects of such a measure.

A number of studies have examined the employment effects of various policy initiatives. For example, Department of Employment surveys show that there were 71 jobs (32 full-time and 39 part-time) in every 100 EAS businesses surviving after 18 months (34 per cent had already failed by that point). However, these figures do not take account of deadweight or indirect effects. The Department of Employment itself estimates deadweight at 44 per cent and negative indirect effects ('displacement') at 50 per cent.

Surveys of the SBLGS participants suggest that after allowing for deadweight, but not indirect effects, about three jobs per loan or 5.1 jobs per firm are created in survivors within four to six years. Survivors over this period represented just under 60 per cent of the total number of firms receiving loans under the scheme. Similar analyses for other measures could be quoted. There is some evidence to suggest that these measures tend to favour the more prosperous regions, since it is the latter regions which tend to have the highest formation rates (and also the highest take-up rates) – see the evidence quoted in Mason et al. (1988).

It is not possible here to undertake a full evaluation of policy-induced job generation in new firms. However, it is important to note that even if a measure does generate significant employment, such an outcome does not of itself provide a sufficient justification for that measure. Only when benefits and costs are assessed is an answer to this issue possible. Such an exercise raises very substantial measurement problems; however, one social cost-benefit study (Johnson and Thomas, 1984) suggested a social internal rate of return on a training course for potential founders of over 19 per cent, a return which compares very favourably with other forms of human investment and which suggests that more funds should be put into this area.

CONCLUSIONS

There has been a substantial increase in formation activity in the 1980s. Although this has been accompanied by more industrial turbulence, the stock of businesses has been increasing. Formation rates vary substantially across industries; not surprisingly, it is the service sector which has enjoyed the highest net increases. Variations across regions are in part explained by variations in regional industrial structure (see also Chapter 13).

The employment impact of new firms is difficult to measure. However, the evidence suggests that over-heavy reliance should not be placed on new firms as a source of jobs; such firms must be seen as one mechanism only for alleviating unemployment. Some estimates of the employment effects of new firms' policies are available.

Evaluations of this kind are, however, of limited value unless they take into account deadweight and indirect effects and the costs of the policies involved.

12

REDISTRIBUTION UNDER CONSERVATISM

Past and future

Ken Richards

INTRODUCTION

It was tempting to choose an alternative title for this chapter, namely 'The economic effects of Mrs Thatcher', with apologies to John Maynard Keynes, who wrote an essay in 1931 under the title 'The economic consequences of Mr Churchill'. That essay by Keynes was written soon after Britain, with Winston Churchill as its Chancellor of the Exchequer, went back to the Gold Standard in 1925. The exchange rate chosen to return Britain to the Gold Standard proved to be substantially out of line with economic reality, with disastrous consequences for export industries in general and the coal industry in particular. As Keynes (1931) wrote:

> On grounds of social justice, no case can be made out for reducing the wages of the miners. They are the victims of the economic Juggernaut. They represent in the flesh the 'fundamental adjustments' engineered by the Treasury and the Bank of England to satisfy the impatience of the City fathers to bridge the 'moderate gap' between $4.40 and $4.86. They (and others to follow) are the 'moderate sacrifice' still necessary to ensure the stability of the Gold Standard. The plight of the coal miners is the first, but not – unless we are very lucky – the last, of the Economic Consequences of Mr Churchill.

It seems doubtful that we have seen the last of the economic consequences of Mrs Thatcher, since the kingdom over which she until recently presided has undoubtedly been divided into two nations, the 'haves' and the 'have-nots' (see also Chapter 13). In Thatcher's Britain, it was not so much the meek who inherited the earth, but the 'yuppies' of the City and the South-East of England. The effects of the

227

economic policies of the Tories since 1979 on the distribution of income and wealth are startling. I intend to analyse them under three headings:

1 measures affecting the taxation of income and capital gains;
2 measures dealing with the taxation of wealth, or rather the transfer of wealth;
3 a brief look at the changes which were brought about in the wake of the replacement of local rates by the Community Charge or 'poll tax' and the possible future effects of the new Council Tax due to be introduced from 1993.

Before turning to these fiscal changes, it may be worth noting the unfortunate position of the unemployed in our society – a figure which has grown from 1 million in 1979 to remain persistently between 2 and 3 million ever since. Indeed, the true unemployment totals may be higher still: Johnson (1987) estimated the true figure of unemployment (at the time about 3 million) to be nearer 4 million, on the grounds that about 800,000 people were being removed from the unemployment register in various ways which did not reflect reality.

The causes of this vast increase in unemployment have been analysed in detail by the *Charter for Jobs* (Employment Institute, 1985), which concluded that the main factor contributing to the rise in unemployment in the early 1980s was a deficiency of aggregate demand, caused mainly by the fiscal and monetary policies followed in Britain (but see Chapter 4). Other factors included the worldwide depression and, particularly in 1981, an exchange rate which was overvalued – the same problem that created so much misery for the miners in the 1920s following the return to the Gold Standard. Although the authors acknowledge that other factors on the supply-side, such as rigidities in the labour market, contributed to the rise in unemployment, they do not place as much emphasis on these as do other economists.

To make matters worse, the Conservative government has made life substantially less amenable for the unemployed; the real level of unemployment benefit has been cut, the earnings-related supplement abolished and the benefit itself, which was formerly untaxed, is now brought into the tax net. (It remains true, however, that anyone living on unemployment benefit alone for the whole tax year is unlikely to be receiving enough to pay income tax.) There is no doubt, therefore, that the unemployed have faced a substantial reduction in their standard of living since 1979.

CHANGES IN TAXES ON INCOME AND CAPITAL GAINS

Every civilised nation these days accepts responsibility for the underprivileged in society and recognises the need to redistribute income from the rich towards the poor. The income tax system, in particular, seeks to achieve this end, but it is recognised that governments of different political complexions will vary in the extent to which they wish to see a large public sector, in their assessment of the amount of tax necessary to pay for it, and indeed of the best way of distributing the tax burden amongst the taxpayers. All three administrations of Mrs Thatcher and that of Mr Major have been, or are, particularly concerned to reduce the burden of income taxation. At the Conservative Party Conference in October 1991, the Chancellor, Mr Norman Lamont, reiterated the aim of the government to reduce the basic rate of income tax to 20 per cent.

Before we discuss the particular measures introduced by various Conservative governments since 1979, it may be worth noting that there are two main ways of reducing income tax, one of which tends to lead to greater fairness, or more redistribution, and the other to less. A simple model of the tax system will illustrate these points.

In a simple tax system the progressiveness, or fairness, of the system depends on two principal factors, namely (i) the level of the personal allowance, that is, the income which can be earned before tax starts to be paid and (ii) the basic rate of income tax. (We will ignore higher rates of income tax at the present moment.) To illustrate this important point, take a simple example. If the personal allowance were, say, £666 and the basic rate of income tax 40 per cent, then someone on an income of £2,000 would have to pay £534 in taxes, leaving a net income of £1,466. Someone with an income of £1,000 before tax on the other hand would have a net income of £866. This simple system has achieved a degree of redistribution in the sense that the ratio of incomes before taxation was 2 to 1 (£2,000/£1,000), whereas after tax the ratio has been reduced to 1.69 to 1, (£1,466/ £866). The disparity in incomes has therefore been reduced as a result of the operation of the tax system.

If the government were now to cut income tax by reducing the basic rate to 30 per cent, other things being equal, the system would become less redistributive because the ratio of net incomes would rise from 1.69 to 1.77. On the other hand, if the reduction in taxation were achieved by raising the personal allowance, say, to £800, with the

Table 12.1 Ratio of after-tax incomes

Personal allowance £	Marginal rate of tax	
	40%	30%
666	1.69	1.77
800	1.65	1.75

basic rate remaining at 40 per cent, the ratio would be reduced from 1.69 to 1.65, indicating an increasing amount of redistribution. These figures are shown in Table 12.1.

As a general principle then, and other things being equal, increasing allowances is a more redistributive way of reducing taxes than reducing tax rates. Since 1979 the Conservatives have introduced numerous measures which have had the effect of reducing taxes on the rich:

1 The basic rate of income tax has been reduced from 33 per cent to 25 per cent.

2 Higher rates of income tax have been reduced from a maximum of 83 per cent on earned income to 40 per cent.

3 The investment income surcharge of 15 per cent has been removed entirely. This was a tax which affected only about 200,000 of the wealthiest taxpayers.

4 Development Land Tax (DLT) has been abolished and replaced by Capital Gains Tax (CGT). The former tax bore quite heavily on gains made through developing land for uses other than agricultural land, for example, but its replacement is much less severe in its impact. DLT raised £81m at its peak in 1984/5.

5 CGT has been reduced substantially in severity over the period in question, particularly by the 1988 budget. Apart from the indexation of gains to take account of inflation, CGT does not, in the present financial year (1991/2), begin to bite until gains of £5,500 have been realised, and is levied only on real gains made since 1982 at the investor's marginal rate of tax. CGT has also been completely abolished on gains made on gilt-edged (government) stocks; gains made over a period of twelve months or more had been exempted by a previous Labour government.

6 The emphasis of the tax system has been shifted from income tax towards less progressive taxes such as Value Added Tax (VAT) and National Insurance contributions. As far as VAT is concerned, the important change came in 1979, when the twin rates of 8 per

cent and 12.5 per cent were abolished and replaced by the single rate of 15 per cent, subsequently raised to 17.5 per cent in the 1991 budget. Although employer-based National Insurance contributions are now levied on the whole of the employee's income, an upper limit of £390 per week remains for employee contributions, so that someone on that income level pays the same absolute amount as other employees earning substantially greater salaries.

7 Owner-occupied housing, which has always enjoyed substantial taxation advantages, has been given a further boost under the Tories. The ceiling for tax relief on mortgage interest payments, which stood in 1979 at £25,000, where it had remained since 1974, was in 1983 raised to £30,000. It remains true, of course, that the value of tax relief has fallen in real terms over time, while the 1988 budget confined the relief to £30,000 per residence rather than per mortgagee. Moreover, the 1991 budget provided for interest relief to be at the basic rate only from 1991/2 onwards.

8 The introduction of independent taxation of husband and wife from April 1990, with a view ostensibly to remove discrimination of the tax system against married women, has in effect resulted in the creation of a number of winners and losers (Richards, 1991). The winners tend on the whole to be couples where a non-working wife has a large investment income against which she is now able to set her own personal tax allowance. Moreover, husband and wife now each have a tax-free Capital Gains Tax allowance instead of sharing one as previously. Some better-off families stood to gain well over £6,000 a year from these changes alone. The losers would include families where the husband was unemployed and the wife the sole breadwinner.

The cumulative effect of a number of these changes on the distribution of income may be seen by taking two imaginary individuals – a stockbroker and coal miner, for example – and comparing their positions in the tax year 1978/9, immediately before the Tories came to power, with the tax year 1990/1. Details of these two imaginary individuals are shown in Table 12.2.

In order to simplify the situation, we assume that their respective incomes do not change between the two periods, and that the only tax allowance they have in 1978/9 is the married man's allowance of £1,535. In 1990/1, we assume that the husband has his own personal allowance of £3,005 and the married couple's allowance of £1,720 and that the wife receives all the investment income against which she can

Table 12.2 Income and mortgage details

	Coal miner	Stockbroker
Earned income	£10,000	£40,000
Investment income	–	£20,000
Mortgage	–	£30,000

set her own personal allowance of £3,005. Mortgage interest of £4,200 is assumed to be paid.

In 1978/9, whereas before tax the income of the broker and his wife is six times that of the coal miner, his net-of-tax income is only 2.66 times that of the miner. However, by 1990/1 the net income ratio has increased to 5.34:1, indicating that the situation had changed substantially in favour of the broker. Had the incomes of these individuals doubled between the two periods in question, the ratio would have changed to 5.13:1.

A somewhat wider perspective is given in a study made by the Institute of Fiscal Studies (IFS) of the major changes in all taxes between 1978 and 1983. Dilnot and Morris (1983) came to the conclusion that although the system was still progressive, it was less so than previously:

> Progressivity has declined. Between 1978 and 1983 the tax rate faced by the lowest income groups has increased more quickly than that of the highest. This has occurred as regressive indirect taxes, and broadly neutral National Insurance contributions have increased in importance relative to progressive income tax.

And again, in a further study in 1987 for the IFS, Dilnot *et al.* (1987) found:

> The great bulk of the population has gained from the tax and benefit changes introduced since 1983, although losses are concentrated amongst the poorer groups. However, it is still the case that the tax burden for much of the population is greater than it was in 1978–9.

An official study (Central Statistical Office, 1987) confirms these trends. Before tax, the top 1 per cent of income recipients increased their share of total income from 5.3 per cent in 1978/9 to 6.4 per cent in 1984/5, while after tax their share increased from 3.9 per cent to 4.9 per cent. For the top 10 per cent, the gross and net changes were respectively from 26.1 per cent to 29.5 per cent and from 23.4 per cent to 26.5 per cent. By contrast, the bottom 10 per cent of income recipients saw their share of income before tax fall from 2.4 per cent in 1978/9 to 2.3 per cent in 1984/5, and after tax from 2.9 per cent to 2.7 per cent. More recent studies by the IFS have analysed separately the change in incomes before tax and those that have resulted purely from policy changes in the field of taxes and benefits. Jenkins (1991) looked at gross changes in the distribution of income in the 1970s and 1980s and came to the following conclusion:

> while inequality has increased, so too have average incomes, with the gains most marked in the 1980s and amongst the rich; the poorest have gained little.

The poor have been the subject of a separate study, in which Johnson and Webb (1990) concluded that between 1979 and 1987 the number of families with incomes below the Supplementary Benefit level – the official poverty line – increased by 18 per cent. Moreover, the benefit itself has remained virtually static in real terms in a period of fast income growth for the population as a whole. Johnson and Stark (1989) examine the effects of discretionary changes to the tax and benefit system between 1979 and 1989 by keeping the real level of earnings, unemployment and structure of the population constant. They conclude that only one group – the single unemployed – lost on average as a result of these changes, by some £2.16 a week. Though some individuals within other groups also suffered, most household groups gained from the changes, most noticeably in the case of the single-earner couple who gained the most on average, namely £13.25 per week, whereas an unemployed couple without children gained a mere £0.34 per week. In terms of categories of income ranges, those in the income range of £1,000 a week and over gained on average £286.53, whereas the least gain at £0.33 per week was recorded by households in the £10 to £50 per week range. This study therefore provides further evidence that the gains from tax and benefit changes were concentrated in the hands of the extremely high-income receivers.

Besides these general measures, the Conservative government has introduced numerous tax incentives designed primarily to foster particular policy objectives (see, for example, Chapters 1 and 8), but which have had the effect of providing further tax-shelters for higher-rate taxpayers in particular. These include the Business Expansion Scheme (BES) (formerly the Business Start-Up Scheme), Enterprise

Table 12.3 Net yields from BES investments

Tax rate	Growth in share price (% p.a. compounded)		
%	0%	5%	10%
27	6.5	17.1	22.5
45	12.7	24.0	29.6
60	20.1	32.1	38.1

Zones to stimulate regional development in depressed areas, and the Personal Equity Plan scheme (PEP), introduced in January 1987 to further the cause of wider share ownership.

The BES allows individuals to deduct from their taxable income the cost of investment in shares of certain companies up to a maximum of £40,000 per annum, subject to certain restrictions on the type of company. Initially designed to improve the flow of investment funds into new high-technology companies, most of the companies raising funds in the early years appeared to be low risk, in the sense that they were involved in ventures with substantial asset backing such as farming and property development, though these types of investments have now been disqualified from being able to participate in BES. In retrospect, the fall in land prices in recent years has raised the risk level of such ventures. In order to secure tax relief for the investor, the companies must not engage in any activities that would prejudice their qualifying status, whilst the investor must retain his shares for a minimum period of five years. The potential rate of return from these investments is substantial, particularly since the 1987 budget removed any gains on such shares from liability to Capital Gains Tax. Most companies in BES do not pay out dividends, but reinvest to foster the growth of the firm. Table 12.3 above shows the rate of return on the assumption that the share price shows different compound rates of growth over the five-year period.

The gross equivalent yields, which apply to tax rates in force in 1987/8, are of course substantially higher. A 60 per cent taxpayer in an investment which effectively stood still over a five-year period would need to obtain a gross yield of 50 per cent per annum elsewhere to gain a comparable amount to the net rate of 20.1 per cent he obtained from the PEP. A study of the IFS confirms this favourable position. Hills (1984) evaluated the extent to which the tax system favours certain types of investment – the 'degree of fiscal privilege'. Of the BES, Hills concluded:

For a top tax-payer [then 75 per cent] selling up after five years it [the degree of fiscal privilege] amounts to 1100–1200 per cent – that is, the tax advantage is eleven or twelve times the size of the underlying pre-tax real return on the shares purchased. In such circumstances the rate of return becomes practically immaterial provided that the company does not fail altogether.

In the 1988 budget, the government made BES rather less attractive by reducing the top marginal tax rate to 40 per cent and limiting the amount an individual company could raise to £0.5m, though this has been partly counterbalanced by allowing the scheme to be used for asset-backed ventures in the form of providing homes for rent under the Assured Tenancy system. The risk of failure is, of course, ever present, but this can be reduced by diversification either between different BES investments or by investing in other non-BES equities. A recent survey of BES investors by one of the largest sponsors showed that about one-fifth invested in two companies, and about 14 per cent in between six and ten companies. Almost one-fifth invested over £20,000 a year, while more than four-fifths of the investors were higher rate taxpayers, 8.5 per cent earning more than £125,000 a year.

While a maximum limit of £40,000 a year is imposed on BES investments, no such limit applies to investment in industrial and commercial property in Enterprise Zones, which have been established over the last twelve years under the 1980 Local Government Planning and Land Act (see also Chapter 13). To facilitate investment by individuals, various trusts and funds have been formed to divide the investment between units in a number of different Enterprise Zones and between different individuals. Not only is full tax relief available on practically the whole of the cost of the investment (the cost of the land is not deductible), but the investor can expect to receive an annual rental income, increasing over time, from this investment. If the property (or share of) is subsequently sold within twenty-five years, there is a balancing charge equal to the difference between the sale value or the purchase price (whichever is the lower) and the written-down value – effectively zero after a 100 per cent initial allowance. Furthermore, the profit on an eventual realisation of the property may be assessable to CGT, the base cost being the original cost after allowing for indexation and disregarding tax allowances. For a 60 per cent taxpayer, the rental yield on the net of tax cost can be around 15–16 per cent per annum, without any appreciation in the value of the property. Again, the 1988 budget changes which reduced the maximum rate of tax to 40 per cent will have reduced the attractiveness of this scheme for those previously paying tax at 45 per cent or more.

Finally, the PEP scheme, designed to widen the number of shareholders, has in fact achieved only very limited success in spite of subsequent improvements. This may be partly owing to the fact that although basic rate taxpayers can benefit to some extent, the advantages primarily accrue to higher rate taxpayers, since dividends are reinvested tax-free within the plan (maximum £6,000 per annum) while capital gains made by the plan are also free of CGT, a benefit which accrues to shareholders who regularly use up their tax-free capital gains allowance on other investments. Compared to the 11 million or so individuals who own shares, in 1989/90 the number of PEP plans opened amounted to only 450,000. As significant share ownership is confined mainly to the wealthy, the less well-off members of society would be unlikely to reap any benefit from these plans.

CHANGES IN THE TAXES ON WEALTH

Unlike many European countries, Britain does not have a tax on wealth as such. Rather, wealth is potentially liable to tax only when it is transferred, either by means of a lifetime gift or by means of inheritance at death. Since March 1986, the medium of taxing such transfers has been Inheritance Tax. The Conservatives, when they came to power in 1979, inherited Capital Transfer Tax (CTT), which had been introduced in 1974 by the Labour government to remedy some of the deficiencies of the old Estate Duty. CTT sought to tax lifetime gifts, as well as gifts passed down at death. CTT proved to be substantially less harsh than had been originally foreshadowed, with substantial privileges being retained by farming and business interests and reduced rates for lifetime gifts. Even so, the Conservatives came to power pledged to remove it, and indeed started the process in 1981 with quite radical reforms. These have been analysed by Sutherland (1981), who began thus:

> In the Budget of March 1981 the Chancellor made changes which would produce a dramatic reduction in the real burdens of most potential payers of CTT. Even without sophisticated tax avoidance, over 99 per cent of wealth owners will be able to pay

zero CTT when they hand on their assets. The burden to be borne by most of the remaining 1 per cent has also been greatly reduced.

That budget saw the introduction of new limits on the amount of gifts that could be made annually without charge, a significant reduction in taxes on lifetime gifts and reductions in taxes on property owned by farmers, businesses and agricultural landlords. But the major change was the introduction of the 'ten-year rule', by means of which all gifts made ten years previously ceased to count in the cumulative total of lifetime gifts. By 1981, an individual could give away £50,000 at one time, in addition to £3,000 annually, and if he lived for another ten years he could give away another £50,000 entirely free of CTT.

In 1986, the introduction of Inheritance Tax carried this tax-reducing process substantially further by abolishing tax on lifetime gifts almost totally and reducing the period of accumulation to seven years. If someone made a gift known as a Potentially Exempt Transfer and lived for seven years, then that entire gift ceased to be counted in the cumulative lifetime total. If he survived for between four and seven years, on the other hand, a proportion of the full tax became payable, varying from 100 per cent for death within the first three years to 20 per cent in the seventh year. Commenting on these changes at the time, the *Financial Times* said:

> The greatest beneficiaries of all from this change will be the ultra wealthy. Britain's wealthiest man, the Duke of Westminster, whose estate is estimated to be at least £2bn, will save a minimum of £600,000,000 at a stroke as a result of Mr Lawson's statement.

By 1991, the tax threshold had been raised to £140,000. The effects of some of these changes can be seen by examining the effect on the average rate of tax paid by different estates. Whereas between 1979 and 1991 inflation was about 100 per cent, the value of assets capable of being transferred tax-free at death had increased more than fivefold, from £25,000 to a figure of £140,000. In 1979 an estate of £110,000 would have suffered taxes of £28,250 – an average tax rate of about 25 per cent. By 1991, an estate which had increased in value roughly in line with inflation to £220,000, would have suffered taxes of £32,000, a little over 14 per cent. Again, on estates of £165,000, in

Table 12.4 Transfer taxes and wealth

	Transfer taxes £	% of total tax revenue	Household wealth £
1976/7	383m	1.8	314bn
1981/2	497m	1.2	696bn
1984/5	664m	1.3	1,028bn

Source: Inland Revenue Statistics, 1990

1979 and £330,000 in 1991, the average tax rates were, respectively, 35 per cent and 23 per cent.

It can be seen, therefore, that even had rich individuals omitted to take measures to avoid taxes during their lifetimes, the tax on death would have been substantially reduced over the period in question. The results of these changes are apparent in the national figures for estate taxes shown in Table 12.4, where the growth in receipts is substantially less than the growth in wealth over this period. As a percentage of total taxes raised by the Inland Revenue, transfer taxes fell from 2.8 per cent in 1976/7 to 1.3 per cent in 1988/9. Comparing 1988 (the latest year for which figures are available) with 1979, the top 50 per cent of wealth owners now own 94 per cent of marketable wealth, as opposed to 91 per cent, while the top 5 per cent own 38 per cent, compared to 36 per cent.

THE COMMUNITY CHARGE

In April 1990, the government, committed to reforming the system of local rates in order to try to exercise more effective control over local government, introduced the Community Charge or 'poll tax'. In the new regime, every adult would have to pay the Community Charge, though there was some help for poor individuals through the social security system. Although it is generally acknowledged that local rates were regressive with respect to income, it could be argued that they were in fact proportionately related to the wealth which is inherent in owner-occupied houses. Moreover, the Community Charge is even more unfair in terms of income than the rating system. It should be mentioned that the rebates for the poorest are restricted, under the Community Charge, to 80 per cent of the tax due, whereas a 100 per cent rebate was obtainable under the rates. A study carried out by

Smith and Squire (1987) for the IFS just before the introduction of the new system came to the following conclusion:

> It can be seen . . . that a poll tax would be an even more regressive tax than are domestic rates. Poorer households would pay a higher proportion of their income in tax, and richer households would pay a lower proportion of income in tax than with domestic rates.

Substantial redistribution would occur from poorer areas to richer areas. To take an example in Wales, in the Rhondda Valley, an economically deprived community, it was estimated that a family of three adults would be faced with an increase of £423 a year in local taxes whereas a similar family in the suburbs of Cardiff would enjoy a reduction of £52 in their charges. Faced with a massive public outcry against the system and the events which eventually led to the removal of Mrs Thatcher as leader of her party in November 1990, the government of Mr Major sought to ameliorate the worst effects of the poll tax in the 1991 budget by reducing the amount of the charge by £140 per person and raising VAT to 17.5 per cent to compensate for the loss of revenue.

From April 1993, a new Council Tax is due to be introduced based on the value of properties in eight (originally seven) different bands, though the upper band in England extends only to houses worth £320,000 and over, so that the rich will not suffer unduly. Moreover, the charge will be based on the assumption that the property is occupied by two people. If the property is, in fact, in single occupation, the householder can apply for a rebate of 25 per cent. For English properties worth over £320,000, the tax rate will be three times that applying to properties in the lowest tax band which reaches to £40,000, at least eight times cheaper. Thus, although this system is obviously fairer than the poll tax, it is still regressive with respect to wealth and not as fair as the old rating system, which related the tax more precisely to the rateable value of the property.

CONCLUSIONS

The standard argument for cutting income tax is that it will improve incentives to work and to save. Empirical evidence on this issue is, however, extremely shaky, and indeed numerous studies such as those of Brown (1983) have come to the conclusion that far from working harder as a result of a cut in income tax, some people actually work less. More recent studies, particularly those in the United States, appear to provide more hard evidence of a disincentive effect, though the position is by no means clear-cut. The reduction in income tax rates did, however, help to remove investment distortion which, with an 83 per cent top rate plus 15 per cent Investment Income Surcharge, was considerable.

It is also difficult to accept redistribution of wealth in favour of the wealthy since, on balance, rich people have acquired their wealth, not because they have worked hard or have built up a business, but because they have inherited the wealth from their predecessors. The distribution of wealth in Britain is substantially more uneven than in the United States, for example. As we have mentioned earlier, in terms of marketable wealth, the 10 per cent richest individuals in Britain own nearly half of the wealth, whereas the 50 per cent most wealthy individuals own nearly 94 per cent of the wealth. It is hard to see therefore the justification for creating further inequity in an already unequal distribution.

Finally, was there a need to change the system of local taxation? Although all political parties have expressed dissatisfaction with the previous rating system of local government finance, the IFS argued that there was no need to abolish rates since they played a significant role in taxing the services of housing and it would be possible to supplement them by means of a local income tax which would be much fairer and would avoid the need to establish a new complex system to compensate those too poor to afford the Community Charge.

13

THE 'NORTH–SOUTH DIVIDE'

Has regional policy failed?

Nigel M. Healey

INTRODUCTION

During the 1980s, the term 'north–south divide' – first coined by the Brandt Commission to describe the difference in living standards between the 'First World' of the northern hemisphere and the 'Third World' of the southern – became increasingly associated with the phenomenon of de-industrialisation, poverty and mass unemployment in the north of Britain coexisting with economic growth, labour shortages and escalating house prices in the south. While the 1990–2 recession has fallen disproportionately hard on the southern part of the country, temporarily reducing the width of regional 'divide', most commentators expect the gap to rewiden as economic recovery takes place. This chapter delves beneath the political rhetoric and examines the nature of the north–south divide and the economic policies that the Conservative government have brought to bear on the problem.

IS THERE A 'NORTH–SOUTH DIVIDE'?

A conventional point of departure for any assessment of regional differences is to focus on a range of standard economic indicators. For statistical purposes, the government divides the country into eleven regions (see Figure 13.1). Table 13.1 shows that in terms of average incomes (measured in various ways) and registered unemployment (but see Southworth, 1987), there are marked regional disparities. The three regions most commonly regarded as constituting the south, namely the South-East, South-West and East Anglia, dominate the top three rankings on almost all indicators of economic performance. For example, the South-East has the highest average incomes on any definition and the second lowest level of unemployment; East Anglia has the second highest average incomes on the average earnings definition and (with the South-West) the lowest incidence of long-term unemployment; and the South-West has the second highest average incomes on the household definition and the lowest level of long-term unemployment. In contrast, the figures for the north – those regions which lie above the imaginary line between the Severn Estuary and the Wash – are unambiguously worse on all counts.

A common criticism of using employment and income data to illustrate the north–south divide is that it is unduly simplistic: in the north there are areas of affluence and low unemployment, while certain parts of the south are blighted by industrial decline and poverty. Redrawing the national unemployment picture by county rather than by region confirms that what is true of the whole is not true of all the parts. In January 1987, for example, the unemployment rate in Grampian and Tayside was lower than that in Kent; in North Yorkshire and the Borders, it was lower than in the Isle of Wight and Devon; and almost everywhere in the north it was lower than in Cornwall.

Inner-city degeneration also pock-marks the British map with unemployment scars that afflict major urban conurbations in north and south alike, with several London boroughs having more in common with Merseyside than the nearby Thames Valley area. On this basis, it is argued that it is more constructive to imagine a national patchwork of economic prosperity than to present the discussion in terms of a 'Chinese Wall' separating a uniformly affluent south from a uniformly impoverished north.

There is clearly great force in this point of view. Yet attempts to delve beneath the regional statistics suggest that the differences between regions tend to swamp those within regions. Armstrong and Taylor (1987), for example, investigated the distribution of unemployment within different regions by focusing on the dozens of 'travel-to-work areas' within each (official statistics use the labour 'catchment' areas of towns and cities, rather than counties or council districts, as their basis for disaggregating employment data). Their results are summarised in Table 13.2. It shows that, contrary to the notion of poverty amidst plenty, in the south less than 10 per cent (and less than 3 per cent in the South-East and South-West) of the workforce was then concentrated in areas of high (15 per cent plus) unemployment. In contrast, most regions in the north had at least 75 per cent of their workforces resident in areas with 15 per cent or more unemployment. The clear implication is that in the south, the pockets of high unemployment experienced in some inner-city areas

Figure 13.1 Standard regions.

Table 13.1 Economic indicators of regional differences

	Gross domestic product (UK = 100)	Household income[1] (UK = 100)	Average weekly earnings[2]	Unemployment[3]	Long-term Unemployment[4]
			£	%	%
The 'south':					
South-East	117.9	113.8	344	5.2	20.3
South-West	94.9	103.1	277	6.1	17.8
East Anglia	97.9	98.6	281	5.1	17.8
The 'north':					
East Midlands	96.5	95.0	269	6.1	24.4
West Midlands	91.5	91.0	269	6.9	27.8
Yorks and Humbs	92.2	94.1	267	8.0	27.0
North	89.5	91.0	265	9.6	29.6
North-West	92.6	93.1	274	8.4	31.5
Wales	84.6	86.0	259	7.8	23.7
Scotland	94.5	96.9	276	8.5	32.0
N. Ireland	77.5	82.2	253	14.1	50.3

Source: CSO *Regional Trends*

Notes: [1] Average pre-tax weekly earnings per household, 1987
[2] Average pre-tax weekly earnings per male worker, April 1990
[3] As a percentage of working population, January 1991
[4] Persons unemployed for more than one year as a percentage of registered unemployed, January 1991

were tiny in terms of the numbers of people they affected. Similarly, in the north (with the notable exception of the East Midlands), the notion of 'islands of jobs in a sea of joblessness' proved largely illusory: in Wales, for example, there was not one single travel-to-work area in which the unemployment rate was below 10 per cent.

Despite the recent fall in house prices, which have slumped hardest in the south, housing market statistics confirm that there is a continuing chasm between north and south. Table 13.3 shows that house prices in the south remain well above those in the north. This phenomenon has arisen mainly because higher incomes in the south have afforded potential buyers greater purchasing power, but also because better employment prospects in the south have attracted mobile (house-buying) labour down from the north (Healey, 1987d). In 1989, for example, 250,000 people resettled in the South-East. While a slightly larger number moved out of the South-East, this

Table 13.2 Percentage of regional workforces in high unemployment localities

| | Percentage of workforce in 'travel-to-work areas' with unemployment rates of: | | | |
	0–10%	10–15%	15–20%	20%+
The 'south':				
South-East	39.1	59.2	1.2	0.5
South-West	11.8	82.6	1.8	0.8
East Anglia	42.2	44.3	13.5	0.0
The 'north':				
East Midlands	30.3	51.7	14.2	3.8
West Midlands	6.9	24.1	66.5	2.5
Yorks and Humbs	4.4	32.2	49.1	14.3
North	2.0	21.5	41.4	35.4
North-West	2.3	45.6	34.0	18.1
Wales	0.0	25.6	60.3	14.1
Scotland	9.0	27.2	47.7	16.1

Source: Armstrong and Taylor, 1987

outward migration was dominated by elderly people moving to cheaper housing areas to retire. The growing numbers of young house-buyers, with ever-larger amounts of money to spend, thus served to bid up house prices in the south during the 1980s, reflecting the south's increasing prosperity at the expense of the slowly depopulating north.

One final statistical indicator of economic performance is provided by the Department of Employment's records of new business registrations for VAT (see Table 13.4). Over the period 1982–9, net registrations (i.e. new registrations less deregistrations) amounted to 35 per cent of the outstanding total in 1981 for the South-East, 26 per cent for the South-West and 26 per cent for East Anglia. In contrast, the comparable figures for the north averaged only 18 per cent, with Yorkshire and Humberside, the North and Northern Ireland (the worst performing regions) managing only 16 per cent, 14 per cent and 16 per cent respectively.

'DEINDUSTRIALISATION' AND THE 'NORTH–SOUTH DIVIDE'

The north–south divide is intimately intertwined with the wider problem of 'deindustrialisation' (see Cairncross, 1978; Thirlwall,

Table 13.3 Regional house price trends

	Average house price in 1989[1]	Increase 1981–9
	£	%
The 'south':		
South-East	94,300	185
South-West	79,400	189
East Anglia	71,900	174
The 'north':		
East Midlands	75,700	168
West Midlands	78,000	196
Yorks and Humbs	62,500	147
North	58,300	135
North-West	70,100	159
Wales	64,900	152
Scotland	55,700	106

Source: CSO *Regional Trends*
Note:[1] New dwelling

Table 13.4 Business registrations and deregistrations (1982–9)

	Stock end 1981	Registrations	Deregis-trations	Net change
The 'south':				
South-East	441.4	640.4	488.3	152.1
South-West	128.3	143.8	110.9	33.0
East Anglia	54.5	59.4	45.5	13.9
The 'north':				
East Midlands	91.7	104.9	83.1	21.8
West Midlands	116.9	134.2	110.1	24.1
Yorks and Humbs	105.2	117.6	99.1	18.5
North	53.8	57.1	48.5	8.6
North-West	131.5	154.5	136.8	17.7
Wales	73.0	68.7	56.6	12.2
Scotland	96.2	100.5	83.4	17.1
N. Ireland	44.8	28.8	22.0	6.8

Source: CSO *Regional Trends*

1982). The tendency of developing economies to expand first their secondary sector (manufacturing and construction) at the expense of their traditional primary sector (agriculture and raw material extrac-

Table 13.5 Employment by sector in Britain (000s)

	1966	1971	1979	1984	1989
Primary Sector					
Agriculture	580	432	368	340	300
Extraction and Energy	1,002	797	721	630	471
Secondary Sector					
Manufacturing	8,587	8,085	7,260	5,517	4,557
Construction	1,648	1,207	1,248	984	1,062
Tertiary Sector					
Services and Distribution	11,441	11,600	13,562	13,691	15,687

Source: CSO *Social Trends*

tion) and then later their tertiary sector (services and distribution) at the expense of their secondary sector is well documented. But in Britain, the latter stage of de-industrialisation, involving the shift out of manufacturing into services, has taken place more rapidly and to a much greater extent than in other advanced economies. Between 1975 and 1985, manufacturing's share of gross domestic product shrank from 30.4 per cent to 23.2 per cent, while that of services grew from 32.6 per cent to 36.1 per cent. Over the same period, manufacturing shed jobs relentlessly, with employment falling by as much as 9.8 per cent per annum in some years. Table 13.5 illustrates the scale of the labour shake-out in manufacturing which took place between 1966 and 1985, when the deindustrialisation was most pronounced.

Many reasons have been offered for the more dramatic onset of deindustrialisation in Britain than elsewhere: the short-termist attitude of British managers; the reluctance of British manufacturers to invest in new capital equipment and training for their workforces; the poor state of industrial relations, which inhibits the introduction of new techniques and processes; and an archaic class system which encourages the country's most able young people to shun manufacturing in favour of a 'profession' in the service sector.

The unusually large presence of transnational corporations in the domestic economy may also have played an important role. In terms of both the number of British-owned companies that have overseas operations, and the number of British-based companies that are subsidiaries of overseas corporations, Britain is second only to the United States and Canada respectively (Healey, 1991b). Giant, global companies have grown enormously in size and importance over the postwar period and have increasingly shunned Britain as a base for their activities, preferring instead to relocate gradually in the newly industrialising countries of South-East Asia. As a result, the natural run-down of the so-called 'sunset' manufacturing industries has been sharply accelerated by the withdrawal of transnational corporations from these activities.

If the process of deindustrialisation were no more than the smooth transfer of productive capacity (labour and capital) from manufacturing into the new service industries, there might be little reason to fear it. But, in practice, it generates a range of short- to medium-term adjustment problems, of which the intensification of regional imbalances is one of the most serious. There are two links in the chain between deindustrialisation and the consequent creation of a north–south divide.

The first is that deindustrialisation in Britain has taken place at such a rapid pace that the service sector has been unable to expand sufficiently quickly to absorb the resources, especially labour, being released by manufacturing (Johnson, 1985). In fact, over the period 1979–86, the growth in service employment was only just enough to offset the natural increase in the working population which took place, leaving the so-called 'shake-out' of workers from manufacturing to be almost exactly mirrored by the rise in unemployment.

Second, neither the decline in manufacturing (and hence the associated unemployment), nor the only partially offsetting growth in the new service industries is uniformly distributed across the regions. Rather, it is the case that manufacturing accounts for a disproportionately larger share of employment and output in the north than it does in the south (see Table 13.6). For example, the three regions which suffered the worst job losses during the 1980s, namely Wales, the North and the North-West, had roughly one-third of their workforces in manufacturing in 1979; in contrast, none of the regions that make up the south had more than a quarter (see also Cornelius and Shields, 1987).

Moreover, the type of manufacturing activity in north and south is somewhat different. Although manufacturing overall in Britain is in relative decline, within this sector the spectacular collapse of the older, 'sunset' industries (e.g. auto production, textiles, heavy engineering, shipbuilding, etc.) contrasts sharply with the growth of the newer, high-tech 'sunrise' sector. Again, the former are concentrated primarily in the north, while the latter have tended to develop in the south. In other words, not only has the north a greater dependence on manufacturing, it also relies disproportionately heavily on the type of manufacturing most vulnerable to the deindustrialisation disease.

THE 'CORE-PERIPHERY MODEL' AND THE 'NORTH-SOUTH DIVIDE'

A related dimension of Britain's regional problem – which is likely to get worse, rather than better, as the pace of European integration accelerates over the 1990s – concerns the tendency of businesses to cluster at the 'core' of a region, country or continent, leaving the 'periphery' underdeveloped. The reasons for this phenomenon are complex and not well understood, but they have to do with the economic principle of externalities (or spillover effects). Whenever a firm sets up in a particular locality, it lowers the costs of other firms in the area; i.e. they enjoy a positive externality. Suppliers experience a reduction in the transactions costs associated with delivering goods to the relocating firm; its customers similarly benefit from the improved delivery and better communications that closer geographical proximity promotes; and its competitors may find that by increasing the demand for industrial services in the region, the arrival of the relocating firm attracts additional suppliers to the area, benefiting the industry as a whole. By grouping together, therefore, firms can collectively reduce their costs.

A good example of this phenomenon is the concentration of computer firms in the Thames Valley area. By clustering together in such a tight, geographical area, each hardware manufacturer has easy access to other specialists – system analysts, software houses, etc. – which, in turn, find their location is convenient for the largest number of potential customers. A software house which set up in, say, Durham, would find that the extra costs of sales and marketing (to create and maintain a profile amongst its target customers) and transport costs would outweigh the cost savings it enjoyed from cheaper land and labour.

In the past, when bulky raw materials (e.g. coal) were a major productive input into many processes (e.g. steel production), the core of industrial Britain was the north. Steel producers could not afford to locate far from the coalfields of Wales, Scotland and northern England; similarly, heavy users of steel (e.g. automobiles, shipbuilding) were, in turn, tied to their suppliers. Today, the new growth industries of the service sector and light, high-technology manufactur-

Table 13.6 The regional importance of manufacturing

	Manufacturing as % total employment in 1979	Percentage change 1979–86 in total employment in:	
		Manufacturing	*Non-manufacturing*
The 'south':			
South-East	25.0	–25.4	+6.2
South-West	27.5	–14.8	+3.2
East Anglia	29.3	–2.4	+13.1
The 'north':			
East Midlands	39.0	–18.0	+7.5
West Midlands	44.0	–28.6	+4.9
Yorks and Humbs	35.2	–35.0	+1.1
North	32.9	–34.1	–3.7
North-West	36.3	–34.7	–4.5
Wales	30.5	–35.9	–8.6
Scotland	28.7	–31.8	–1.5

Source: Armstrong and Taylor, 1987

ing need a well-educated labour force and access to continental markets, so that in many sectors the core area for activity is the South-East. Indeed, this same trend is apparent for the European Community as a whole. There now exists a 'golden triangle' connecting London, Milan and Frankfurt, within which the core of the EC's production and income is contained. The core–periphery model suggests that as the process of deindustrialisation continues, the new industries are likely to be ever-more concentrated in the south generally and in the South-East specifically.

HAS REGIONAL POLICY FAILED?

Establishing that Britain suffers from a genuine north–south divide begs the crucial question: does this mean that regional policy in Britain has failed? Successive governments have operated active regional policy aimed at reducing spatial differences in employment and economic activity since the 1930s. The gulf between north and south certainly appears *prima facie* evidence that half a century of intervention has proved largely ineffective. Traditionally, regional policy has relied on 'taking work to the workers', by inducing manufacturing firms to locate new operations, or to relocate existing operations, in depressed areas. These inducements have included financial incentives like grants and subsidies, as well as differential planning controls which made it much easier to obtain a licence for industrial expansion in the assisted regions.

There are three major flaws in this approach (Livesey, 1984). One is that much of the government money may well have been wasted in 'bribing' firms to do what they would in any case have done. The second is that most of the government money was handed out in the form of investment grants, which were, in turn, often used to purchase new, labour-saving manufacturing technologies, so creating few, if any, additional jobs. And the third, and most damning of all, is that by concentrating aid on manufacturing, successive governments merely enticed ultimately doomed industries from the south to the north without doing anything to address the root cause – namely, deindustrialisation.

The last point may be illustrated by considering the analogous example of a gardener who uproots terminally blighted shrubs from the most fertile parts of the garden, where they were dying relatively slowly, and replants them in the most barren, where the existing stock is dying rapidly. Not only is this strategy ultimately futile, but it actually serves to concentrate the problem in the least-advantaged area. Far better to replace the blighted shrubs with a new, resilient strain, or in the case of the British economy, to replace the sunset industries of the north with the sunrise, service jobs that were naturally springing up in the south.

On the other hand, it might be argued that regional policy brought to the north many manufacturing companies which have so far resisted the deindustrialisation disease, so preventing regional imbalances from becoming more pronounced than they might otherwise have been. Table 13.7 shows that, with the exception of the West Midlands (which only 'joined' the north during the 1979–81 depression after decades of relative prosperity), the north enjoyed a net inflow of manufacturing establishments over the period 1960–81: discounting the West Midlands, 77 per cent of all remaining moves were into the north, which has only 52 per cent of the workforce. Overall, research by Moore et al. (1986) for the Department of Trade and Industry suggests that approximately 600,000 net jobs (i.e. after

Table 13.7 Interregional movements of British manufacturing 1960–81

| | Number of manufacturing establishments | | |
	Moving in	Moving out	Net movement
The 'south':			
South-East	195	1,842	–1,647
South-West	423	107	+316
East Anglia	426	72	+354
The 'north':			
East Midlands	335	274	+61
West Midlands	96	430	–334
Yorks and Humbs	261	255	+6
North	420	55	+365
North-West	336	318	+18
Wales	626	40	+586
Scotland	367	64	+303

Source: Armstrong and Taylor, 1987

allowing for job losses), were created in the designated 'Assisted Areas' between 1960 and 1981 as a result of regional policy.

Should the process of deindustrialisation continue at its present rate, however, the north may not thank central government for temporarily propping it up with more of the same doomed species. Certainly, the present Conservative government has been convinced by the argument that, in its traditional form, regional policy has been far from successful. Since 1979, it has introduced a number of reforms which have radically altered the thrust of regional policy in Britain (see Harrison, 1986).

THE CHANGING FACE OF REGIONAL POLICY

Since 1979, there have been three major changes in the way central government has sought to tackle the north–south divide:

1 modification of existing regional policy to address criticisms of the traditional approach;
2 a new set of policies to tackle the particular problems of the 'inner cities', almost all of which are in the north;
3 a change in the way that businesses pay local rates, which has benefited the north.

Taking the changes in regional policy proper first, the overriding aim has been to improve its cost-effectiveness in terms of 'real' jobs created, in the main by making assistance discretionary rather than automatic. Specifically, this has involved alterations to both the structure and geographical coverage of assisted areas. A new category – the 'Enterprise Zone', in which incoming firms are exempt from rates, development land taxes and various planning restrictions – was added to the inherited hierarchy of Special Development Areas, Development Areas and Intermediate Areas. Special Development Areas were subsequently all downgraded to Development Areas, while Regional Development Grants, previously 22 per cent in all assisted areas, were first cut to 15 per cent and finally abolished altogether in January 1988. Instead, a new discretionary scheme to subsidise consultancies for all companies, operating in both the manufacturing and service sectors, was introduced. This is available nationwide, but attracts higher rates of grant in the assisted regions. Conventional grant aid has only been retained for the smallest firms in the assisted regions: enterprises with fewer than twenty-five employees are now eligible for grants of up to £15,000 for investment and £25,000 for innovation, again on a discretionary basis.

At the same time as regional policy has been extended to the service sector and gradually made more selective, new central government initiatives like the Urban Development Corporations (UDCs), City Action Teams and Task Forces have introduced an even more tightly targeted element into the policy framework. These initiatives have become an increasingly important arm of regional policy in its broadest sense.

Finally, the recent reforms of local government finance resulted in a considerable redistribution of resources between north and south. As part of the package, which also introduced the Community Charge (which is due to be replaced by a new Council Tax), the rateable values of business premises were reassessed in 1990 and all firms charged a nationwide, uniform rate poundage. This means that firms operating in the prosperous south on balance found their rates bills increasing, while those in the north benefited from a corresponding fall. Table 13.8 illustrates that the size of these changes compares favourably with the allocations being made under the formal regional programme.

TOO LITTLE, TOO LATE?

Whether the changes in regional policy, or in regional, inner-city and business rates policies taken together, will do much to close the gap

Table 13.8 Effect of business rates reforms on regional business rates bills

	Estimated full-year changes in rates bills (1987–8 prices) £
The 'south':	
South-East	+120m
South-West	+170m
East Anglia	–20m
TOTAL CHANGE	+270m
The 'north':	
East Midlands	–50m
West Midlands	+180m
Yorks and Humbs	–160m
North	–130m
North-West	–110m
TOTAL CHANGE	–270m

Source: Centre for Local Economic Strategies

between north and south is highly debatable. Certainly, there is a case to be made for each and, in this sense, these developments might be interpreted as steps in the right direction. Yet they are such tiny steps. The improvements in regional policy that took place in the 1980s were largely negated by the cuts in funding that accompanied them (Armstrong and Taylor, 1986). Between 1983–4 and 1987–8 alone, spending on regional policy fell from £700m to £400m, a reduction of approximately half in real terms. The hidden agenda underlying the new inner-city initiatives appears to have as much to do with wresting control of urban regeneration from local authorities (Healey, 1987b), as it does with genuinely increasing the flow of resources to particularly depressed areas. And although the transfers generated by the new uniform business rating system are not insignificant, there is little evidence that business rates have any effect on the location of companies.

Most important of all, however, is the fact that none of these measures addresses the fundamental, underlying problem of deindustrialisation. The Conservative government's curt dismissal of the report of the House of Lords Select Committee on Overseas Trade (see Aldington, 1986), which highlighted the growing difficulties faced by the British economy as its industrial base declines, revealed a deep-rooted reluctance to face up to the issue. Systematic, coherent industrial policy, the prerequisite of any serious attempt to arrest Britain's economic decay, is conspicuous by its absence. In its intellectual commitment to free markets, the Conservative government instead spent the 1980s standing idly by as both British-owned and foreign-owned transnational corporations deserted the industrial heartlands of the north in favour of offshore production in the newly industrialising countries of Southern Europe and South-East Asia, leaving behind only their London-based head offices and the service jobs these strategic management centres require in the south.

In the absence of concerted government action to tackle the immanent causes of the north–south divide, rather than simply redistributing an increasingly small pool of mobile business with increasingly less appetising fiscal carrots, the prospects for the twenty-first century must be grim. As Cusick (1986), a northern academic, grimly observed:

> the north is turning into a third world economy. If I was a foreigner travelling north, I think I would believe I was travelling into another country . . . we [the north] are a lost colony.

CONCLUSIONS

Although the term 'north–south divide' is an over-simplification of a geographically complex phenomenon, from the statistical data considered above it is clearly meaningful to make a distinction between the regions to the north of the Severn Estuary–Wash dividing line and those to the south. The emergence of this gulf between the two is part of the wider problem of deindustrialisation which traditional regional policy has done little to address. Recent developments in this policy area have sought to make regional policy more cost-effective, but taken in the context of a greatly reduced expenditure total, they are unlikely to make more than a marginal impact on the problem which may, if anything, intensify in the 1990s as further European integration spurs the development of the core south at the expense of the peripheral north.

REFERENCES

Aldington, Lord (1986), 'British manufacturing industry', *The Royal Bank of Scotland Review*, no. 151, September.

Armstrong, H. and Taylor, J. (1986), 'Regional policy: dead or alive?', *The Economic Review*, vol. 4, no. 2, November.

—— (1987), *Regional Policy: The Way Forward*, London: Employment Institute.

Artis, M. (1991), 'The European monetary system', *Economics*, vol. XXVII, no. 113, Spring.

Ashton, P. (1987), 'Tackling long-term unemployment: an assessment of Restart', *Quarterly Economic Bulletin*, March.

—— (1988), 'Tax-benefit reform and incentives', *Quarterly Economic Bulletin*, December.

Ashton, P. and Minford, P. (1987), 'What is the effect on tax revenue of cutting top rates of tax?', *Quarterly Economic Bulletin*, March.

—— (1988), 'Labour supply response and the effects of tax rates', *Quarterly Economic Bulletin*, March.

Ashton, D., Green, F. and Hoskins, M. (1989), 'The training system of British capitalism: changes and prospects', in F. Green (ed.), *The Restructuring of the UK Economy*, Brighton: Harvester Wheatsheaf.

Averch, H. and Johnson, L. (1962), 'Behaviour of the firm under regulatory constraint', *American Economic Review*, vol. 52.

Bank of England (1988), 'Real rates of return', *Bank of England Quarterly Bulletin*, August.

Barro, R. J. and Gordon, D. B. (1983), 'Rules, discretion and reputation in a model of monetary policy', *Journal of Monetary Economics*, vol. 12, no. 2.

Beenstock, M. (1979), 'Taxation and incentives in the UK', *Lloyds Bank Review*, no. 134, October.

Bishop, M. and Kay, J. A., (1988), *Does Privatization Work? Lessons from the UK*, London: London Business School.

Blackaby, D. H. and Hunt, L. C. (1989), 'The manufacturing productivity "miracle": a sectoral analysis', in F. Green (ed.), *The Restructuring of the UK Economy*, Brighton: Harvester Wheatsheaf.

Blanchflower, D. G. and Millward, W. (1988), 'Trade unions and employment change: an analysis of British establishment data', *European Economic Review*, vol. 32, nos. 2/3, March.

REFERENCES

Blanchflower, D. G. and Oswald, A. (1988), 'The economic effects of Britain's trade unions', Discussion Paper no. 324, Centre for Labour Economics, London School of Economics.

Boakes, K. (1988), 'Britain's productivity miracle – more to come', Greenwell Montague Gilt-Edged Economic Research Paper, May.

Borcherding, T., Pommerhene, W. and Schneider, F. (1982), 'Comparing the efficiency of private and public production: the evidence from five countries', *Zeitschrift für Nationalokonomie*, vol. 42, supplement 2.

British Business (1987), 'Business trends: industrial R&D', London: HMSO, February 27.

Brown, C. V. (1983), *Taxation and the Incentive to Work*, Oxford: Oxford University Press.

—— (1988), 'Will the 1988 income tax cuts either increase work incentives or raise more revenue?', *Fiscal Studies*, vol. 9, November.

Brown, C. V., Levin, E. J., Rosa, P. J., Rafell, R. J. and Ulph, D. T. (1987), *Taxation and Family Labour Supply*, Fiscal Report of HM Treasury Project, London: HMSO.

Buiter, W. and Miller, M. (1983), 'Changing the rules: economic consequences of the Thatcher regime', *Brookings Papers on Economic Activity*, vol. 2.

Cairncross, A. (1978), 'What is deindustrialisation?', in F. Blackaby (ed.), *Deindustrialisation*, London: Heinemann.

Campbell, M., Hardy, M. and Healey, N. M. (1989), *Controversy in Applied Economics*, Brighton: Harvester Wheatsheaf.

Casson, M. (1982), *The Entrepreneur: An Economic Theory*, Oxford: Martin Robertson.

CBI (1988), *UK Productivity: Closing the Gap*, London: CBI.

—— (1990), *Economic Priorities for 1990: Investing for the New Decade*, London: CBI.

Central Statistical Office (1985), *United Kingdom National Accounts: Sources and Methods*, (3rd edition), Central Statistical Office Studies in Official Statistics, no. 37, London: HMSO.

—— (1987), 'The distribution of income in the United Kingdom, 1984/85', *Economic Trends*, no. 409, November, London: HMSO.

—— (1990), *Economic Trends*, no. 435, January, London: HMSO.

Cook, M. and Healey, N. M. (1990), *Current Topics in International Economics*, Prudhoe: Anforme.

Cornelius, M. and Shields, J. (1987), 'Employment losses and the north–south divide', *Charter for Jobs Economic Report*, vol. 2, no. 3, January.

Cross, M. (1981), *New Firm Formation and Regional Development*, Aldershot: Gower.

Cusick, J. (1986), 'The great divide', *Manchester Evening News*, March 18.

Daly, A., Hitchens, D. M. N. and Wagner, K. (1985), 'Productivity, machinery and skills in a sample of British and German manufacturing plants', *National Institute Economic Review*, no. 111, February.

Davies, S. and Caves, R. E. (1987), *Britain's Productivity Gap*, Cambridge: Cambridge University Press.

Department of Trade and Industry (1984), *A Study of Businesses Financed under the Small Business Loan Guarantee Scheme*, London: Department of Trade and Industry.

Devereaux, M. (1987), 'On the growth of corporation tax revenues', *Fiscal Studies*, vol. 8, no. 2, May.

—— (1988), 'Corporation tax: the effect of the 1984 reforms on the incentive to invest', *Fiscal Studies*, vol. 9, no. 1, February.

Dilnot, A. and Kell, M. (1988), 'Top rate tax cuts and incentives: some empirical evidence', *Fiscal Studies*, vol. 9, no. 4, November.

Dilnot, A. and Morris, C. N. (1981), 'What do we know about the black economy?', *Fiscal Studies*, vol. 2, no. 1, March.

—— (1983), 'The tax system and distribution 1978–83', *Fiscal Studies*, vol. 8, no. 2, May.

Dilnot, A. and Stark, G. (1986), 'The poverty trap, tax cuts, and reform of social security', *Fiscal Studies*, vol. 7, no. 1, February.

Dilnot, A., Stark, G., Walker, I. and Webb, S. (1987), 'The 1987 budget in perspective', *Fiscal Studies*, vol. 8, no. 2, May.

Dornbusch, R. (1976), 'Expectations and exchange rate dynamics', *Journal of Political Economy*, vol. 84.

Dunn, N. S. and Gennard, J. (1984), *The Closed Shop in British Industry*, London: Macmillan.

Dunsire, A. and Hood, C. C. (1989), *Cutback Management in Public Bureaucracies: Popular Theories and Observed Outcomes in Whitehall*, Cambridge: Cambridge University Press.

Eatwell, J. (1982), *Whatever Happened to Britain?*, British Broadcasting Corporation, London: Duckworth.

Edwards, J. (1984), 'The 1984 corporation tax reform', *Fiscal Studies*, vol. 5, May 1984.

Edwards, P. (1987), *Managing the factory*, Oxford: Basil Blackwell.

Elwell, C. K. (1983) 'Supply-side economics: a general perspective', in B. Bartlett and T. P. Roth (eds), *The Supply-Side Solution*, London: Macmillan.

Employment Institute (1985), 'We can cure unemployment', *Charter for Jobs*, May.

Firn, J. and Swales, J. K. (1978) 'The formation of new manufacturing establishments in the Central Clydeside and West Midlands conurbations 1963:72: a comparative anlaysis', *Regional Studies* 12(2): 199–213.

Fothergill, S. and Gudgin, G. (1979) *The Job Generation Process in Britain*, Centre for Environmental Studies, Research Services 32, London: CES.

Freeman, R. B. (1989), *Labour Markets in Action*, Brighton: Harvester Wheatsheaf.

Freeman, R. and Medoff, J. (1984), *What Do Unions Do?*, New York: Basic Books.

Friedman, M. (1968), 'The role of monetary policy', *American Economic Review*, vol. 58, March.

—— (1980), 'Memorandum' in Treasury and Civil Service Committee, *Memoranda on Monetary Policy*, Cmnd 720, London: HMSO.

Gallagher, C. C. and Stewart, H. (1986), 'Jobs and the business life cycle in the UK', *Applied Economics*, vol. 18.

Ghatak, S., Healey, N. M. and Jackson, P. (1992), *The Macroeconomic Environment*, London: George Weidenfeld & Nicolson.

Gilbody, J. (1985), 'The public sector borrowing requirement and the money supply: a simple descriptive account of the UK institutional mechanisms', *Economics*, vol. XXI, no. 91, Autumn.

Glyn, A. (1989), 'The macro-anatomy of the Thatcher years', in F. Green (ed.), *The Restructuring of the UK Economy*, Brighton: Harvester Wheatsheaf.

Godley, W. (1989), 'The British economy during the Thatcher era', *Economics*, vol. 25, no. 108, Winter.

Goodhart, G. (1989), 'The conduct of monetary policy', *Economic Journal*, vol. 99, June.

Green, F. (1989), *The Restructuring of the UK Economy*, Brighton: Harvester Wheatsheaf.

Gudgin, G. (1978), *Industrial Location Processes and Regional Employment Growth*, Farnborough: Saxon House.

Gutmann, P. M. (1983), 'Taxes and the supply of national output', in B. Bartlett and T. P. Roth (eds), *The Supply-Side Solution*, London: Macmillan.

Harrison, B. (1986), 'Recent developments in regional policy', *Economics*, vol. XXII, no. 93, Spring.

Hartley, K., Parker, D. and Martin, S. (1991), 'Organisational status, ownership and productivity', *Fiscal Studies*, vol. 12, no. 2, May.

Healey, N. M. (1987a), 'Whither monetary targeting?', *Economics*, vol. XXIII, no. 98, Summer.

—— (1987b), 'Government inner city regeneration plans will bypass councils', *Local Government Chronicle*, no. 6282, November.

—— (1987c), 'The 1979–82 UK monetarist experiment: why economists still disagree', *Banca Nazionale del Lavoro Quarterly Review*, no. 163, December.

—— (1987d), 'The widening price of a home', *Town and Country Planning*, vol. 56, no. 12, December.

—— (1989), 'Is monetarism at last dead?', *Economic Affairs*, vol. 10, no. 2, December/January.

—— (1990), 'The British "monetarist experiment": what lessons for the rest of the world?', *Indian Economic Journal*, vol. 38, no. 1, July–September.

—— (1991a), 'Do current account deficits matter?', *The Economic Review*, vol. 8, no. 4, March.

—— (1991b), 'The role of multinational corporations in the British economy', *British Economy Survey*, vol. 20, no. 2, Spring.

—— (1992a), 'The British "economic miracle": myth or reality?', *American Economist Survey*, vol. xxxvi, no. 1, Spring.

—— (1992b), 'European monetary integration', in Griffiths, A. (ed.), *European Community Survey*, London: Longman.

Healey, N. M. and Levine, P. (1990), 'Britain's deficit: an employment-friendly remedy', *Employment Institute Economic Report*, vol. 4, no. 10, January.

Healey, N. M. and Parker, D. (1990), *Current Topics in Economic Theory*, Prudhoe: Anforme.

Hemming, R. and Mansoor, A. M. (1988), 'Privatization and public enterprises', IMF Occasional Paper 56.

Hills, J. (1984), *Saving and Fiscal Privilege*, IFS Report Series no. 9.

Jarvis, V. and Prais, S. J. (1989), 'Two nations of shopkeepers: training for retailing in France and Britain', *National Institute Economic Review*, no. 128, May.

Jenkins, S. P. (1991), 'Income, inequality and living standards: changes in the 1970s and 1980s', *Fiscal Studies*, vol. 12, no. 1, February.

Johnson, C. (1985), 'Mismatch of jobs and jobless', *Lloyds Bank Economic Bulletin*, no. 77, May.

—— (1987), 'The Meaning of Unemployment', *Lloyds Bank Economic Bulletin*, no. 105, September.

Johnson, P. and Stark, G. (1989), 'Ten years of Mrs Thatcher: the distributional consequences', *Fiscal Studies*, vol. 10, no. 2, May.

Johnson, P. and Webb, S. (1990), 'Low income families, 1979–87', *Fiscal Studies*, vol. 11, no. 4, November.

Johnson, P. S. (1986), *New Firms: an Economic Perspective*, London: Allen & Unwin.

Johnson, P. S. and Thomas, R. B. (1984), 'Government policies towards business formation: an economic appraisal of a training scheme', *Scottish Journal of Political Economy*, vol. 31, no. 2.

Kay, J. A. and Thompson, D. J. (1986), 'Privatisation: a policy in search of a rationale', *Economic Journal*, vol. 96, March.

Keegan, W. (1989), *Mr Lawson's Gamble*, London: Hodder & Stoughton.

Keynes, J. M. (1931), *Essays in Persuasion*, London: Macmillan.

Knowlman, N., Pointon, G. and Watkins, D. (1985), *The Operation and Effectiveness of the Business Expansion Scheme*, London: Small Business Research Trust.

Laidler, D. (1987), 'The political control of inflation: a sceptical view', *Economic Affairs*, vol. 7, no. 3, February/March.

Layard, R. and Nickell, S. (1985), 'The causes of British unemployment', *National Institute Economic Review*, no. 111, February.

—— (1987), 'The performance of the British labour market', in R. Dornbusch and R. Layard (eds), *The Performance of the British Economy*, Oxford: Oxford University Press.

—— (1989), 'The Thatcher miracle?', *American Economic Review (Papers and Proceedings)*, vol. 79, no. 2.

—— (1990), 'Mrs Thatcher's miracle?', *Economic Affairs*, vol. 10, no. 2, December/January.

Leibenstein, H. (1966), 'Allocative efficiency versus x-efficiency', *American Economic Review*, vol. 56, June.

Livesey, F. (1984), 'Regional economic policy', *Economics*, vol. XX, no. 86, Summer.

Lloyd, P. and Dicken, P. (1981), *Industrial Change: Local Manufacturing Firms in Manchester and Merseyside*, Inner Cities Research Programme, Department of the Environment.

Machin, S. (1987), 'The productivity effects of unionisation and firm size in British engineering firms', Economic Research Papers, no. 293, Warwick: University of Warwick.

McWilliams, D. (1988), 'The renaissance of British management', the IBM Lecture, Kingston Business School, May 25.

REFERENCES

Mason, C., Harrison, J. and Harrison, R. (1988) *Closing the Equity Gap? An Assessment of the Business Expansion Scheme*, London: Small Business Research Trust.

Matthews, K. G. P. and Minford, P. (1987), 'Mrs Thatcher's economic policies, 1979-87', *Economic Policy*, October.

Matthews, K. G. P. and Rastogi, A. (1986), Little M0 and the moonlighters', *Quarterly Economic Bulletin*, June.

Matthews, K. G. P. and Stoney, P. (1987), 'The black economy: the evidence from Merseyside', *Quarterly Economic Bulletin*, June.

—— (1990), 'Explaining Mrs Thatcher's success', *Economic Affairs*, vol. 10, no. 2, December/January.

Matthews, R. C. O. (1988), 'Research on productivity and the productivity gap', *National Institute Economic Review*, no. 124, May.

Maynard, G. (1988), *The Economy under Mrs Thatcher*, Oxford: Basil Blackwell.

Mendis, L. and Muellbauer, J. (1984), 'British manufacturing productivity 1955-1983: measurement problems, oil shocks and Thatcher effects', Discussion Paper no. 32, London: Centre for Economic Policy Research.

Metcalf, D. (1988), 'Trade unions and economic performance: the British evidence', Discussion Paper no. 320, London: Centre for Labour Economics, London School of Economics.

Millward, N. and Stevens, M. (1986), *British Workplace Industrial Relations, 1980-1984*, Aldershot: Gower.

Millward, R. and Parker, D. (1983), 'Public and private enterprise: comparative behaviour and relative efficiency', in Millward, R., Parker, D., Rosenthal, L., Sumner, M. T. and Topham, N., *Public Sector Economics*, London: Longman.

Minford, P. (1979), 'Memorandum', in Treasury and Civil Service Committee, Memoranda on Monetary Policy, Cmnd 720, HMSO.

Minford, P., Marwaha, K., Matthews, K. G. P. and Sprague, A. (1984), 'The Liverpool macroeconomic model', *Economic Modelling*, vol. 1.

Moore, B., Rhodes, M. and Tyler, R. (1986), *The Effects of Government Regional Economic Policy*, Department of Trade and Industry, London: HMSO.

Muellbauer, J. (1984), 'Aggregate production functions and productivity measurement: a new look', Discussion Paper no. 34, London: Centre for Economic Policy Research.

Muellbauer, J. (1986), 'Productivity and competitiveness in British manufacturing', *Oxford Review of Economic Policy*, vol. 2, no. 3.

Niehans, J. (1981), 'The appreciation of sterling: causes, effects and policies', ESRC Money Study Group Discussion Paper, ESRC.

Niskanen, W. A. (1971), *Bureaucracy and Representative Government*, Chicago: Aldine.

Nolan, P. (1989), 'The productivity "miracle"?', in F. Green (ed.), *The Restructuring of the UK Economy*, Brighton: Harvester Wheatsheaf.

O'Doherty, R. and Flegg, T. (1991), 'The impact of changes in interest rates on consumers' expenditure in the UK', *Economics*, vol. XXVII, no. 116, Winter.

Oulton, N. (1987), 'Plant closures and the productivity "miracle" in manufacturing', *National Institute Economic Review*, no. 121, August.

Parker, D. (1990), 'The 1988 Local Government Act and compulsory competitive tendering', *Urban Studies*, vol. 27, no. 5.

Patel, P. and Pavitt, K. (1987), 'The elements of British technological competitiveness', *National Institute Economic Review*, no. 122, November.

Peacock, A. T. and Wiseman, J. (1961), *The Growth of Public Expenditure in the UK*, Boston, Mass.: National Bureau of Economic Research.

Pearce, B. (1991), 'Whatever happened to the personal saving ratio?', *Economics*, vol. XXVII, no. 4, December.

Peltzman, S. (1976), 'Towards a more general theory of regulation', *Journal of Law and Economics*, vol. 19.

Podolski, T. (1987), 'Financial change and monetary policy in the 1990s', *Economics*, vol. XXV, no. 100, Winter.

Prais, S. J. (1987), 'Qualified manpower in engineering: Britain and other industrially advanced countries', *National Institute Economic Review*, no. 122, November.

Prais, S. J. and Steedman, H. (1986), 'Vocational training in France and Britain: the building trades', *National Institute Economic Review*, no. 116, May.

Prais, S. J. and Wagner, K. (1988), 'Productivity and management: the training of foremen in Britain and Germany', *National Institute Economic Review*, no. 123, February.

Price, R. and Bain, G. S. (1983), 'Union growth in Britain: retrospect and prospect', *British Journal of Industrial Relations*, vol. XXI, no. 1, March.

Pryke, R. (1981), *The Nationalised Industries: Policies and Performance since 1968*, Oxford: Martin Robertson.

Richards, K. (1991), 'Winners and losers: the pluses and the minuses of independent taxation', *Planned Savings*, July.

Riddell, P. (1989), *The Thatcher Decade*, Oxford: Basil Blackwell.

Robins, P. C. (1984), 'Keynesian economic policy and the "crowding-out" hypothesis', *Economics*, vol. XX, no. 87, Autumn.

—— (1985), 'What is the government's employment policy?', *Economics*, vol. XXI, no. 91, Autumn.

Sandford, C. T. (1978), *The Economics of Public Finance*, Oxford: Pergamon.

Sargent, J. R. and Scott, F. G. (1986), 'Investment and the tax system in the UK', *Midland Bank Review*, Spring.

Smith, S. and Squire, D. (1987), *Local Taxes and Local Government*, IFS Report Series, no. 25, May.

Smith-Gavine, A. N. and Bennett, A. J. (1988), 'Percentage utilisation of labour', *Labour Bulletin*, March.

Southworth, M. (1987), 'Counting the jobless', *Economics*, vol. XXIII, no. 97, Spring.

Spencer, P. (1987), 'Britain's productivity renaissance', *CFSB Economics*, Credit-Suisse First Boston, June.

—— (1988), 'Britain's productivity renaissance – an update', *Shearson Lehman Hutton Economics*, December.

Steedman, H. (1988), 'Vocational training in France and Britain: mechanical and electrical craftsmen', *National Institute Economic Review*, no. 126, November.

Steedman, H. and Wagner, K. (1987), 'A second look at productivity, machinery and skills in Britain and Germany', *National Institute Economic Review*, no. 122, November.

—— (1989), 'Productivity , machinery and skills: clothing manufacture in Britain and Germany', *National Institute Economic Review*, no. 128, May.

Stewart, N. (1987), 'Collective bargaining arrangements, closed shops and relative pay', *Economic Journal*, vol. 97, March.

Stigler, G. (1971), 'The theory of economic regulation', *Bell Journal of Economics and Management Science*, vol. 1.

Storey, D. J. (1982), *Entrepreneurship and the New Firm*, London: Croom Helm.

—— (ed.) (1985), *Small Firms in Regional Economic Development*, Cambridge: CUP.

Sutherland, A. (1981), 'Capital transfer tax: an obituary', *Fiscal Studies*, vol. 2, no. 4, November.

Thirlwall, A. (1982), 'Deindustrialisation in the UK', *Lloyds Bank Review*, April.

Thompson, G. (1986), *The Conservatives' Economic Policy*, London: Croom Helm.

Treasury, HM (1987), 'Productivity and employment', *Economic Progress Report*, no. 188, January–February, London: HMSO.

—— (1988), 'Productivity in the 1980s', *Economic Progress Report*, no. 201, April, London: HMSO.

—— (1991), *Economic Briefing*, no. 2, May.

Ture, N. B. (1983), 'The economic effect of tax changes: a neo-classical analysis', in B. Bartlett and T. P. Roth (eds), *The Supply-Side Solution*, London: Macmillan.

Venables, A. (1989), 'Productivity change in the UK', *Economic Review*, vol. 7, no. 1, September.

Wadhwani, S. (1989), 'The effect of unions on productivity growth, investment and employment: a report on some recent work', Discussion Paper no. 356, London: London School of Economics.

Walters, A A. (1986), *Britain's Economic Renaissance*, Oxford: Oxford University Press.

Whitmarsh, D. (1982), 'Productivity – the concept and its uses', *Economics*, vol. 18, no. 78, Summer.

Wilkinson, M. (1988), 'Is there a 'natural rate' of unemployment?', *Economics*, vol. XXIV, no. 102, Summer.

Williams, N. (1988), 'Productivity: will the UK close the gap?', *CBI Economic Situation Report*, October.

Wilson, N, (1987), 'Unionisation, wages and productivity: some British evidence', Discussion Paper, University of Bradford Management Centre, February.

INDEX

adaptive expectations 21–2
Advisory, Conciliation and Arbitration Service (ACAS) 201
advisory/information services 222
aggregate demand 38–9; anticipated and unanticipated changes 24–5; anti-inflation strategy 145–6; 45-degree line diagram 9–13; growth and inflation 30–1, 132, 159–60; inflationary expectations 28, 29, 30; money supply and 31–2, 132; rational expectations 24; tax cuts and inflation 159–60; unemployment 25–8, 228; see also demand-management policy
aggregate production function (APF) 15–16, 17, 35, 36, 37
aggregate supply 14, 38–9; 45-degree line diagram 9, 10, 10–13; inflationary expectations 28, 29, 30; long-run aggregate supply schedule 15–18, 34–7; short-run aggregate supply schedule 18–21, 22, 25
Aldington, Lord 254
Armstrong, H. 242, 245, 254
Ashton, D. 125
Ashton, P. 78, 80
assisted regions 251–3
Associated British Ports (ABP) 178, 184, 185
attitudinal changes 55, 76, 81
auto industry 62–3
Averch, H. 190

Bain, G. S. 201
balance of payments: deficit 97–8, 104, 105–7, 142; manufacturing decline 103–5; North Sea oil and 66, 96; reasons for deterioration 68–9; trends 52, 53, 67–8
'balanced budget' fiscal expansion 155–6
banking system 31–2, 55, 136

bargaining, collective 198
Belgium 63
Bishop, M. 184
black economy 80–1, 158–9
Blackaby, D. H. 119
Blanchflower, D. G. 205–6, 206–7
Boakes, K. 120
borrowing: consumer see credit boom; foreign 96, 105–7; public sector see public sector borrowing requirement
British Aerospace 178, 187, 188
British Airports Authority (BAA) 178, 182, 191
British Airways 178, 180, 182, 187, 188
British Gas 178, 179, 182, 184, 185; regulation 190, 191, 192
British Steel 62, 178, 182
British Telecom (BT) 178, 179, 182, 193; performance 184, 185; regulation 189, 190, 191, 192; see also Post Office
budget deficits 132, 156; see also public sector borrowing requirement
Buiter, W. 77, 87
business 'deaths' 213, 214, 217, 221; by region 246; by sector 216, 217
Business Expansion Scheme (BES) 222–3, 224, 233–5
business formation see new firms
business sector 115, 118
business taxation: local rates 252, 253, 254; new firms 222–3; redistribution 233–6; reforms 169–71, 172

Canada 62, 98, 116, 118
capital account deficit 104
Capital Gains Tax 163, 230, 231, 234, 235, 236
capital intensity 61; see also labour shedding
capital investment 37, 67, 69, 70, 101
capital markets 175–8, 179, 180–1